Castle to Fortress

Castle to Fortress

Medieval to Post-Modern Fortifications in the Lands of the Former Roman Empire

J.E. Kaufmann and H.W. Kaufmann

Pen & Sword
MILITARY

AN IMPRINT OF PEN & SWORD BOOKS LTD.
YORKSHIRE – PHILADELPHIA

Frontispiece: *Caen: Porte des Champs Gatehouse, the eastern entrance to the Château of Caen.*

First published in Great Britain in 2019 by
PEN & SWORD MILITARY
An imprint of
Pen & Sword Books Ltd
Yorkshire - Philadelphia

ISBN 978 1 52673 687 1

A CIP catalogue record for this book is
available from the British Library

Typeset in Ehrhardt 11/13.5
by Aura Technology and Software Services, India

Printed and bound in India
by Replika Press Pvt. Ltd.

Pen & Sword Books Ltd incorporates the Imprints of Aviation, Atlas,
Family History, Fiction, Maritime, Military, Discovery, Politics, History, Archaeology,
Select, Wharncliffe Local History, Wharncliffe True Crime, Military Classics,
Wharncliffe Transport, Leo Cooper, The Praetorian Press, Remember When, Seaforth
Publishing and Frontline Publishing.

For a complete list of Pen & Sword titles please contact

PEN & SWORD BOOKS LTD
47 Church Street, Barnsley, South Yorkshire, S70 2AS, England
E-mail: enquiries@pen-and-sword.co.uk
Website: www.pen-and-sword.co.uk

Or

PEN & SWORD BOOKS
1950 Lawrence Rd, Havertown, PA 19083, USA
E-mail: Uspen-and-sword@casematepublishers.com
Website: www.penandswordbooks.com

Contents

Preface

During the period covered in this volumes and its predecessor *Castrum to Castle*, thousands of forts, castles and city walls were built in Europe, many of which remain today either in ruins or intact, but heavily modified through the ages. It is not possible to cover all of them, or even only those of significant historical importance in a few hundred pages. This volume covers the fortifications of Iberia from the time of the Islamic invasion through the Reconquista. Next, it continues with France after the era of Philippe Augustus through the Hundred Years War (1337–1453) in which small castles were replaced by large castles and fortified cities. The age of gunpowder artillery brought dramatic changes to warfare and fortifications. However, long into the Renaissance, sieges continued to be more frequent than battles in the field as armies and fortifications grew in size.

During the latter part of the Middle Ages, fortifications retained archaic basic features such as the moat and the high wall, usually made of masonry. The advent of the cannon brought significant changes to the height and width of the walls and altered the role of towers, which were converted into or replaced with bastions. Siege methods such as mining or breaching walls became increasingly refined and complex. Rome, the 'Eternal City', continued to modernize its fortifications as it was a frequent target of invading armies. Many older fortifications throughout Europe were frequently updated, which makes it difficult to date them based on their present condition.

This work includes historical background associated with the fortifications in addition to their descriptions. The reader should have an atlas or maps of Western Europe available for finding certain locations referred to in the text since illustrations in the book may not have them all marked. For more detailed descriptions of medieval fortifications and a general survey that covers all of Europe we recommend our earlier publication titled *Medieval Fortress*, Sidney Toy's *Castles* and E.E. Viollet-le-Duc's *Military Architecture*. For the best description of warfare covering castles, military organization, logistics, technology, combat and strategy during the Middle Ages we recommend Bernard and David Bachrach's *Warfare in Medieval Europe c.400–c.1453*.

Acknowledgements

We would like to thank the following people and organizations for their assistance in preparing this project: Miguel Andújar (photo of model), Arnaud Bouis (photos), Pierre Etcheto (photos and data), Martyn Gregg (photos), Rupert Harding (photos), Lorenzo and Roberto Mundo (photos), Bernard Lowry (photos and data), and Wojciech Ostrowski (illustrations). Special thanks to Pierre Etcheto for providing us with a key reference book on French fortifications and other materials on castles in addition to his valuable assistance.

Chapter One

Iberia: Crusading for Conquest

Brief History of Iberia

After Tariq invaded and destroyed the Visigothic kingdom in 711, the Islamic forces swept across most of the Iberia Peninsula. Later, friction arose between Tariq's Moroccan Berbers and two different Arab ethnic groups led by Musa ibn Nusayr that followed them.[1] In 714, the new Caliph in Damascus removed both Tariq and Musa. Musa's son Abd al-Aziz seized Pamplona, Tarragona and Barcelona and crossed into Septimania. He remained in charge in Iberia until the Caliph had him assassinated in 716 to prevent him from becoming independent from the caliphate.[2] In 732, the Franks, led by Charles Martel, defeated Emir Abd al-Rahman at the decisive battle of Tours. Between 740 and 742, conflict broke out again between the Berbers, whose only reward had been the poorest Iberian lands, and the Arabs. In 750, the Abbasids seized the Caliphate and Abd al Rahman I escaped to Iberia where he founded the Umayyad Emirate of Córdoba in 755.

After stopping the Islamic northward advance in 740, Alfonso I, sovereign of the Christian kingdom of Asturias, launched the Reconquista. In 778, Charlemagne, in league with the Abbasids, crossed the Pyrenees, but met defeat at the hands of the Basques at Roncesvalles. By the end of the eighth century, even though the king of Asturias seized Lisbon for a short time, the Christians remained confined to the north. The Franks established the Spanish March, helping the Catalonians who had fled across the Pyrenees to return by driving the Moors from Gerona in 797 and Barcelona in 801. Rebellions fomented by the Christian kings shook the emirate. At the death of Alfonso III in 910, the kingdom of Asturias was divided among his three sons, creating León, Galicia and Castile. Abd al-Rahman III launched a punishing campaign against the new kingdoms in 920, but even though he returned home victorious, the Christians continued to resist. In 929, Abd al-Rahman III ended the emirate and claimed the title of caliph. The tide turned in favour of the Christians who forged an alliance with the governor of Zaragoza (Saragossa). The self-proclaimed caliph launched a new campaign during which he destroyed Zaragoza in 937. In 939, he suffered a major defeat in several days of battle at Alhandega (in front of the city walls of Simancas[3]) at the hands of Ramiro II of León. This battle secured the Duero river line for León.

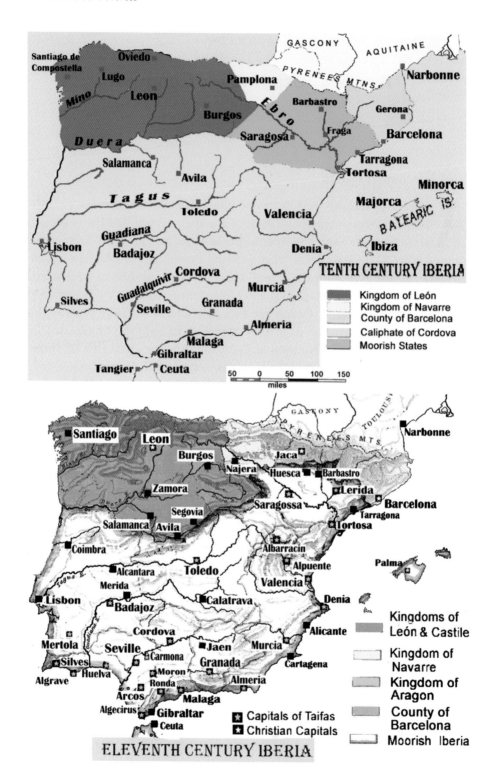

TENTH CENTURY IBERIA

Kingdom of León
Kingdom of Navarre
County of Barcelona
Caliphate of Cordova
Moorish States

50   0   50   100   150
miles

Kingdoms of León & Castile
Kingdom of Navarre
Kingdom of Aragon
County of Barcelona
Moorish Iberia

✪ Capitals of Taifas
✚ Christian Capitals

ELEVENTH CENTURY IBERIA

The struggle between Christian and Islamic forces continued until a de facto Arab ruler, the Yemenite Almanzor, took over. Cordoba prospered and Al Andalus flourished. The high massive walls surrounded this most culturally sophisticated city in the West. A few kilometres to the north-west, Abd al-Rahman III built his exquisite city/palace of Medina al-Zahra (Madinat az-Zahira). Construction began in 936 and took over fourteen years. The complex endured until 1010 when it was ravaged during a civil war. Three of its four sides had double walls with three levels and with square towers.[4] An alcázar was within the compound on its north side. Almanzor established a formidable military machine that dominated the peninsula and launched punishing assaults against the Christian kingdoms of the north and Catalonia. During his campaigns, he even took Barcelona, Pamplona and León. He brought down the massive walls and towers of León. On his last campaign, he razed the church of Santiago to the ground, but spared the shrine of St. James. He employed both Berber and Christian mercenaries to ravage the lands of those who resisted. His death in 1002 destabilized the caliphate as civil wars erupted against succeeding caliphs. In 1031, the caliphate broke up into about two dozen small states called taifas, which consisted of Berbers, Arabs and muwallad (mixed ancestry, i.e. Hispanic with Arab or Berber blood). Although they were relatively large, these taifas easily succumbed to Christian forces until 1086 when the Almoravids – Muslim Berber rulers of north-west Africa – crossed into Iberia under the leadership of Yusuf. By 1091, Yusuf had taken over all the taifas except Saragossa and restored order to Islamic Iberia.

During the European Dark Ages before the death of Almanzor, the Islamic world was culturally on the ascendant while the Christian world was in decline. In Iberia and throughout the Middle East, the Arabs advanced in mathematics, sciences, medicine, agriculture and even literature. They did not exclude people of other faiths from taking part in this intellectual flowering, which shows a greater deal of sophistication on the part of the Arabs than found in Christian Europe.

The León/Castile Front

The Iberian Peninsula, almost square like a boxing ring, became an arena where the Islamic world of the East and the Christian world of the West fought for control for almost 800 years. Since the Muslims failed to clean out the last pockets of resistance in Asturias in the Dark Ages, several Christian states slowly emerged and by the end of that period began reconquering the northern part of the peninsula relying on fortifications to maintain their hold. León, which led the way in the eleventh century, controlled the county of Castile ('Land of Castles') until they formally merged in the twelfth century. Catalonia and Aragon came together and held close connections with France. Islamic Iberia was not a homogenous unit since its population consisted of Berbers, several Arab ethnic groups,[5] converted Christians and non-converted Christians known today as Mozarabs. The taifas emerged from the collapse of the Caliphate of Córdoba in 1031. At one time during the eleventh century, there were up to two dozen taifas in Al Andalus. Before 1080, however, constant warfare between them reduced their number as some of the larger taifas absorbed the smaller ones.[6] The large taifas of Badajoz, Toledo and Zaragoza, and the smaller Tortosa faced the Christian kingdoms and counties. The larger taifas, however, occupied sparsely populated regions and could only field small armies. The smallest, mostly urban, taifas often could barely muster a guard force. The dominant taifas, which included Valencia, Almería, Granada, Córdoba, Seville, and Málaga, often fought each other. The Christian kingdoms in the north fought each other as well. Both sides employed Christian and Muslim mercenaries. The Christian monarchs often forced the taifas on their borders to pay tribute.

King Sancho III Garcés 'the Great' (1000–35) took the throne of Navarre before the break-up of the Caliphate of Córdoba and the creation of the taifas. He dominated both Aragon and Castile and proclaimed himself King of Spain. His united Christian kingdom only lasted until his death in 1035 whereupon it was divided among his sons, Garcia III of Navarre (1035–54), Fernando I of Castile (1035–65), Ramiro I of Aragon (1035–63), Vermudo III of León (1035–7), and Gonzalo (1035–43) who got the counties of Sobrarbe and Ribagorza, both of which were annexed to Aragon after Gonzalo's assassination. Fernando I established Castile as the dominant power and he reunited it with León in 1037 after Vermudo died in a battle against him. Fernando dominated the neighbouring taifas. In the meantime, Ramón Berenguer I, count of Barcelona (1035–76) turned Catalonia into a formidable power, forcing tribute from the taifa of Zaragoza.

The large frontier taifas of Badajoz, Toledo, and Zaragoza with relatively small populations, were unable to prevent the Christians from raiding beyond their ribats – frontier outposts.[7] King al-Muqtadir of Zaragoza (1046–81), whose taifa faced several Christian kingdoms and suffered the most, tried to play Castile against Aragon. By 1055, Fernando I of Castile had pushed south of the Duero River. In 1063, he campaigned against Seville, forcing its ruler to pay tribute. Next, his victory over the Moors in the six-month siege of the city of Coimbra in July 1064 led to the establishment of Portugal.

In 1065, when Zaragoza refused to pay tribute, Fernando launched a campaign that took him as far as the Júcar River, south of Valencia where he took ill and returned home to die at the end of the year. His son, Alfonso VI (1065–1109), inherited the crown of León upon his death. Fernando had left Castile to Sancho II, and Galicia to Garcia. Sancho II forced Zaragoza to pay tribute, which gave rise to friction with the Christian kings of Navarre and Aragon. He turned against his brothers, driving Garcia from Galicia and forcing Alfonso to flee to Toledo. When Sancho was assassinated in 1072, Alfonso VI returned to the north after nine months of exile to claim both Castile and León. Alfonso expanded his empire and forced the rulers of Seville, Granada, Badajoz and Toledo to pay tribute. In 1080, while the leaders of the taifas were at each other's throats, al-Qadir, the ruler of Toledo, sought Alfonso's help. Alfonso marched south and restored al-Qadir to the throne of Toledo in exchange for control of the castles that protected the city. In 1081, Alfonso banished his ablest lieutenant, Rodrigo Díaz de Vivar – nicknamed 'El Cid Campeador'('The Lord [Arabic] Campaigner [Spanish]') and the military commander of Castile.[8] El Cid offered his services to the Muslim king al-Muqtadir of Zaragoza and his son. Meanwhile in 1084, Alfonso VI raided so far south that he reached the coast while plundering the taifa of Seville. Next, late in the summer, he laid siege to Toledo. Finally, in May 1085, when Toledo, the key position on the Meseta (the large high plateau of central Iberia), surrendered, Alfonso established his capital there and proclaimed himself the ruler of Spain. He installed al-Qabir as ruler of Valencia, which he turned into a protectorate. Toledo was strategically located in the centre of Iberia and on the southern Meseta within range of key Islamic cities.

By the late eleventh century, conflict between the Christian kings had simmered down. As the Christians now threatened to overrun Muslim Iberia, the petty taifa monarchs turned for help to the Almoravid (al-Murabitun in Arabic) Berbers of North Africa who had conquered Morocco in 1069 and had advanced eastward along the North African coast during the following decade. Before they answered the appeals of the taifa kings, the Almoravids had to secure their own position and take Ceuta,[9] the key port for crossing the straits where the Muslim governor of Gibraltar had built a fort in 1068, fearing an invasion from this radical sect. Finally, in 1085, after Alfonso took Toledo and threatened Seville, the leader of the Almoravids, Yusuf, crossed the straits and marched north to crush Alfonso's army at the battle of Zallaca (Sagrajas) in October 1086. He returned from Morocco in 1089 to subjugate the taifas. By the end of the decade, he had checked the advance of León/Castile and withheld the tribute paid to the Christian king by the taifas.

Alfonso VI had brought El Cid out of exile before this change of fortune and appointed him protector of al-Qabir, the Muslin ruler of Valencia and former king of Toledo. Meanwhile in March 1091, Yusuf took control of Córdoba and threatened Seville's Muslim ruler, al-Mu'tamid, who had helped him during the battle of Zallaca in 1085. Yusuf laid siege to Seville in June, and defeated Alfonso VI who tried to rescue al-Mu'tamid. Seville fell to Yusuf in September 1091. Later that year, El Cid joined forces with Alfonso in an attempt to stop Yusuf at Granada, but no battle resulted. Another rift emerged between El Cid and his lord. El Cid travelled north and negotiated a peace between Zaragoza and Aragon. Shortly after Badajoz fell to Yusuf in 1094, most of the remaining taifas succumbed as well. Meanwhile, the Moors of Valencia overthrew al-Qabir in October 1092 and awaited the arrival of the Almoravids. However, El Cid reacted quickly. He took Cebolla and refortified it to use it as a base against Valencia.

He also used the fortified position of Benicadell to the south of the city in the foothills of the mountains, which he had taken in the abortive campaign against Granada in 1091. He ravaged the countryside from these two sites. His forces were not strong enough to attack Valencia, but he effectively blockaded the city during the winter of 1093–4. Negotiations began in May and El Cid occupied the city on 15 June taking up residence in the alcázar where he played the role of king. Yusuf who was still at Badajoz in the west, sent his nephew Muhammad against El Cid. In October 1094, the Almoravids appeared before Valencia, black kettledrums pounding and camels towering over the battlefield. The noise sent the Christians' horses into a panic. Until this point, no Christian army had stopped them. According to an Arab geographer who wrote in 1085, 'no city in Al-Andalus has more perfect or more elegant walls' than Valencia, which had six gates (actually seven). There are no other descriptions of the fortress, but only Seville was said to rival it as a major fortified site in Iberia.[10] El Cid, instead of waiting for the enemy to lay Valencia under siege, sallied forth in October, caught the Islamic army on the plain of Cuarte (16km [10 miles] west of Valencia), and dealt Muhammad a resounding defeat.[11] He also tried to create a defensive ring. To the north, he took the castle of Olocau to block the northern approaches. According to historian Richard Fletcher, the garrisons of these outlying castles were not only meant to protect Valencia but also to intimidate the population and confiscate their harvests and herds to support his occupation. Muhammad returned in 1096 and almost trapped El Cid and Pedro I of Aragon at the fortress of Benicadell,[12] which El Cid had rebuilt in 1091. However, El Cid and the king escaped the trap and soundly defeated the Almoravids again at the battle of Bairén later that year.

In 1097, El Cid learned that the city of Játiva had joined Muhammad's forces as the Muslims cut through Valencian territory north of the city to the coast.[13] When the Muslim forces approached Murviedro (the former Iberian town of Sagunto), El Cid drove them northward into Almenara where he put them under siege.[14] They surrendered after three months, in the late autumn. El Cid next turned against Murviedro, the strongest natural fortress on the east coast, which included older Roman/Iberian fortifications along the heights above the town and against the coast. It included seven enclosures with Muslim-built walls. The Moors built cisterns to maintain a large water supply. El Cid laid siege to the city in 1098 and used psychological warfare against its Muslim defendants.[15] They arranged a truce and agreed to surrender if a relief force did not arrive. Their appeals to Yusuf, Alfonso VI, al-Musta'in, and the ruler of the taifa of Albarracan fell on deaf ears. Only the count of Barcelona agreed to help by undertaking a siege of the castle of Oropesa in the north to divert El Cid. However, that castle belonged to King Pedro of Aragon, which complicated the situation. Since Yusuf did not show up, Murviedro surrendered. The Almoravids returned to besiege Valencia where El Cid remained until his death in July 1099. His wife, Jimena,

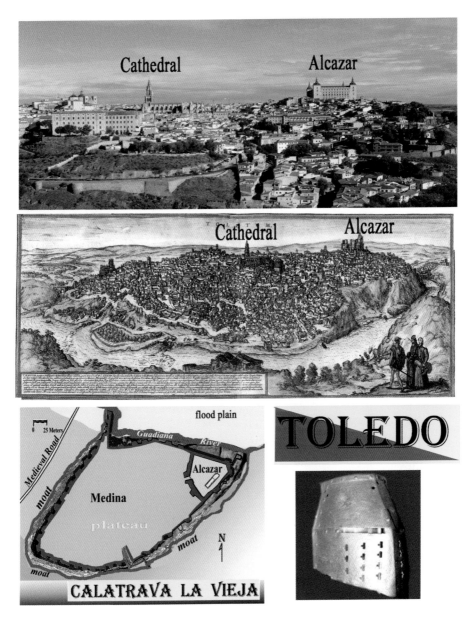

Top: View of city of Toledo and the Alcázar courtesy of Bernard Lowry. Middle: 1572 painting of the city of Toledo. Bottom: Calatrava la Vieja was a Moorish fortress taken by the Christians and used to protect the south-west approach to Toledo.

held the city until 1101, when the Almoravids besieged the city for seven months, only lifting it when word reached them that Alfonso VI was on the march. Alfonso ordered the city evacuated and the Almoravids occupied it in May 1102. Only the taifa of Zaragoza kept its independence, as the Almoravids and Christians divided the Iberia Peninsula amongst them.

Walls of Toledo

TOLEDO

Alcantara Bridge

Photo of Gate courtesy Bernard Lowry

Castillo
San Servando

Top left: Walls of Toledo and illustration from Codex of 976 AD. Top right: Moorish Gate photo by Bernard Lowry. Middle: Old photo of Alcántara Bridge and statue of El Cid. Bottom: Old photo of San Servando and Alcántara Bridge.

Fortifications of Medieval Iberia

When the Muslims invaded Iberia, the local fortifications left much to be desired. Some cities, like Zaragoza and Tarragona, relied on their old Roman walls for defence. Most fortifications consisted of towers and many small watchtowers located between forts. For centuries, Muslims and Christians added to the older works, modified them or built new ones. Detailed descriptions are few so it is impossible to describe many of the most important ones adequately because during and after the turbulent centuries of the High Middle Ages they were repeatedly repaired and modified.

For centuries, fighting in Iberia followed the same pattern. Most belligerents sent mobile raiding forces of up to a few hundred men into enemy territory, bypassing frontier defences and avoiding major battles and sieges, seeking only to plunder livestock, slaves or prisoners for ransom. The objectives of invading armies, on the other hand, were fortified towns and cities. As time passed, the number of castles and fortified towns grew to deter raiders and invaders and provide refuge from enemy armies. As heavily fortified towns and cities emerged in Muslim Iberia, they became greatly coveted prizes because they offered luxuries and sophisticated lifestyles not found in Christian Iberia. The Christian leaders developed a procedure for negotiating during sieges. If the enemy capitulated quickly, the citizenry was usually given the right to remain and maintain its traditions, but if the siege dragged on for too long, they were only given the option to leave only with whatever possessions they could carry. If they continued to refuse, their defeat often meant enslavement or death. The Muslims responded in kind. During and after the eleventh century, the Christians continued to push southward, sending their own people to resettle towns or to establish new ones, which were usually fortified or had a castle for refuge. This procedure secured the expansion of the Catholic kingdoms. These frontier towns formed their own militias to secure the surrounding area. The Muslims, on the other hand, created ribats held by religious volunteers to cover the frontier.[16] They also built many coastal ribats on the south and east coast to protect against piracy.

In the tenth century, the Moors developed a type of concrete known as 'tabby' or 'tapia' that replaced mud and straw in fortification building. It consisted of a mixture of gravel, earth, lime, straw and animal bones that had great strength when it set. Some characteristics of Islamic architecture include arched or horseshoe entrances, square towers, and bent entranceways with a sharp turns usually of 90 degrees after passing through the gate. The Moors also made extensive use of brick. The torre (tower) albarrana (Arabic for exterior) was a Moorish tower located outside the curtain walls and linked to them by a bridge, arcade or coracha, which allowed the defenders to occupy a position from which they could give enfilading fire against an attack on the walls. These towers could be square or round. The Tower of Gold of Seville, a twelve-sided twelfth-century tower, and the Malmuerta in Córdoba (built by a Christian king in the early fifteenth century over a Muslim structure) are two of the most famous examples. Another Moorish feature was the coracha, a short wall connecting an albarrana tower to the curtain walls. It could also be used to cover the short distance to a well or water source, or some other feature important to the defence located outside the curtain walls. The Moors also built alcázars, fortresses cum castles and sometimes palaces, in or near a city. The Moorish architects also built subterranean cisterns or corachas up to 100m (328ft) long with some type of bastion to protect water sources.

The Troubadour Tower at Zaragoza was built in the tenth century as a quadrangular watchtower and defensive position consisting of five levels. The Aljafería fortified palace with the tower was built during the next century. Its square outline was 70m by 70m (229.6ft by 229.6ft) and included round towers projecting along the walls.[17] The palace, which underwent many alterations after it was taken by the Christians, is famous for its Mudejar[18] decoration. The city included a typical Roman wall begun in the first century, which extended for 2,650m (2888.5 yds) with a height of up to 10m (32.8ft). This concrete wall was up to 7m (22.9ft) thick and faced on both sides with ashlars. It included four entrances and about 120 semicircular towers about 15m (49ft) apart.[19] Some Moorish enceintes had several closely spaced square towers.

Not only did the Muslims improve their fortifications, but at the end of the tenth century Al Mansur (Almanzor), the de facto ruler of Andalus, launched dozens of devastating raids from Barcelona to Santiago de Compostela where he levelled the famous church. His campaign of terror against the Christian lands ended in 1002 after he sacked Burgos and became fatally ill. The Christians responded by building forts or castles to protect their holdings and by pushing into unoccupied areas between Christian and Muslim lands to establish towns where the settlers were responsible for defence. In Iberia, the term 'castillo' refers not only to forts but also to freestanding towers, an increasing number of which appeared during the tenth century and later as people settled into lightly occupied regions. It is estimated that up to 10,000 castillos, Moorish and Christian, were built on the Iberian Peninsula during the Middle Ages. About 60 per cent still stand today, giving Iberia the greatest number of medieval fortifications in Europe. These fortifications sported features such as machicoulis, concentric walls, and barbicans that are thought to have originated in the Holy Land.

During the tenth century, the Catalonians built impressive towers that are unusual because they are round and made of stone while in France the first stone castles did not appear until late in the century and round towers not until a century or more later. One of these early keeps was built above a narrow valley at Vallferosa. It is rather large with a diameter of 38m (126.6ft) and over 30m (98ft) high and dominates the nearby village. Large, roughly surfaced ashlars face its concrete walls. A few, narrow openings provide light to the interior; access to the upper levels was by ladder. There is no evidence that this tower served as a residence. Another tower in the county of Bages dates from 960 and is similar to the others. It had three floors and still has its battlements. The towers built during the mid-eleventh century appear to

PENAFIEL

Peñafiel, built during the thirteenth, fourteenth and fifteenth centuries over an older Moorish fortress. Top: View of the ship-like castle, about 150m (492ft) long and 10m (32.8ft) wide, with a large keep in the middle. Centre: Entrance. Bottom: View across one of the baileys towards the keep.

Torre del Oro & Walls of Seville
Photos Courtesy of Arnaud Bouis

Seville's early thirteenth-century Torre del Oro and city walls. (Photos courtesy of Arnaud Bouis)

Almansa Castle was built over an Almohad castle captured by James of Aragon in the thirteenth century. It was rebuilt in the fourteenth century and modified in the next century. Three views of the castle.

be more standardized. They were either round or square, made of limestone or sandstone, and their floors had vaulted ceilings. In a few cases, enceintes were built around the towers. In these cases, however, these slightly enlarged fortifications appeared further south than the freestanding towers and marked the line of expansion.

More impressive styles and types of fortifications appeared in the twelfth century with the introduction of new features imported from other parts of Europe and the Middle East. The Moors may have introduced machicoulis as an improvement over wooden hoardings. In the twelfth century, as the Christian

Top: Castle of Ferdinand and Isabel at Segovia in the shape of a ship. Work began in the late eleventh century and continued through the sixteenth century. Bottom: Estepa, a Moorish fortification lost to the Christians in the thirteenth century. In the fourteenth century, the square Tower of Homage, 13m (42.6ft) on each side and 26m (85.3ft) high, was built on the site.

kingdoms advanced southward, they took over many Moorish fortifications and added their own modifications. In the late Middle Ages, Franco-Italian designs began to dominate, but the Moorish influence still persisted.

Castles and even city walls dominated heights as well as plains of Iberia. Those built on heights often had no moats. Some castles built along ridges like Peñafiel and the larger Almansa and Segovia Castles had a ship-like shape. Castles built on heights, like in other regions, were often very irregular in shape, but those built on level land were often rectangular and later in the Middle Ages acquired concentric walls. Most Iberian castles served as outer defences for cities or dominated lines of communications like river crossings, passes, etc. In other parts of Western Europe, however, this was not always the case because feudal lords often chose remote and easily-defended locations to protect themselves from their overlords. Fortifications dominated war in Iberia, even more so than in other parts of Europe, and sieges were far more common than grand battles.

Aledo and the Forgotten Fortresses

As he recoiled from the thrashing he received at the battle of Zallaqa in 1086 and from his failed siege of Zaragoza, Alfonso VI tried to rebound by taking advantage of Yusuf's return to Morocco. As he re-established his position in central Iberia and marched on Granada, one of his knights ventured into the rugged south-east towards Murcia where he seized the key fortress of Aledo.

Aledo, whose importance fluctuated through history, is not listed among the great fortresses of the world. The ebb and flow of conquest in Iberia, especially between the eleventh and thirteenth centuries, resulted in changing frontiers, which in turn changed the strategic importance of many fortresses like Aledo. The site is located 9km (5.6 miles) north-west of Totana and about 32km (20 miles) south-west of Murcia. Before 896, fortifications located on an outcrop on the foothills of the Sierra Espuña at an elevation of about 125m (490ft) commanded the Guadalentín Valley, one of the largest in Spain. They were destroyed in 896 by the Moors who replaced them with a new fortress that consisted of a walled city and a citadel in typical Moorish style. Aledo was one of many fortresses and watchtowers in this region. When the Castilian army occupied the site in 1086, it took on a new importance and became a thorn in the side of Islamic Spain. From here, Christian forces could dominate the trade routes running from Valencia through Murcia to Cartagena and Almería. The fortress at Lorca afforded similar advantages, but its location in the valley left it exposed. The nearby crossroads town of Totana, with ancient defences on a small hill, was too exposed to be of military value. From Aledo, Castilian raiders threatened and plundered the lands of Murcia, Jaén, Almería, and even Granada.

According to some chroniclers, the Christians' depredations caused Yusuf to return from Morocco and send an army to besiege Aledo. The Moors built siege engines and bombarded the walls in 1092. By the time Alfonso VI at the head of a relief contingent forced the Muslims to break off the siege and retreat. The walls of the fortress had sustained heavy damage and the king judged it impractical to hold the outpost without making major and costly repairs to its defences. Thus, he opted to abandon Aledo and ordered his men to destroy what remained of the site. Subsequently, the Moors built new fortifications. Meanwhile, El Cid concentrated his efforts on taking Valencia while Alfonso dealt with other difficulties. Some fortresses and castles around Valencia such as Olocau, Liria, Cebolla, Murviedro, Almenara, Atalaya and Benicadell, which seldom find mention in most histories of the Reconquista, had their moment in the sun during this period.[20]

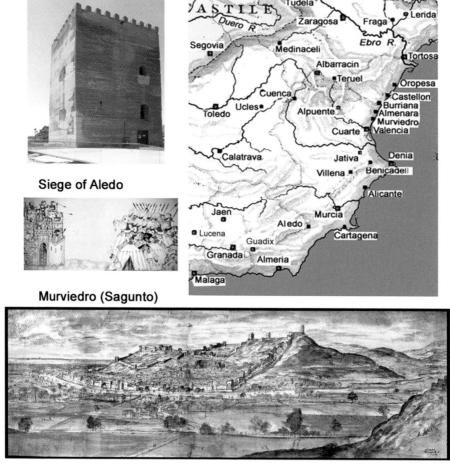

Keep at Aledo

Siege of Aledo

Murviedro (Sagunto)

Tower of Aledo, 20m (65.6ft) high and built in the thirteenth century. Illustration of the 1088 siege. Map of Eastern Spain. Bottom: Painting of fortified town of Sagunto (medieval Murviedro).

Model photo by Miguel Andujar

Atalaya Castle at Villena: View of the twelfth-century Moorish castle with its concentric walls and keep. Captured by James I of Aragon in 1240 and later turned over to Castile. The upper sections was built in the mid-fifteenth century (a distinct separation can be see in the top photo). Centre left: Entrance Gate. Centre right: View from keep of inner and outer wall, with towers with walls averaging 3.5m (11.5ft) thick. Bottom: Model of the castle courtesy of Miguel Andújar and photo taken between the inner and outer walls.

The castle of Atalaya at Villena is representative of these significant but minor fortifications. In 1092, El Cid was supposed to rendezvous there with Alfonso to relieve Aledo, but he failed to show up. In the next century, the Moors built a castle with their typical tapia walls and twelve round towers at the location. In the thirteenth century, it served as a northern fortress for the emirate of Córdoba and it was put under siege three times by Jaime I of Aragon who finally took it in 1239. Jaime passed it by treaty to the crown of Castile in 1244. Eventually Atalaya was given to the Order of Calatrava. A Muslim revolt in the 1260s returned it briefly to Moorish control. By the 1480s, the Castilian crown reclaimed possession. During the fifteenth century, it became an impressive and formidable castle when a concentric wall was added to it. The Moors built the two lower levels of the square keep and the Christians increased its height by two levels and added turrets to its top. The completed castle never served in a major role in war.

The Aragonese/Catalan Front

Before the death of Fernando I of Castile in 1065, some crucial events turned the Reconquista into a crusade. Thanks to the Cluniac Order,[21] the plight of the Christians in the Peninsula came to the attention of Pope Gregory VII, who appealed for help to the rest of Christendom. Burgundians, Normans, and Italians joined the Catalans and the Aragonese in the First Crusade, which actually preceded those in the Holy Land. The first encounter between Crusaders and Muslims was the siege of the Moorish fortress of Barbastro (east of Huesca) in 1064. After forty days, the besiegers gave the defenders a guarantee of safe conduct if they surrendered, but they broke their word and massacred them instead. Nine months later, when most of the Crusaders went home, the army of Zaragoza recaptured Barbastro, and the Reconquista became a holy war.

Sancho I Ramírez (1063–94) invaded Navarre after the assassination of its king in 1076. He placed Aragon under the protection of the pope since Alfonso VI (1065–1109) of León/Castile threatened his kingdom. El Cid, exiled from Castile, served the Muslim ruler of Zaragoza, holding off the forces of Aragon and Catalonia. Alfonso VI besieged Zaragoza in 1085 and El Cid took no action against the king since he still considered him his liege lord.[22] The arrival of the Almoravids in 1086 forced Alfonso to lift the siege and move south to meet the new threat. Sancho declined to help Alfonso against the Almoravids. Alfonso was defeated at Zallaca that year. In 1089, Sancho continued his advance, taking Monzón, the gateway into the Cinca valley located between Lérida and Huesca on the Cinca River. Next, he sent his forces deep into Zaragoza territory where he built the fortress of El Castellar.[23] In 1094, Sancho died in the siege of Huesca. His son Pedro I (1094–1104) continued the fight and even defeated a relief force from the taifa and Castile. The lead in the Reconquista went from Castile to Aragon. That victory resulted in the surrender of Huesca in 1096, and by 1100, Pedro wrested Barbastro from the Moors. In 1101, Pedro led a crusade against Zaragoza and he built the hilltop fortress of Juslibol, also known as Picote de San Martín, outside of the city of Zaragoza in preparation for a siege. This stronghold may have already existed as a Moorish rectangular tower with supporting features. It was protected from attack up the vulnerable south slope with walls that followed the contours of the hill giving an irregular pattern. Alfonso I 'the Battler' took the throne of Aragon on Pedro's death in 1104 and pushed his borders across the Ebro west of Zaragoza. Finally, a combined force of French from the Midi (south France), Aragonese, Navarrese, Catalans, and veterans of the First Crusade who brought their experience in siege warfare from the Holy Land, marched on Zaragoza in 1118. The city, which occupies a site on the south bank of the Ebro, was defended by Roman walls 3,000m (9,800ft) long that consisted of a standard concrete core faced with ashlar stones. It was about 10m (32.8ft) high and up to 7m (22.9ft) thick with 120 semicircular towers about 15m (49ft) apart. West of the city, there was an eleventh-century aljafería or castle-palace. The Moors capitulated on 18 December 1118 after an eight-month siege. Alfonso turned the city into the new capital of Aragon and the palace became the royal residence of the kings of Aragon. In the thirteenth century, the Christians added a brick wall that began at both ends of the Roman wall along the river and encircled the expanded city.

By 1120, Alfonso had pushed the Muslims out of most of the Ebro valley to the south of Zaragoza. A defensive line of about 20km (12.4 miles) that included several Muslim fortifications stretched along the Ebro. He cleared the Jiloca and Jalón basins to the south-east of Zaragoza and pushed the borders across the former taifa. In Catalonia, Count Ramón Berenguer III (1097–1131) led a fleet of French, Pisan, and Catalonian Crusaders into the Balearic Islands in 1114 and besieged the town of Palma, which fell to an assault in April 1115, but he lost the islands a year later.

In 1125, Alfonso I of Aragon launched a major offensive deep into Muslim territory with his fast-moving army. The size of his force, like most others, is unknown. This type of operation required mounted noblemen – knights – and lighter cavalry of free men who had sufficient funds to own horses. Alfonso slipped past the Muslim strongholds of Valencia, Denia, Murcia, and Guadix, struck out towards Granada, and defeated an Almoravid army at Lucena. On his return trip to the north in 1126, he gathered thousands of Mozarabs to settle new colonies in the Ebro valley. In 1129, his siege of Valencia failed. In 1134, Alfonso was defeated at Fraga by the Almoravids and died shortly afterward leaving his kingdom to three military orders: the Templars, Hospitallers, and the Holy Sepulchre. This inheritance did not last, since his brother Ramiro II, a former Benedictine monk who had renounced his vows, took the throne in 1134.[24]

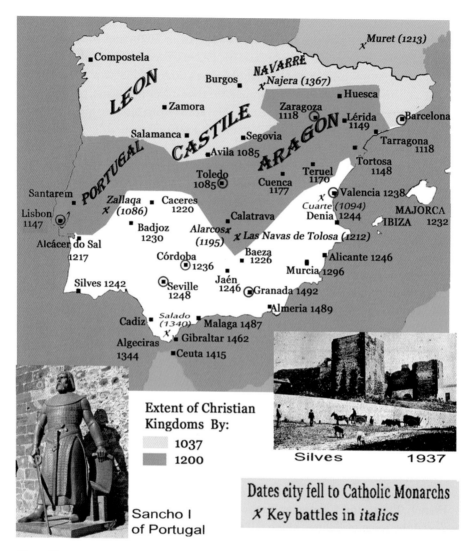

Map of Spain with dates when cities fell to Catholic monarchs and key battles. Photo of Silves from January 1937 magazine Costa de Oiro (public domain). Photo of statue of Sancho I in front of Castillo Silves by Ricardo Liberato. (Wikimedia Commons)

The Tide Turns

As the power of the Almoravids waned, taifa states reappeared and lasted until 1146. Meanwhile, Alfonso VII of Castile renewed the Reconquista in 1139 with the siege of the castle of the town of Oreja about 50km (31 miles) up the Tagus River from Toledo that lasted from April to October. The Moors surrendered after his siege engines destroyed the towers.[25] Alfonso's wife, Berengaria of Barcelona, remained at Toledo when the Muslim army arrived. Nearby, a former monastery converted into the castle of San Servando by Alfonso VI in 1085, fell

to the Muslims. It was located on a hill to defend the other side of the Bridge of
Alcántara. Queen Berengaria sent a message to the Muslim leaders[26] informing
them that they were waging war on a woman and that rather than dishonour
themselves by such an action, they should go to Oreja and engage her husband.
Next, she gathered the women of her court and climbed to the top of the alcázar
where they began to sing in defiance. Either out of humiliation or chivalry, the
Moors departed.[27]

In 1146, a new group of Muslims, the Almohads, entered the Peninsula. The
Almohads, who were even more fanatical than their predecessors, had formed
in the Berber regions of Morocco and overthrown the Almoravids in Africa.
By 1172, they ruled Muslim Iberia. The Christian kings did not sit idly by.
The shifting fortified frontier between Islamic and Christian Iberia included a
number of ribats that protected the approaches to Moorish Spain. The Moors
also built a number of towers that served as signalling stations by using fire or
some other means to send out an alert. These stations gave warning of fast-
moving mobile raiders plundering livestock and/or taking slaves. Both sides
engaged in these raiding expeditions since they could strike quickly and depart
before the enemy could react. On the Christian side, the military orders founded
their own fortified sites, which included a sprinkling of Christian towns formed
to hold newly won conquests. Each of these towns had a nearby castle, its own
set of walls, or both.

In 1147, the knights of the Second Crusade stopped in Iberia en route to the
Holy Land. That same year, the Pope authorized Alfonso VII of León/Castile
to launch a crusade against the Moors. The 13,000 Crusaders from northern
Europe joined 7,000 Portuguese in the siege of Lisbon between 1 July and
25 October. The defenders destroyed the Crusaders' siege engines and foiled
their efforts to mine beneath the walls. Although they were well protected within
their fortifications, the 15,000 Moors of Lisbon were forced to surrender by
starvation. The Crusaders sacked the city before they departed. King Afonso
I, who had taken Santarém in March 1147, went on to capture the impressive
hilltop fortress of Sintra about 24km (15 miles) to the west.[28] Built sometime
during the tenth century, Sintra had walls that wound around rocky crags and
included its own citadel.

Meanwhile, Alfonso VII of Castile launched his own crusade, advancing deep
into enemy territory against the coastal fortress of Almería. First, he besieged
Córdoba. He asked the Genoese to blockade Almería by sea and invited Ramón
Berenguer IV of Catalonia and others to join him. In July 1147, the Genoese fleet
joined Alfonso's 400 knights and 1,000 infantry. Despite the small size of this
army, Alfonso took Almería on 17 October 1147 and laid siege to Jaén the next
summer. The taifas looked to be on the verge of being divided and conquered by
Christian forces, when the Almohads started crossing the Straits of Gibraltar.
The Christian monarchs divided their efforts once more. On 31 December

1148, Berenguer, with help from the Genoese and French, took Tortosa after a five-month siege. Other fortified sites including Fraga, Mequinenza, and Lleida fell by October 1149 and the Christians secured much of the lower Ebro up to Tortosa.

Fearing the Almohads, Ibn Mardanish, the ruler of Murcia, whose taifa also controlled Valencia and Denia, sought the protection of Aragon and Catalonia in 1147. The Almohads took Seville in that year while Almoravids abandoned the Peninsula. In the 1160s, Alfonso II of Aragon seized Teruel and prepared to take Valencia. Shortly after that, he and Alfonso VIII of Castile forced Ibn Mardanish to pay tribute. However, when Ibn Mardanish died in 1172, the Almohads overran his lands. During the twelfth century, crusading reached new heights as the Templars and Hospitlars appeared in Iberia, and the Spanish formed their own monastic military orders such as the Orders of Calatrava, Alcántara, and Santiago. The Christian monarchs endowed these orders with castles to form defensive barriers from the Ebro to the Tagus River valleys. At the time these orders were founded, the Almohad Caliph Abu Ya'qub Yusuf I (1163–84) advanced through central Spain and laid siege to Huete (between Toledo and Teruel) until he was chased away by Alfonso VIII of Castile in 1172. A few years later, the Castilian king and Fernando II of León called a truce with Abu Ya'qub Yusuf who turned west and laid siege to Santarém in 1184.[29] The caliph's four-month siege failed. The tide turned for Afonso I of Portugal when Fernando II of León came to his rescue five days later and the Caliph withdrew to Seville where he died from a wound he suffered when he ended the siege. Across the Mediterranean, Jerusalem fell to Saladin and the Pope called for a third crusade.

In 1189, Sancho I of Portugal began a three-month siege of Silves with the help of Crusaders bound for the Holy Land. The town of Silves had grown rapidly during the eleventh century. When it became the capital of the Taifa of Silves (1027–69), the Moors enclosed it with a tapia wall covered with local sandstone. The city and the castle had three gates and quadrangular towers. The alcaçova (citadel) of Silves, which stands on the remains of Roman fortifications on the heights above the town, has eleven towers, including a keep, two of which are albarrana towers linked by arched passages. The main gateway of the alcaçova leads to the adjacent town, which also had two towers and the third gate. The second gate of the citadel, on the north wall, leads to open terrain. The city became a centre of wealth in the next century, which led to Sancho I's attack. During the siege, Sancho employed a variety of siege engines like towers, catapults, and rams with which he succeeded in destroying several towers and sections of the walls. The town surrendered on 2 September, whereupon it was sacked. The new caliph, Ya'qub al-Mansur, launched a relief expedition, which did not reach Silves until early 1190. However, al-Mansur's army had to withdraw due to lack of supplies.[30] Al-Mansur returned in April 1191, captured Alcaçer do Sal and took Silves three months later. He also took back the territories the Christians had occupied south of the Tagus River except for Evora. At the end of the twelfth century, Silves became the most important city in Iberia and a major city in the Islamic world thanks to its wealth. Sancho I returned to the attack in 1198, this time with German Crusaders. Since he could not hold the site, he destroyed the castle. In 1242, the Order of Santiago recaptured Silves and its castle, which had been rebuilt, and later modified the Moorish fortifications.

In 1195, Alfonso VIII of Castile engaged the Almohads in one of the rare major battles, but he was defeated at Alarcos and the Arabs' advances continued. In 1211, the Almohad caliph decided that Salvaterra Castle, a stronghold of the Order of Calatrava from which raiders ventured into his lands, was a thorn in his side.[31] He seized key positions around the castle from which he could bombard it with his siege engines and forced the defenders to surrender after a ten-week siege. Later, Pope Innocent III called for a new crusade. On 16 July 1212, a mixed force from León, Castile, Aragon, Navarre, and Portugal with French Crusaders totalling up to 14,000 men surprised the Almohad army of 22,000 to 30,000 men at Las Navas de Tolosa. The resulting battle was a decisive turning point in the Reconquista. His army routed, Caliph Muhammad al-Nasir escaped. The Christian force captured several castles and took the town of Baeza after its Muslim population had fled. Next, Alfonso VIII laid siege to Úbeda, a short distance from Baeza, which fell after three days. However, he had to abandon Baeza and Úbeda when disease and lack of supplies put an end to his campaign. Meanwhile, the Almohad caliph fled first to Seville and finally to Morocco where he died at the end of 1213. The Christian frontier had been pushed further south, to the borders of Andalusia.

At the end of July 1217, knights of the Fifth Crusade landed in Lisbon and joined the Portuguese king in the siege of the hilltop castle (probably originally a ribat) of Alcácer do Sal, which overlooked the port and the Sado River. The castle included a large keep and a curtain wall with twenty to thirty irregularly-spaced towers built mostly in the previous century by the Moors. Some of the walls, mostly of tapia, ran along the cliffs. The Crusaders tried to tunnel under the walls, but they brought down only one tower by the end of August. After they beat back a Muslim relief force, the defenders surrendered in mid-October.

The Muslim collapse continued as Alfonso IX of León laid siege to Cáceres in 1222. The Almohads had improved the fortifications of this town in the late twelfth century adding six albarrana (detached) towers made of tapia. As Alfonso's men brought down the towers of the fortress and surrender appeared eminent, the caliph offered tribute, which the king accepted.[32] It was not until 1229 that the Leonese took back the city, which had changed hands repeatedly during the previous century. By this time, the Almohads had to deal their own civil war since they had little control over their Iberian governors.

Ibn Hud, the governor of Murcia, revolted against his Almohad overlords and ruled most of Islamic Spain by 1228 as the Muslim rulers of Seville, Córdoba, Granada, and Jaén rallied behind him. However, Cáceres and other fortified cities continued to fall to the Christians. Even though Jaime I of Aragon failed to take Peñíscola, the intimidated Valencians decided to pay him tribute. In 1230, the kingdoms of León and Castile merged under Ferdinand III. In 1233, Ferdinand defeated Granada and forced the surrender of Córdoba in 1236. Although Ibn Hud was able to crush his rivals, he could not stop the Christian monarchs. He died at the hands of an assassin at Almería in September 1238. Valencia fell to Aragon after a siege and Jaén surrendered in 1246. Granada became a vassal state

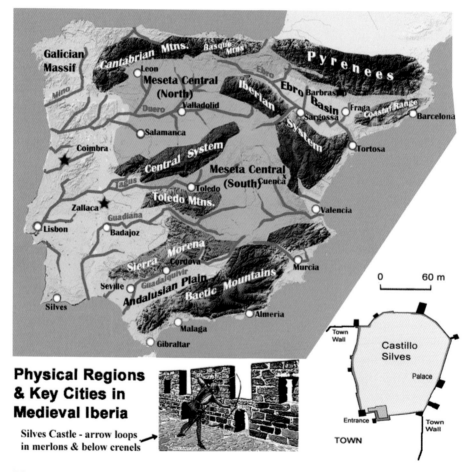

Physical Regions & Key Cities in Medieval Iberia

Silves Castle - arrow loops in merlons & below crenels

Physical map of Iberia. Bottom: plan of the Moorish Castle of Silves which is linked to the town walls. Also a graphic view of the unusual arrow loops not in the merlons but just below the crenel allowing the archer a protected angled view to the area in front of the castle walls.

of Castile. Seville, which capitulated in 1248, was ringed with forts and had its own twelfth century Almoravid walls that spanned over 7km (4.3 miles) and included 166 towers and 13 gates. An alcázar was part of the city defences. The Almohads had modified the fortifications and added the famous Tower of Gold (Torre del Oro) in 1220. A chain extending from this twelve-sided, three-level albarrana tower to the other shore blocked the river. A 16-month blockade by Castilian ships and troops forced the city to surrender. Islamic Iberia continued to dwindle in size during the latter half of the thirteenth century. Alfonso X, son of Ferdinand III, took Cádiz in 1262 and King Jaime I of Aragon conquered Murcia in 1266. Only the emirate of Granada remained as a bulwark of Islamic Iberia.

Meanwhile in North Africa, the Marinids, another Berber group, overthrew the Almohad dynasty in 1244. Their takeover in Africa was not complete until 1269.

Siege and Conquest of Lisbon 1147

Watercolor of siege of Lisbon by Alfredo Roque Gameiro (1917)

Siege of Lisbon 1147 illustrated in watercolour by A.R. Gameiro in 1917.

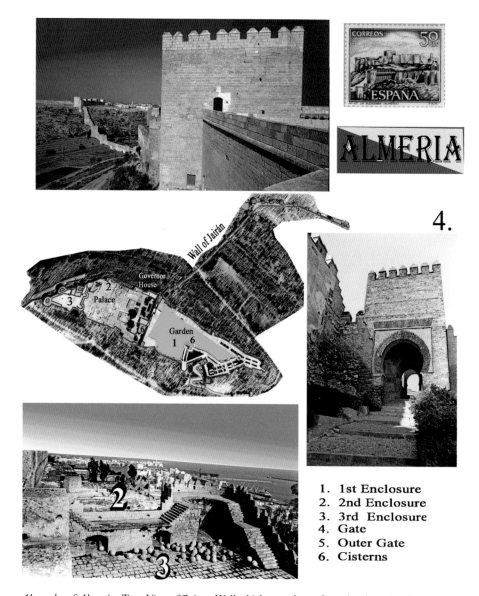

1. 1st Enclosure
2. 2nd Enclosure
3. 3rd Enclosure
4. Gate
5. Outer Gate
6. Cisterns

Alcazaba of Almería. Top: View of Jairan Wall which extends out from the alcazaba. Centre: Plan and photo of entrance. Bottom: View from citadel (#3) of the other enclosures.

They took control of Algeciras and occupied Gibraltar in 1294. Earlier, they had fought off Castilian attacks on Morocco. Castilian troops took Gibraltar in 1310 (but lost it to Granada in 1333). The Marinids bolstered the remaining Islamic states of Iberia, but a combined Portuguese and Castilian army defeated them at the battle of Rio Salado (or Tarifa) in October 1340 forcing them out of Iberia. The Christian monarchs next fought among themselves. A civil war that broke out in Castile culminated in 1367 when the English supported Pedro of

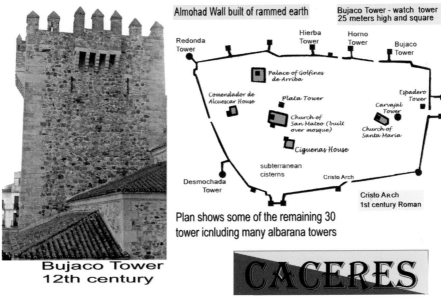

Almohad Wall built of rammed earth   Bujaco Tower - watch tower
25 meters high and square

Redonda
Tower

Hierba
Tower

Horno
Tower

Bujaco
Tower

Palace of Golfines
de Arriba

Comendador de
Alcuescar House

Plata Tower

Espadero
Tower

Carvajal
Tower

Church of
San Mateo (built
over mosque)

Church of
Santa Maria

Ciguenas House

subterranean
cisterns

Cristo Arch

Desmochada
Tower

Cristo Arch
1st century Roman

Plan shows some of the remaining 30
tower icnluding many albarana towers

**Bujaco Tower
12th century**

CÁCERES

Cáceres. Top: View of town walls. Bottom left: The 25m (82ft) high twelfth-century Moorish Bujaco Tower. Ashlars can be seen on corners and brick merlons (these may have been part of the restoration work). Bottom right: Plan of city walls.

Castile who defeated his French-supported rival at the battle of Nájera. In 1469, Isabel of Castile and Ferdinand of Aragon married and directed the final thrust of the Reconquista against the last Iberian Muslim state from their residence at Córdoba.

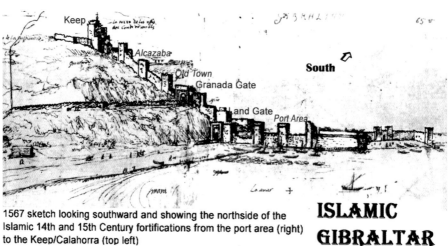

1567 sketch looking southward and showing the northside of the Islamic 14th and 15th Century fortifications from the port area (right) to the Keep/Calahorra (top left)

ISLAMIC GIBRALTAR

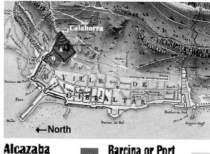

1879 photo looking up from old port area to the Keep

Alcazaba (12th to 14th Century)	A	**Barcina or Port** (13th to 14th Century)	B
Old Town (12th to 14th Century)	O	**Turba or City** (13th to 15th Century)	T

1799 Map of Gibraltar with Islamic Medieval positions highlighted.

PLAN DE GIBRALTAR . PAR J.D. BARBIÉ DU BOCAGE.

Islamic Gibraltar. Sketch of fortifications, old photo and 1799 map.

Córdoba and Islamic Iberia

Andalusia, the southern part of Spain, includes Córdoba, Seville, Granada, Malaga, Almeria, and Jaen, forming the core of Islamic Spain. The Sierra Morena, which separates the Guadalquivir Valley and the Andalusian Plain from the high plains of the Meseta Central, was the last major barrier that protected the region from the Catholic monarchs. Seville, its main cultural centre, dominates the lower Guadalquivir Valley. Córdoba, a rival city further up the river, controlled the main crossing leading north with its Roman-era bridge. In the eighth century, the Arabs rebuilt the bridge and added water mills for irrigation, which allowed the economy of the valley to diversify from grain and grape production to a greater variety of crops, which, in turn allowed the region to thrive.

As Córdoba thrived, its Islamic rulers built an impressive Alcazaba and one the largest mosques in the West. This Great Mosque, which is an architectural masterpiece, was built in the tenth century. When Fernando III of Castile/León took the city in 1236, he appropriated the Alcázar as his residence and converted the mosque into a cathedral. The Castilian army continued its relentless advance. Seville and Jaén fell before 1250, effectively pushing the Moors out of the Andalusian Plain and leaving them cling to the Baetic Mountains and their coastal fortresses. Only Granada stood as the main centre of Moorish resistance.

In 1327, Alfonso XI changed the complexion of Córdoba. The Alcazaba was converted and divided. Sections of it went to the Order of Calatrava and the bishops. Alfonso converted the remainder into the Alcázar or Castle of the Catholic Kings, a showcase of Gothic architecture. It has a square plan with sides of about 64m (210ft) and includes four square towers. The octagonal Tower of Homage occupies the north-east corner and used to house the royal residence on the first floor in a vaulted hall. The Lion Tower, named for one of its gargoyles, is on the north-west corner. The square tower, built in the Almohad style, includes two floors with high vaults and pointed arches. The three-level Gardines Tower on the south-east corner on the river side, is newer than the other three. This octagonal tower sat on a circular base. Finally, the Paloma (Dove) Tower stood on the south-east corner, but there is little information about it since it was destroyed.[33] The castle courtyard consists of two separate parts.

Alfonso XI added an Arab-style bathhouse with dressing rooms to the castle. The bathhouse included cold and warm rooms and a hot room for steam and hot baths. In 1482, Isabel and Ferdinand took up residence at the castle from which they engineered the final campaigns of the Reconquista for eight years. In 1492, they approved Columbus' expedition from this castle. That same year, they turned it over to the Inquisition, which remodelled the place by adding cells and torture chambers. Finally, in 1812, the king took it from the Inquisition. It served as a prison between 1822 until the early twentieth century when it became an army headquarters until 1955.

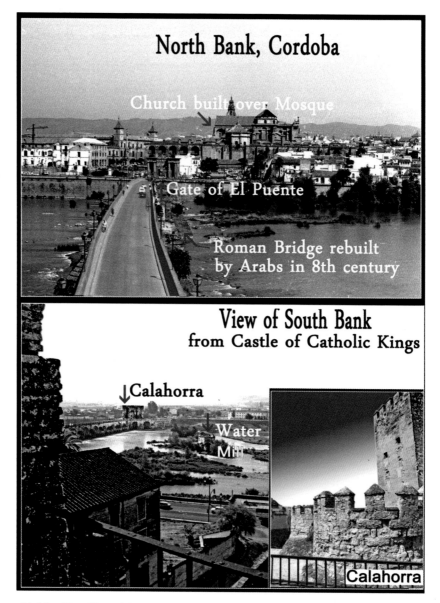

Córdoba: Top: View of Córdoba and Roman Bridge. Bottom: View of Roman Bridge and its Tower (the Calahorra) from the Castle of the Catholic Kings.

The Almohads built the Tower of La Calahorra, at the south end of the Roman bridge, which had two towers. King Enrique II of Castile modified it and added a third tower in 1369 to defend the city from attack by his brother Pedro I the Cruel.[34] It is surrounded by a deep moat except on the north side, which faces the bridge.

View of Gardens & Lion Tower

View from Tower of Homage of Lion Tower

Tower of Homage on NE corner & Lion Tower on NW corner

CORDOBA

Córdoba Royal Castle built on a Moorish Alcázar by Alfonso XI of Castile in 1328: Top: Views of Lion Tower. Bottom: View of Tower of Homage.

The Last Islamic Bastion

Whereas during the eighth century, the Moors had pushed the Christians of Iberia into the Cantabrian Mountains in the north, by the end of the fourteenth century, they became confined to the Baetic Mountains in the south-east. For much of the fifteenth century, only the Emirate of Granada remained as the last Islamic bastion on the Iberian Peninsula. It stretched from Gibraltar to Granada to the old borders of the taifas of Jaén and Murcia and included the ports of Málaga and Almería. There were major fortifications at Gibraltar, Málaga, Almería, and Granada. Most of the cities in the Emirate had defences and there were many castles/forts throughout the region. Although Gibraltar fell to Castile in 1462, the definitive campaign to push the Moors out of Spain did not begin until 1482. On 26 December 1481, the Moors broke the Truce of 1478 in response to Spanish raids. Under the cover of darkness and a roaring storm, a Muslim force scaled the walls of the small frontier town of Zahara, south-west of Ronda, overwhelmed the unwary garrison, and enslaved the townspeople.

In retaliation, the Spanish sent 2,500 cavalrymen and 3,000 infantrymen to strike into the heart of the emirate with the intent of taking the wealthy city of Alhama, a fortress on top of a rocky height protected by a city wall with a watercourse at its base, which gave the defenders a false sense of invincibility. Don Rodrigo Ponce de León, Marquis of Cádiz, who led the expedition, became Granada's greatest nemesis.[35] On 28 February 1482, he sent a detachment of about thirty escaladores (scalers) two hours before dawn to climb the heights quietly and place their ladders against the walls of the citadel of Alhama. The men reached the top of the battlements, came across a sleeping sentry, quickly dispatched him, took out the garrison, and threw open the gates. No one had expected such a brazen assault on so formidable a position deep in the heart of the emirate. The alarm was raised in the city as the Marquis of Cádiz triumphantly entered the citadel, trumpets blaring. Securing the city was more difficult. The Moorish handgunners and crossbowmen held the Castilians off until the Marquis intervened. He destroyed part of the fortifications that faced the town and charged in. His men sacked the city. On 5 March, the emir appeared before the walls of Alhama with 3,000 cavalry and 50,000 foot soldiers. After he lost 2,000 men attacking the city, he decided to lay siege to it. He diverted the river, which left Alhama with a single well for its water supply. However, when news of King Ferdinand's imminent arrival reached the emir, he lifted the siege on 29 March. As soon as Ferdinand got word of this, he returned to Córdoba. When he realised that no relief force was coming, the emir returned, this time with cannons, and prepared to resume the siege of the city. He sent forty men over the city walls, but the defenders wiped them out before they could reach the gates. Ferdinand led another relief force and the Granadans withdrew once more. This time however, the king completed his trip and entered Alhama on 14 May. Fortune did not always smile on the Castilian army, however. In July 1482, Fernando was defeated trying to take Loja, between Alhama and the frontier.

Granada was racked with internal and external problems. In 1415, the Portuguese had seized Ceuta, the main port in Africa serving Islamic Iberia. Ceuta successfully resisted a siege by Arab forces in 1418. The Spanish had neutralized support from Morocco, denying Granada help from that quarter except from religious volunteers. The emirate was flooded with refugees from areas conquered by the Spanish. In addition, raids had devastated the countryside driving more people into the cities. A palace revolt ousted emir Abu l-Hassan-Ali of Granada in February 1482. His son, Muhammad XII, Boabdil, made a bid for power, but he had to face his uncle Muhammad XIII, al-Zagal, sparking a civil war. In 1483, the Spanish captured Boabdil while he was leading a raid. In 1485, the Marquis of Cádiz took Ronda, which is perched on top of cliffs and is divided by a deep gorge spanned by a Roman bridge. At the time, the city was surrounded by walls and had an alcazaba.[36] Its commander was on a raid and he was unable to break the Spanish siege. The Castilians tightened the siege by cutting the aqueduct that supplied the city with water while their cannons battered the walls. Ronda surrendered in May. According to the nineteenth-century historian William Prescott, despite the fall of Ronda, after 1483 'no siege or single military achievement of great moment occurred until . . . 1487, although in the intervening time a large number of fortresses and petty towns, together with a very extensive tract of territory, were recovered from the enemy'.[37]

Ferdinand and Isabel released Boadbil who returned to Granada where he had to face his uncle in 1485. He sought help from Castile. In September 1486, with the help of Castilian troops, he retook Granada but his uncle held the Alhambra until he lost the support of his subjects. By 1487, the Spanish troops had captured additional important cities in the emirate and put Málaga under siege.

Warfare had changed drastically during the fifteenth century as firearms and heavy artillery became more sophisticated and required more reliable gunpowder than the earlier mixtures. The Spanish monarchs imported specialists from other regions, following the example of the Ottomans who had built heavy cannons to smash Constantinople in 1453. In Iberia, the belligerent armies (not the raiding forces) were normally accompanied by siege trains since most of their objectives were cities. By the fifteenth century, the Christian armies also included an artillery train. Although the Moors also had guns and cannons, they were outgunned. Throughout Europe many arrow slits in castles and forts were modified to accommodate guns with the addition of a circular opening for small gunpowder weapons. Large cannon embrasures also began to appear. Some walls lacked the strength to resist heavy artillery. Both sides were prepared for gunpowder-age warfare whose value in reducing fortifications had been demonstrated earlier in the century during the Hundred Years War in France and the destruction of Byzantium by the Ottomans. During the campaign against Granada, the Spanish artillery was hindered by the lack of roads and the difficult terrain, which forced the Spanish to employ thousands of pioneers to prepare the lines of communications. The Moors had armed the city of Málaga with its own artillery, and like at Alhama they had numerous handgunners.

In April 1487, Ferdinand led his army across difficult terrain to Vélez-Málaga, between Málaga and Granada. Since his pioneers did not have enough time to prepare the roads for heavy artillery, he came with only light cannons. El Zagal tried to attack the Spanish camp, but the Marquis of Cádiz drove him back.

Although a hilltop castle/fortress dominated the area from 80m (262ft) above the town, the Spanish fleet and army blockaded the small port by land and sea forcing its surrender on 27 April 1487. The Spanish had already occupied the lands south of Málaga by 1485. After they took Vélez in 1487, they seized several other towns between Loja and the coast thus isolating Málaga.[38]

Málaga, which was second only to Granada in the emirate, had an impressive alcazaba, which served as a palace and citadel and was built in 1279 at the foot of the mountain, adjacent the city and port. The alcazaba had three sets of walls that included the palace and linked with the city walls, located at sea level. There were over 100 towers, about 75 of which were in the city walls. Most of the towers were rectangular and the gates were well protected. The Malagans strengthened the walls, which were made of brick and stone. A stream flowing from the mountains formed a partial moat on the west side of the town. The city was surrounded by mountains except on the side facing the Mediterranean. In 929, the Caliph of Córdoba built the Castle of Gibralfaro, the key to the defences of the city, on the site of an ancient Phoenician lighthouse about 130m (426ft) above the city. It had two sets of walls and a large tower on the north-east side. Gun ports were added to its towers. The castle, which could hold 5,000 men, had a 40m (131ft) deep well, three large underground cisterns, and several underground chambers that served as storage rooms and prisons. Yusuf I, the ruler of Granada, enlarged it early in the fourteenth century by adding a 600m (1,968ft) long double-walled coracha that linked the alcazaba to the castle. The coracha descended from the hill in a zigzag fashion to allow the defenders to cover the walls with flanking fire without towers. The bottom of the coracha walls consisted of stone and the upper part was made of tapia.

Al-Zagal placed Hamid al-Zagri (Hamete Zeli) – the very man who had lost Ronda in 1485 – in command of Málaga. Ferdinand with an army of 30,000 men reached the city on 7 May and laid siege to the castle. The Christian contingent grew to 60,000 to 90,000 by the end of the siege. Hamete Zeli tried to ambush the Christians in the hills, but he was forced back into the castle. Ferdinand offered liberal terms of surrender, but Hamete Zeli turned him down because he had faith in his garrison, which had been reinforced with volunteers from other towns and with African mercenaries. Ferdinand laid down a fortified camp in his siege lines and moved his cannons into position under the cover of darkness to avoid fire from the accurate Muslim handgunners and crossbowmen. His field fortifications of earthen mounds and timber walls, sometimes with trenches, encircled the city. Spanish ships blockaded the port. The Marquis of Cádiz positioned his 2,500 knights and 14,000 infantrymen near the castle on commanding heights.

The Moors sallied more than once in almost suicidal attacks while the Spanish artillery pounded the walls, but inflicted significant damage only from close range. The Moors valiantly contested every breach and worked day and night to plug gaps with wood and stone, but they could not match the Castilian heavy artillery. The continuous bombardment led to a shortage of stone and iron cannon balls forcing the Castilians to bring ammunition from all over the kingdom. The overcrowded city soon began to run out of supplies while the besieged watched Spanish ships unloading fresh provisions. The summer heat depressed morale on both sides and many men deserted from the besieging army. The rumour of plague further lowered the soldiers' spirits and only the arrival of Queen Isabel boosted morale. An assassination attempt against her and Ferdinand failed. The body of the assassin was hacked to pieces and catapulted into the city. Ferdinand ordered the construction of mobile siege towers.

Finally, Ferdinand began sapping operations to undermine the walls, but the garrison opened counter mines. One of his mines reached a tower that guarded access to a bridge leading into the city. As was the custom in the fifteenth century, this mine was filled with gunpowder. The resulting explosion brought down the tower causing panic inside the city, which continued to hold out. The heat of August increased the misery of the people who were resorted to killing pets and rats for food. The demoralized citizens demanded Hamete surrender. Thus, Málaga surrendered unconditionally on 19 August after a three-month siege and its population was enslaved. Hamete holed up in the castle with the last 9,000 defenders and refused to surrender.

The remainder of the war passed without great sieges like the one at Málaga. Several fortresses including Granada and Almería remained in the hands of the Moors. The alcazaba of Almeria, which was built on a ridge parallel to the sea, dated from 955. It is claimed that it was only second in size to the alcazaba of Granada. Supposedly established by Abd-ar Rahman III, Caliph of Córdoba, the city took its name from a watchtower. The alcazaba consisted of three enclosures, the largest of which was on the east end and served as the military site and refuge. It had a 70m (229.6ft) deep well. The middle enclosure had a palace, public baths, and a mosque. The third, which was at the highest point and surrounded a triangular area, had three semicircular towers including the keep. The walls, which spanned 1,450m (1,580.5 yds) and were 5m (16.4ft) high and about 3m (9.8ft) thick, dominated the city and the harbour.[39] In the eleventh century, mulberry trees were planted in the area for the silk industry that brought prosperity to Almería. When Emir Jairan (1012–28) took the city, he strengthened its fortifications and added the Jairan Wall, which crossed the valley and expanded the fortress. It included three square towers. Jarian also built cisterns to withstand sieges. The Templars added four semicircular towers. Alfonso VII captured the city in October 1147, but the Almoravids recaptured it shortly afterward. In the thirteenth century, the city became part of the Narsid Emirate of Granada.

In 1488, Ferdinand's army invaded the eastern half of the emirate and laid siege of the city of Baeza the next year. Al Zagal pulled troops from Almería to defend Baeza. The Spanish surrounded the city with a palisade on one side and

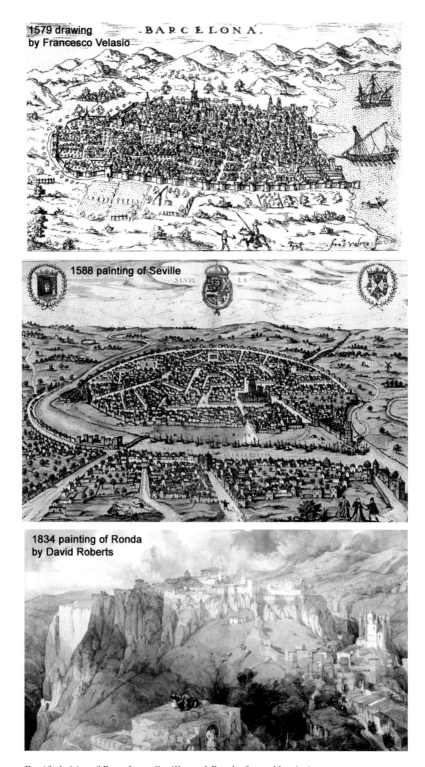

Fortified cities of Barcelona, Seville, and Ronda from old paintings.

Ronda: Top: View of Puerta de Almocábar. Centre: View of two sets of walls. Bottom: West side of city and the new bridge. (Photos courtesy of Arnaud Bouis).

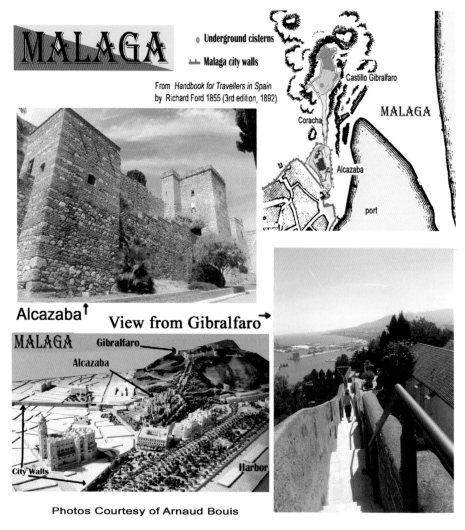

Photos Courtesy of Arnaud Bouis

Málaga's eleventh to fourteenth-century Alcazaba and fourteenth-century Gibralfaro. (Photos courtesy of Arnaud Bouis)

a wet moat, a stone wall, and a dry ditch on the other side. The siege drained the Spanish treasury, but Baeza finally yielded in December after seven months of resistance. Al Zagal withdrew to Almería and signed a treaty with the Spanish, turning the city over to them without a fight on 26 December. Muhammed XII was left with only a small territory and was no longer a vassal of the Catholic monarchs.

The Red City, Granada, home of the famed Alhambra, which dates back to the Neolithic and gained importance during the Roman Empire. Its alcazaba was built during the early eleventh century. The Alhambra, Granada's famous palace complex, was built on a height dominating the city. It is 820m (894 yds) long and

1. Tower of Homage   2. Tower de la Vela   3. Mosque   4. Tower of Comares   5. Tower of the Queen 6. Palace of Principe
7. Tower de los Picos   8. Tower del Cadi   9. Tower de las Infantas   10. Torre del Agua   11. Tower of 7 Floors
12. Tower de las Cabezas   13. Tower de la Justica   14. Tower of Arms   15. Palace & Courtyard of the Lions
16. Palace & Courtyard of Ambassadors 17. Palace of Carlos V   18. Church   19. Entranceway of Carlos V

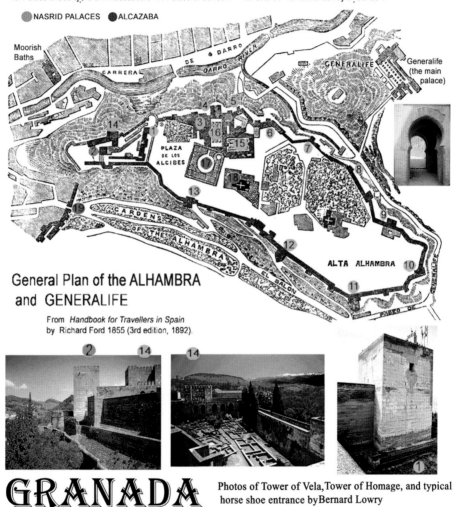

General Plan of the ALHAMBRA
and GENERALIFE

From *Handbook for Travellers in Spain*
by Richard Ford 1855 (3rd edition, 1892).

GRANADA   Photos of Tower of Vela, Tower of Homage, and typical
horse shoe entrance by Bernard Lowry

Granada. Top: Plan of site. Bottom: Alcazaba photos, Tower of Vela and Tower of Homage courtesy of Bernard Lowry.

has a maximum width of 222m (243 yds). Its 2m (6.6ft) thick tapia walls reach an average height of 9m (30ft) and its Comares Tower is 23m (75.4ft) high. It includes palaces, a mosque, and an alcazaba. In 1490, the population of Granada had swollen to over 200,000 souls as refugees fled the devastated countryside.

In June 1490, Muhammed XII struck out from Granada and captured several nearby castles held by the Spanish, and tried, but failed, to reach the coast. That

View from main palace
of Nasrid palaces

GRANADA

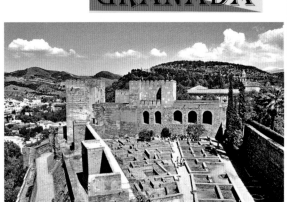

Alcazaba

Palace

Granada. Top: View of Alhambra from main place. Alcazaba photo (bottom left) courtesy of Bernard Lowry.

winter, Fernando and Isabel planned the final campaign and siege. In April 1491, they left Seville for Granada, determined to end the war. In October, they built a permanent siege camp that would serve as winter quarters for the army. The emir began secret negotiations with the Catholic Kings, when he realized that the Granadans were not happy with him. In January 1492, he surrendered the city and the Reconquista was completed.

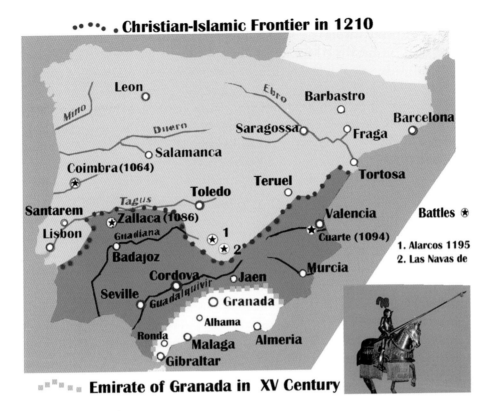

····· .Christian-Islamic Frontier in 1210

Leon
Miño
Duero
Ebro Barbastro
Barcelona
Saragossa Fraga
Salamanca
Coimbra(1064)
Teruel
Tortosa
Toledo
Santarem
Tagus
Zallaca (1086)
Lisbon Guadiana 1
Badajoz 2
Valencia Battles ⊛
Cuarte (1094)
1. Alarcos 1195
2. Las Navas de
Cordova Jaen Murcia
Seville Guadalquivir
Granada
Alhama
Ronda Almeria
Malaga
Gibraltar

▪▪▪▪▪▪ Emirate of Granada in XV Century

Map of the Reconquista.

Ávila and other Spanish Classics

Although most cities in Iberia and Medieval Europe were walled, few have retained all their defences to this day. Ávila, like Carcassonne in France, is one of the few cities to have kept its complete medieval enceinte. Built over an old Roman town, on top of a relatively flat rocky hill, the city was located on the shifting frontier between Christian and Moorish Spain until the late eleventh century when León/Castile finally took control of the area in 1088. Christian settlers repopulated the area around the walled city. Raymond of Burgundy, who came to Iberia to fight the Moors in the 1080s, started the construction of the walls in 1090. The completed enceinte of brown granite spans 2,516m (2,752 yds.) and includes nine gates and eighty-eight towers that are among the earliest round towers in the region. The walls rise to about 12m (39ft) and are 3m (9.8ft) thick. According to tradition, a Gothic cathedral was built into the walls in 1107, but it is now believed that it may have actually been built a few centuries later. The Alcázar Gate or main gate is flanked by a pair of towers linked to each other by a bridge. War largely passed the city by after its fortifications were completed.

The castles of Medina del Campo and Coca represent a transitional style. The village of La Mota (Medina del Campo), located about 50km (30 miles) north of Ávila, was also in the virtual 'no man's land.' It was fortified when it was repopulated in the 1070s. Within a century, however, it grew out of its walls leaving the fortress known as La Mota on the hill. In the fifteenth century, work began on the castle, which was given to the future king of Aragon by the king of Castile in 1390. Enrique IV of Castile took back the town in 1445. In 1460, in one corner of the castle, he began the construction of a large square keep, which is 38m (124.6ft) high and has five floors, 13m (43.6ft) long sides, and corner turrets and machicoulis on its battlements. The other three rectangular towers of the old curtain walls date from about 1433. The concrete used in the construction of the castle is made with lime and chalk. It is finished in brick in the Mudejar style. The castle includes a large barbican and concentric walls. The low outer wall built between 1476 and 1483 replaced relatively high, thin walls damaged by artillery several years earlier. The newer walls are lower than the inner curtain, but high enough to protect the base of the walls from cannon fire.[40] A deep, wide moat lowers the profile of the outer walls, further reducing their exposure. The outer wall rise about 20m (65ft) from the bottom of the moat, but only a small proportion of it is above the level of the moat. This wall, which has three-level round towers, includes gun embrasures and casemates for artillery that the thinner walls of the interior curtain walls could not accommodate. The towers house gun casemates on three levels, one of which is above moat level. The tower battlements could mount mortars. The outer walls and towers have galleries at moat level that were used as listening posts to warn against enemy mining and for countermining operations. The entrance has a special barbican to protect against artillery fire. La Mota, Coca and Salses (which is now in France) are some of the best examples of the transition from castle to fortress at the end of the Middle Ages. During the fifteenth century, the La Mota changed hands several times because of disputes. The castle became better known during the next century when Hernando Pizarro and Cesare Borgia were imprisoned there. Cesare Borgia escaped from the tower of homage by using a rope.

In the fifteenth century a powerful Castilian nobleman built Coca Castle, located about 25km (15 miles) south-east of La Mota, near the border of Segovia and Valladolid. Since the region is sandy and lacks stone, it was built with bricks by Mudejar masons in the same style as Medina del Campo. Its layout is Gothic rather than Islamic. The outer walls have polygonal towers at the corners and semicircular ones between corners. The huge dry moat has a massive brick counterscarp wall, which, like the one at La Mota, was intended for defence against artillery. The main walls have polygonal and round towers and supposedly, all the walls are about 2.5m (8.2ft) thick. Coca represents the epitome of brick military architecture.

View of city walls of Ávila built between the eleventh and fourteenth centuries.

18th century plan

Medina del Campo

1806 plan

La Mota at Medina del Campo with inner walls from the thirteenth century. The castle was rebuilt and extended in the 1440s in Mudéjar style. Top: eighteenth-century plan showing Castillo and the medieval city walls. Photo of La Mota showing ('C') a fausse-braye built as protection against cannon fire and ('B') the original interior walls.

1. Keep
2. Courtyard
3. Dry Moat
4. Buildings

Coca Castle, built in the last half of the fifteenth century as a brick castle with walls up to 2.5m (8.2ft) thick. It is considered one of the best examples of Mudéjar style with concentric walls. The castle was put under siege in 1521.

Torrelobatón ←---

↑ Medina del Campo

Torrelobatón ←---

↑ Medina del Campo

Fuensaldaña ←---

Fifteenth-century castles of Valladolid built on older castles. Torrelobatón has a square plan with three towers and a keep and archery loops and cannon ports. It once had an outer wall with eight towers. La Mota (Medina del Campo) rebuilt in the fifteenth century with an added outer wall, or fausse-braye, and positions for gunpowder weapons. Lower photo shows its 38m (124.6ft) high, five-floor square Tower of Homage. Fuensaldaña has four round corner towers and a large rectangular keep. The castle has been rebuilt and may have had an outer wall.

These castles are attributed to the School of Valladolid, which developed under King Enrique IV of Castile during the mid-fifteenth century. The castles of the School of Valladolid are characterized by a square enceinte that includes three corner towers, a large keep whose height is at least double the height of curtain walls, elaborate bartizan turrets and machicolations on the battlements of the keep and curtains that are often more decorative than functional. After the advent of artillery, most of these castles became palatial residences for status-seeking families. However, some were adapted to artillery.

Barcelona City Wall

1480 Clavero Tower
at Salamanaca

Montealagre

Watch Tower near
Almeria

Spanish fortifications: Barcelona city wall at the thirteenth to sixteenth-century shipyard. Fifteenth-century Clavero Tower of Salamanca, thirteenth-century castle of Montealagre, and typical watchtower found throughout Iberia.

Sax Castle: Top: View of the Moorish castle of Sax built in the tenth century on a limestone outcrop 500m (1,640ft) above sea level and overlooking the town. Main works from the twelfth-century Almohad period with a single-storey stone tower on the north end that was taken from Muslims by James I of Aragon in 1239. Early in the fourteenth century, to the south-west of the Moorish tower, Castilians built the 20m (65.6ft) high great keep of stone with three floors and barrel vault ceilings in the Gothic style. Center: Fifteenth-century swords. Bottom: two views of the Sax Gothic-era keep looking from the south along the ridge.

Ampudia Castle built in the thirteenth century, and heavily modified in the fifteenth century, has a trapezoidal plan and four square corner towers (one was demolished and the largest is the 63m [206.6ft] high keep). A barbican-like feature with cylindrical towers protects half the castle. The castle was captured in 1521 in a revolt against Carlos I. It was used in films including El Cid. *Inset: Statue of El Cid at Burgos.*

Chapter Two

The End of the Age of Castles, Part I

Fourteenth-Century Evolution

In general, castles did not serve as private residences for the nobility in Iberia. Instead, they fulfilled specific military functions such as providing security for urban areas and/or protecting their approaches. Late in the Middle Ages, however, castles became a status symbol for the lesser Spanish nobility. In contrast, in France and England in the High Middle Ages, castles tended to develop as residences of noble families and did not necessarily provide security for a town. They were an expression of the classical feudal system and differed in that respect from the Iberian castles. Whereas in Iberia the king often built or took ownership of castles and made them 'Royal' property to exert his control, in France and England powerful noblemen built them to extend control over their neighbours and even to challenge their monarchs. While Iberian castles served as outposts to protect the frontier and secure royal territorial gains, English and French castles were used in private wars, which resulted in many sieges that involved far fewer troops than similar sieges in the Peninsula. However, Edward I used castles the way the Spanish did in his conquest of Wales. The Hundred Years War between France and England, which began in the mid-fourteenth century, was a departure from previous conflicts in which Richard I and John had fought the French king to maintain lands they theoretically held as vassals of him. Those wars had usually resulted in sieges where the objective was the castle and the lands it dominated. During the Hundred Years War, large armies occasionally engaged each other and cities became the main objectives, like during the Reconquista in Spain.[1] In France, many cities like Carcassonne had maintained and improved their ancient city walls. Some urban areas had allowed their Gallo-Roman walls to decay or quarried them for stone for other structures although the foundations remained. The situation was slightly better in England where feudalism took a different form than in France and where many cities and towns had defences especially after the arrival of the Vikings.

Philippe Augustus began encircling Paris with a wall in 1190. The work began on the Right Bank of the Seine between 1190 and 1209 and continued on the Left Bank between 1200 and 1215. Philippe's wall rose to a height of 6m to 8m (19.6ft to 26.2ft) and was about 3m (9.8ft) thick. It consisted of the traditional rubble and mortar core with ashlar of limestone blocks facings on both sides. It had seventy-seven semicircular towers projecting from the walls at intervals of about 60m (197ft).

At a height of 15m (49ft), the towers rose above the wall and had a diameter of 6m (19.6ft) and walls 1m (3.3ft) thick. A large tower 10m (32.8ft) in diameter and 25m (82ft) high stood at each of the points where the wall reached the Seine (two points on each bank). Chains could be strung across the river between each pair of towers. Fifteen large gates and a number of posterns pierced the wall,[2] which covered about 2,600m (2,834 yds) on the Right Bank and 2,500m (2,725 yds) on the Left Bank.[3]

The Louvre Castle, completed in 1202, reinforced the defences on the right bank at a point most vulnerable to English attack and served as a fortress. It was almost square with sides from 72m to 78m (236.2ft to 255.8ft) in length, and 2.5m (8.2ft) thick and a round tower at each corner. There was an additional tower between the corner towers on the north and west walls and pairs of towers flanked gates on the south and east walls. The Great Tower, which stood slightly off centre in the courtyard, was a large cylindrical keep with a diameter of 15m (49ft), and 4m (13ft) thick walls that reached a height of 30m (98ft). It had its own deep, dry moat. Accommodations and facilities were built into the south and west walls. In the late fourteenth century, Charles V (reigned 1364–80) added similar facilities into the other two walls. The castle was levelled in the sixteenth century to make way for the present palace.

Another citadel outside Philippe's walls was the Temple, a fortified Templar monastery, built in the late twelfth century. In the 1190s, the Templars drained a marshy area outside the city to build the Temple, with a square tower known as Caesar's Tower 10m (32.8ft) wide with three floors and battlements. Other structures, including a hospital, dormitories, kitchens, religious buildings, etc. and a second donjon, the Temple Tower – similar to Caesar's but with an additional floor and four corner towers – were added during the thirteenth century. The wall of this complex had over a dozen towers and bartizans with a heavily-defended gatehouse. In 1312, after Philippe IV, seeking their wealth, disbanded and persecuted the Templars, then turned the site over to the Hospitallers.

In 1356, when his father King Jean was captured in the battle of Poitiers, the Dauphin – soon to be Charles V – began making changes to the walls. At the time, Philippe II's wall was in poor condition and masked by homes that had sprung up outside over the years. Étienne Marcel, the provost of Parisian merchants, ordered ditches to be excavated to improve the position. Charles initiated a new 6km (3.72-mile) long wall built on the Right Bank late in the century and had the old wall on the Left Bank reinforced. He added a moat and installed a system of locks to fill parts of the moat with water. He added conical roofs to the towers and reinforced the gates with barbicans. Some parts of the allure, already 2m (6.6ft) wide, were adapted for artillery. Since the Louvre ended up inside the new wall, he turned the fortress into a palace. Philippe Augustus had used its Great Donjon for a treasury and archives. Work on Charles' new wall took several decades. By 1420, under the reign of Charles VI, the wall was completed and like with the Louvre, it brought the Temple within the enceinte. In April 1370, work began on the famous Bastille.

The Louvre: Top: Etching showing Philippe's Wall; Bottom left: Drawing of the Louvre as a castle by Viollet-le-Duc 1856. Right: A fifteenth-century illuminated manuscript showing the Louvre from the Très Riches Heures du duc Berry.

Paris Fortified

At the time of the Viking raids, the bridges of Paris had formed the main line of defence even though there were some defences on the Ile de la Cité. During the early eleventh century, King Robert II built a palace on the western third of the island. It formed a rectangle 110m by 135m (360.8ft by 442.5ft) and included a great hall, residential and administrative structures associated with a palace, a wall, towers and a 25m (82ft) high keep for the protection of the royal treasure.

During the High Middle Ages, the majority of the estimated 50,000 Parisians lived on the right bank. In 1162, Louis VII launched a period of construction on the island that gave Paris its greatest landmark, the Cathedral of Notre Dame. Philippe II, who ascended to the throne in 1180, ordered the construction of a stone wall for Paris before he went on the Third Crusade in 1190. Philippe's wall, which was finished in 1212, enclosed some sparsely occupied areas to allow for future growth. By this time, the population of Paris had reached about 80,000 souls.

The walls averaged about 3m (9.8ft) in thickness (thicker at the base), were 8m to 10m (26.2ft to 32.8ft) high, and had cylindrical towers with arrow loops for crossbowmen at about 50m (164ft) intervals. They ran in a straight line between the towers allowing the crossbowmen to enfilade attackers. Sockets or putlog holes in the walls allowed the defenders to insert beams for hoardings along the wall in time of danger. Surprisingly, there was no moat even though it was the most common form of defence in lowlands. A dozen gates allowed entry into the city, but it is not known exactly what they included beside a double-towered gatehouse. They may not have had drawbridges since there was no moat.

At the four points where the walls reached the Seine, large towers controlled river traffic. The two main bridges dating back to the Viking attacks in the ninth century had their two end towers as well. In 1130, Louis VI rebuilt the Grand Châtelet on the Right Bank in stone. The structure continued to undergo improvements even though it lost its importance when the enceinte was completed. On the left bank, the Petit Châtelet also turned into an impressive fortification that eventually lost its military significance.

In the fourteenth century, after the battle of Poitiers in 1356 during the Hundred Years War, King Jean II became a prisoner.[4] Charles V took the throne in 1364 and decided to extend and improve the city walls, which must have been in poor condition. According to the Froissart Chronicles,[5] the Parisians became alarmed back in 1346 when Edward III advanced along the Seine and crushed the French army at Crécy leaving their city with its long-neglected fortifications exposed.[6] The disaster at Poitiers ten years later left Charles V no choice but to prepare Paris after he took the throne. He had his new set of walls extend the enceinte on the Right Bank, pushing it outward and enclosing the strongholds of the Louvre and the Temple within them. The wall on the right bank also placed new suburbs (faubourgs) behind the defences. Initially, this wall was a simple earthwork with a ditch

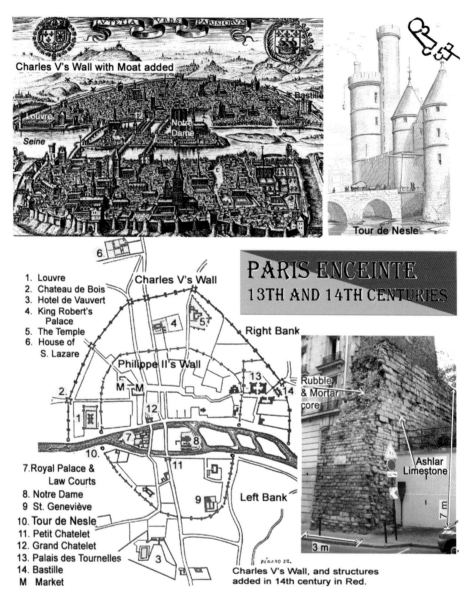

1. Louvre
2. Chateau de Bois
3. Hotel de Vauvert
4. King Robert's
   Palace
5. The Temple
6. House of
   S. Lazare

7. Royal Palace &
   Law Courts
8. Notre Dame
9 St. Geneviève
10. Tour de Nesle
11. Petit Chatelet
12. Grand Chatelet
13. Palais des Tournelles
14. Bastille
M   Market

Charles V's Wall, and structures
added in 14th century in Red.

Paris Enceinte: Top left: Illustration from the 1600s showing Charles V's wall on the Right Bank and improvement of Philippe II's wall on the Left Bank. Right: Tour of Nesle gate on Left Bank with plan of tower in corner from Viollet-le-Duc, 1856. Bottom: Plan of Paris showing both sets of walls and photo of a remaining section of Philippe's Wall showing the rubble-and-mortar core with ashlar facing.

and palisade, but in 1365, Charles began to turn it into a stone wall. The walls were thicker than the old ones ranging from 3m to 6m (9.8ft to 19.6ft) and in some cases were 13m (42.6ft) high. Machicoulis were added to the towers and gatehouses. The crenels were fitted with hinged shutters. In addition to bartizans, échauguettes, and turrets, there were at least sixty (possibly as many as seventy-seven) large and mostly square towers. Barbicans improved the defences of some gateways.[7] An 8m (26.2ft) deep and 20m (65.6ft) wide moat filled with waters from the Seine fed by a system of locks. A smaller, dry, V-shaped ditch in front of the moat completed these defences. The king's Royal Palace, reinforced by several stone towers, occupied the west side of the Ile de Cité. On the Left Bank, Charles added a moat in front of the old walls. The work was completed in 1420 under Charles VI, just in time for a sixteen-year-long English occupation.

The growing bourgeoisie of the city formed a militia to augment the small number of soldiers manning the wall.[8] Most of the regular troops held the towers and gatehouses. Tax collectors were stationed at the gatehouses since almost all traffic had to pass by them, but this was not the case for the posterns. The Grand Châtelet became the headquarters for the Provost who controlled the police force. The worst disaster Paris faced during the Hundred Years war was the Black Death, which wiped out a large number of Parisians in 1348. The city walls offered no defence against it.

Philippe II ordered the construction of walls for other cities, including Laon, Soissons, and Bourges, but work there was rather limited.[9] Over a hundred years later in 1339, Philippe VI was dismayed by the condition of the defences of many towns. The walls were in poor shape at Noyon and they were still unfinished at Saint-Quentin and Reims. The Roman defences of Reims were largely gone and the enceinte did not amount to much more than earth banks and wooden palisades.[10] After the battles of Crécy and Poitiers spurred the construction of city fortifications, the wall was finished in 1358. Diverse structures ranging from houses to hospitals that lay beyond the enceinte were removed and the nearby countryside was cleared. People from the demolished villages in the 'cordon sanitaire' or barren zone around the city, moved into Reims. The work was completed in 1359, just in time to ward off Edward III who besieged the city at the end of the year. The Reims enceinte covered over 6km (3.72 miles) and had over forty towers, but it was not as impressive as the walls of Paris. Like Paris and other cities, the Black Death of the fourteenth century took a heavy toll. Reims remained in an exposed position and its defences were tested several times during the remainder of the Hundred Years War.[11]

In the aftermath of the Arab invasions and the Albigensian Crusade, the towns in south-west France became more strongly fortified than in northern France. The bastide (fortified town) developed during the crusade to secure the Christians' advances against the Moors. Like the Spanish, the French monarchs established militias in these new towns to protect against English expansion during the Hundred Years War. It is estimated that 500 to 700 bastides were built in France between 1200 and 1400. Along with militias, these new towns provided the king with a new tax base to support the cost of war.

Carcassonne, a wealthy city on a pilgrimage crossroads, is one of the finest and best-preserved medieval walled cities. With an enceinte of a little over 1,670m (1,820 yds), it was not very large, but it was probably one of the best-defended cities in France. In the thirteenth century, it had a single set of largely Gallo-Roman walls. In 1218, after Simon de Montfort died in the siege of Toulouse, his son Amaury was unable to resist Raymond VI of Toulouse and the Count of Foix. In 1223, Amaury left for Paris where he gave Languedoc to King Louis VIII who personally led a crusade against the Cathars and their supporters. Most of the towns in Languedoc quickly surrendered to the king.

The defences of Carcassonne underwent a period of reconstruction and expansion and the viscount's home was given defensive walls that turned it into a castle. As a result, new set of walls encircled the old one, creating concentric walls. Semicircular towers were open at the rear, leaving them exposed to defenders on the inner wall should the outer one fall. The area between the walls, the lists, was levelled by cutting down into the foundation of the old wall, which gave an added height to the wall. However, parts of the Roman foundations were too weak to support the new wall causing several sections to collapse. These had to be rebuilt. The inner walls dominated the outer walls and the heavily defended entrances completed the system. A wall linked the large circular barbican on the Aude to the town. The outer wall included thirteen towers, the barbican on the Aude, the Crémade Barbican on the south side, and the main entrance with the Saint Louis Barbican on the east. The inner wall had twenty-two towers including the towers at the Narbonnaise Gate on the east side and the Saint Nazaire Gate on the south side. Except for the steeply-sloped west side, the outer walls were protected by a wide dry moat. The castle complex consists of a dry moat, a barbican, a gate flanked by two towers, six additional towers, and a keep. In 1262, the people who lived outside the city walls had to set up a new town on flat land across the river. This new city prospered within its own walls until 1355 when the Black Prince put it to the torch during a chevauchée.[12] The town was rebuilt. Carcassonne and the Midi played a lesser role in the Hundred Years War than it had in the previous century (see *Castrum to Castle* for the Albigensian Crusade).

Avignon is located in Provence on the Rhône not far from Nîmes, at the emplacement of a Romans fortified rectangular site dating from the first century. In 1226, after a three-month siege, Avignon surrendered to Louis VIII who levelled part of its old walls and filled its moats. He removed a double set of walls and an inner wall that followed the course of the old Roman wall. Between 1234 and 1237, the citizens built new ramparts 30m to 40m (33 yds to 44 yds) in front of the ruins of the old walls. They also completed a new wall in 1248. Between 1305 and 1403, seven popes and three anti-popes took up residence at Avignon.[13] As was often the case in medieval towns, suburbs grew outside the city walls causing Pope Innocent VI to build a new enceinte in 1355 to enclose them.[14] In 1359, before the new walls were completed, Pope Innocent ordered the repair of the old entrances to serve as a second line of defence. This work took place in the aftermath of the Hundred Years War when roving bands of soldiers from free companies that had been broken up after a 1357 truce plundered the region. In November 1365, Charles V sent Bertrand du Guesclin[15] at the head of 30,000 Crusaders to sweep the bandits from the Rhône valley. In 1369, after a dispute ended the 1360 Treaty of Brétigny, France and England resumed the Hundred Years War and brigands returned to the region.

Carcassonne: Left: Plan, and below a view of Narbonne Gate. Right: Top view of concentric walls looking toward old Roman towers from Treasury Tower. Also view of the moat. Middle: View from Narbonne gate looking down the lists. The inner wall dominates the outer which offers no protection to an attack if captured. Bottom: View of gate between two Roman horseshoe-shaped towers (bottom photo by Pierre Etcheto).

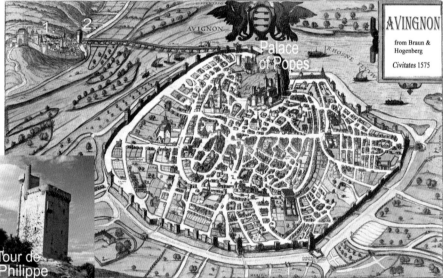

1. St. Andre Fortress   2. Tour de Philippe

*Fortified brick Gothic cathedral of Albi on Tarn River. Construction began in 1287. Avignon: St. André
Fortress and Tower of Philippe IV on the right bank of the Rhône and Avignon on the left bank.*

Pope Innocent's enceinte had a perimeter of 4.33km (2.68 miles) and was 8m
(28.2ft) high. It included seven city gates with drawbridges, thirty-five tall towers,
and fifty medium and small towers. Except for three that were semicircular, all
the towers were square or rectangular and most were open in the rear. In the
fifteenth century, a polygonal tower surrounded by a large 4m (13.1ft) deep moat
filled with waters from the Sorgue and Durance rivers was added to the defences.

Avignon. Top: View of city across the Rhône looking at remains of the old bridge. Top right: Tower and section of wall with machicoulis and below it photo of the towers at the entrance to the city wall. One tower has a turret on it. Bottom right: Back of typical wall tower which was open to the rear. Bottom left: Fortified palace of the Popes.

The old fortified port of Aigues Mortes, one of many small, fortified cities in the area, is occasionally classified as a bastide. It had a 1.6km (1 mile) enceinte built by Louis IX in the thirteenth century. However, by 1300 it ceased to be a seaport when its harbour filled with silt but it remained a trading centre of some importance. Its only claim to fame in the fourteenth century is that its Philippe Constance Tower served to imprison some Templars in 1307. It was occupied by Burgundian troops between 1420 and 1421. Other French ports like Bordeaux on the Bay of Biscay or Calais on the Channel were better fortified than many French cities when the Hundred Years War began.

1 Gatehouse
2 Tower

Fort St. André: Built in the early fourteenth century, its walls enclosed an abbey. It is located on the opposite side of the Rhône from Avignon. 1. The large gatehouse with machicoulis. 2. The only tower in the wall.

The Hundred Years War (1337–1453)

The Hundred Years War was one of the most cataclysmic events in the West. The struggle that pitted England and France against each other threatened to tear France apart. Instead, two strong national states emerged from this conflict to join Spain and Portugal as the leading powers in the West in the fifteenth century. This war not only represented the apogee of the castle but also its decline in the face of the cannon. During this period, knights transitioned from a suit of armour consisting largely of chain mail to the plate armour that we associate with knighthood to this very day.

King Philippe IV, 'the Fair', won control of Flanders and challenged Edward I's control in the south. He stood up to the Church and was instrumental in forcing the Pope to take up residence in Avignon. In 1311, he suppressed the order of the Templars in order to seize their wealth. As his three sons had short reigns and left no male heirs, Philippe VI, a cousin, became the first Valois king in 1328. The new king challenged the English in France and supported their enemy, the Scots. Finally, in 1336, Edward III refused to accept his position as vassal of the French king and declared war the next year claiming his right to the French throne through his French mother, the daughter of Philippe IV. The war lasted over a hundred years, encompassed the reigns of several French and English monarchs. It was punctuated with various truces and outbreaks of the Black Death. Castle building reached its climax during this period. Even though cannons played an insignificant role in the early battles, they helped end the war and the age of the castle in the fifteenth century.

The Hundred Years War was marked by few great battles but numerous sieges as many towns and cities rebuilt their defences or erected new ones. The largest English army during this period numbered only about 10,000 men. The French, on the other hand, mustered three times that number for some of the larger battles. However, their armies were smaller than those participating in the Spanish Reconquista had been. The first major battle of the war was the naval engagement at Sluys in 1340. It was followed in 1342 by a successful English expedition against Brest. A month later in September, 2,400 English soldiers and a number of Bretons attacked the port of Morlaix before they laid siege to it. A French relief force of about 3,000 cavalry and 1,500 Genoese crossbowmen engaged the English. Even though the longbow proved effective against the French, the English had to withdraw. In 1346, Edward III led a campaign that began with the successful siege of Caen – held by over a thousand French troops – and culminated in the battle of Crécy, a month later at the end of August.[16] At Crécy 5,500 English longbowmen, 2,500 men-at-arms, and 1,000 Welsh infantrymen felled about 2,000 French armoured knights from a force of over 25,000.[17] Edward, flush with victory, moved on to Calais where he beat back a French relief force and starved the city into surrender after an eleven-month siege.

The Black Death slowed down the war between 1346 and 1353. Major hostilities resumed in September 1356 when Edward, the Black Prince, spread terror in the region at the head a chevauchée of about 2,000 longbowmen, 3,000 mounted men-at-arms, and 1,000 Gascon infantrymen. King Jean II, with an army of about 8,000 cavalry and 3,000 infantry engaged him at Poitiers. The French suffered another humiliating defeat and their king was captured. The Treaty of Brétigny of 1360 brought almost a decade of peace, ending the first phase of the war. During this period, Bertrand du Guesclin, a Breton knight, led a mercenary force of free companies in 1367 to support Count Enrique de Trastámara against his half-brother, King Pedro the Cruel of Castile. Pedro, on the other hand, got help from Edward, the Black Prince, who came out of Guyenne with his own army of mercenaries. Pedro and his ally came out victorious after the clash at the battle at Nájera, but the Black Prince contracted dysentery and returned to England. Du Guesclin and Enrique cornered Pedro at the fortress of Montiel in 1369. After Du Guesclin lured Pedro into a trap, Enrique stabbed his half-brother multiple times and claimed the throne of Castile. Prince Edward never fully recovered after his Spanish expedition, but one of his last major actions was the siege of Limoges in August 1370. His troops took the city by storm even though their leader was virtually bedridden.

Additional small engagements and sieges took place in the 1370s. In June 1372, an English relief convoy was trapped at the English-held port of La Rochelle. Du Guesclin placed the city under siege and the mayor tricked the English commander into surrendering. When they were faced with English raids, the French withdrew into fortified towns and denied the enemy supplies and battle. The Black Prince, who had never recovered from his bout of dysentery, died in 1376. When his father, Edward III, died the next year, the war slowed once more as England fell into turmoil. During the 1381 Peasant Revolt, the 14-year-old Richard II was trapped in the Tower of London, but managed to ride out past the mob that was after his hated advisors whom it killed after it stormed the Tower. Richard ruthlessly crushed the revolt and became a tyrant. Except for Calais and a strip of coastline on the Bay of Biscay, the English crown lost most of its holdings in France. The new French king, Charles VI 'the Mad' was not much better a monarch than Richard II. Henry IV of Lancaster forced Richard from the throne in 1399, but had to face rebellions at home, the most serious of which was led by the Welsh Owain Glyndwr in 1400.[18] By 1404, Owain, who operated out of Harlech Castle, left only a few Welsh castles under English control. In 1405, he contracted a treaty with the French who launched an invasion of Aquitaine and sent troops to Wales. In 1407, Henry began to regain the upper hand in Wales when Aberystwyth castle surrendered followed by Harlech in 1409. Owain was reduced to leading raids and disappeared in 1412. Henry V, who ascended to the throne in 1413, finally brought peace to Wales in 1415. Meanwhile in France, the Dukes of Orléans and Burgundy vied with each other to run the government of their incompetent king. The struggle culminated in the assassination of the Duke of Orleans in 1407, which led to a civil war that Henry V of England fully intended to exploit.[19]

Henry V renewed the Hundred Years War in 1415 by landing in Normandy, putting the port of Harfleur under siege, and taking it after five weeks. He marched on Calais with about 6,000 troops (about 5,000 longbowmen and 750 men-at-arms). On the way, he engaged the French in at Agincourt where he faced about 30,000 French troops (3,000 crossbowmen, 7,000 knights, and 15,000 dismounted men-at-arms).[20] The battle was a repeat of Crécy, another decisive English victory. In 1417, Henry landed in Normandy once again intending to take the whole province. He stormed Caen on 4 September and forced the city's castle to surrender on 20 September. In July 1418, he laid siege to Rouen, which capitulated in January of 1419. That month the Armagnacs assassinated Jean I, Duke of Burgundy, which led the Burgundians to ally themselves to the English. The Burgundians allowed Henry to take Paris and act as Charles VI's regent as the Treaty of Troyes of 1420 temporarily ended the war.[21]

When Henry VI succeeded to the throne at the age of nine months in 1422, the Duke of Bedford assumed the regency and campaigned against the Armagnacs. In 1424, he defeated the Dauphin's army at Verneuil[22] and drove the Armagnacs back to the Loire. He put Orléans under siege in 1428 while the Dauphin cowered in the castle of Chinon. In 1429, Joan of Arc went to Chinon to urge the King to resist. She was sent with a relief force to Orléans, an event that marked a turning point in the war.[23] She led Charles VII to Reims where he was crowned, but she was captured by the English and burned at the stake on 30 May 1431. The Duke of Burgundy broke with the English in 1435 and joined Charles VII. The year of 1444 saw a new truce, but in 1449 the English attacked and plundered Fougères from their base in Normandy and the war was renewed. The French army reorganized and established a well-armed artillery corps that reduced dozens of English-held castles and broke England's hold over Normandy in 1450 at the battle of Formigny. The next year, the French took Gascony, which led an English army under John Talbot to recapture Bordeaux in 1452. The next year Talbot was defeated at Castillon and retook Bordeaux. When the war ended in 1453, only Calais remained in English hands.

Fortifications and the Hundred Years War

When the Hundred Years War began, the English held a coastal strip of western France that ran from La Rochelle to the Pyrenees, in most of the province of Guyenne.[24] The English constable resided at Bordeaux, a city of about 30,000 souls, similar in size to London. In contrast, Scotland's largest city, Edinburgh, had only 4,000 inhabitants. The economy of Guyenne was closely linked to England with exports of French wine and imports of English wool. In 1337, King Philippe VI reclaimed Guyenne from King Edward III. In 1339, the French army took Blaye, posing a threat to Bordeaux's sea trade; in 1340, they recaptured La Réole and moved towards Bordeaux. Meanwhile, the English gained a foothold in Flanders, while the French launched seaborne raids on English ports. In 1339, Edward resorted to chevauchées to weaken his enemy. The naval battle of Sluys in June 1340 gave the English a victory in the first major naval battle of the war, but did not prevent the French from raiding the English coast. Edward's army of 6,000 English and Flemish troops laid siege to Tournai in July. Edward decided to starve the city into submission, but he lifted the siege after the truce of September 1345. Problems had developed in Scotland after he invaded it in 1333 and occupied Edinburgh Castle in 1335. The Scots, supported by the French, revolted and recaptured Edinburgh Castle by trickery, slaughtering the hundred-man English garrison in 1341. They launched a chevauchée against northern England in 1345. Thus, while Edward used Flanders and Tournai to divert the French from Guyenne, the French used the Scots in a similar manner. In addition, Jean de Montfort and Charles de Blois fought over the succession the duchy of Brittany. After Montfort aligned himself with him and paid him homage, Edward sent an expedition of about 5,000 men in 1342. A few battles ensued and the English faction besieged and captured various cities, including Brest, Dinan, Vannes, and Rennes. In June 1344, Henry of Lancaster, Earl of Derby landed at Bayonne, mustered an English army of 900 men-at-arms and 2,000 archers, swept away the French forces that were threatening Bordeaux and captured many castles and towns.

At first glance, the Hundred Years War seemed to be a typical medieval war fought in a traditional manner, with few field battles, and sieges, small and large, estimated in the hundreds. As was often the case in the Middle Ages, actual combat was not continuous, but the devastation was still massive, especially when chevauchées were involved. Civilians and soldiers were fair game and chivalry existed only in the courts of love. However, significant changes were taking place as well. For instance, the monarchs could no longer call upon their vassals to provide the needed soldiers. Armies required large units that could move beyond their own regions. Men-at-arms and specialized mercenaries such as Genoese crossbowmen required cash payment. Troops had to be fed and specialists such as archers and crossbowmen often had to be provided with supplies. Except for raiding expeditions, armies needed large logistic tails of wagons and or/carts to sustain their movements. For the English the problem was compounded by the fact that they had to transport supplies and men to France by sea.[25] All this cost vast sums of money, which went far beyond feudal obligations. Taxes on certain products had to be increased and other methods had to be devised to raise funds. Some monarchs even resorted to selling the crown jewels. Economy and trade were important for both France and England since they brought prosperity that the crown could tax. Strategy became multi-dimensional more than ever before. Thus, the sale of English wool to Flanders made this region an economic target for the French. In addition, cannons started to appear in engagements as early as 1345, but until late in the century, they still fired stone shot. They were not reliable weapons, but were expensive, even more so when cast-iron shot came into use. Although clashes continued to be seasonal during the Hundred Years War, sieges could be year-round operations during which the besieged and their tormentors often suffered from food shortages, disease, and atmospheric conditions. This war was often punctuated with armistices as both sides became exhausted and needed a break.

War in Brittany: Succession and Sieges

Brittany became an area of contention between the English and the French when John III, duke of Brittany died in April 1341 without a male heir. John de Montfort, the son of John's half-brother, claimed the title. However, his niece, Joan of Penthièvre, who had married Charles, Count of Blois and nephew of the French king, claimed the title as well. There ensued a 25-year struggle for the right of succession to Brittany. John seized Nantes and most of Brittany and sought the support of Edward III of England. Meanwhile, the Count of Blois captured over two dozen of John's soldiers, beheaded them, and catapulted their heads into Nantes. The terrified citizens surrendered. John was taken to the Louvre where he was imprisoned for four years.

Charles took control of most of the duchy and besieged Joan of Flanders, who was leading the resistance, at Hennebont, a town between Vannes and Quimper. In March 1342, Edward III sent Sir Walter Manny to raise the siege, but the sea trip lasted until May. Manny broke into the city and the next day, he captured and destroyed Charles' catapult, which was bombarding the city. In August 1342, the Earl of Northampton and about 3,000 men landed near Brest and forced Charles to lift the siege of Hennebont. In September, the English advanced on Morlaix, which they failed to take and decided to lay under siege. A French army, which heavily outnumbered Northampton's troops, came to the rescue of Morlaix. On 30 September, the two forces clashed at Morlaix; the French failed to break the English lines, and retreated to lay a new siege of Hennebont. The newly-reinforced walls of the city held out against the eighteen large siege engines and Charles withdrew to Nantes for the winter.

While the siege of Morlaix continued, Edward III landed at Brest at the head of a large force on 30 October 1342. After Morlaix fell, an English force of about 5,000 men sailed around the peninsula and landed near Vannes, which it laid siege to. Despite its unimpressive walls, the city held a very defensible position. The English archers cleared the enemy from the battlements at the beginning of the attack, but subsequent charges against the walls throughout the day failed. When night fell, a group of soldiers climbed a section of wall with scaling ladders at a point where the defenders had been pulled back to hold the gates. Once inside the town, they rushed to take down the guards at two of the three city entrances and threw open the gates. A small English garrison remained at Vannes while the rest of army marched out in search of the enemy. Before long, the small English force ran into a much larger French army and had to retreat to Vannes where the townspeople had risen against the garrison and driven it out. The small English army had no recourse but to fight its way to Hennebont.

Before long, Edward III launched a winter campaign across the peninsula with two columns. On 25 November 1342, he laid siege to Vannes at the head of the southern column. At the end of November, he detached a smaller force to besiege Nantes. In December, Northampton's troops placed Rennes under siege while a smaller force headed north to Dinan where it was turned back. After mustering a large army at the fortress of Angers, King Philippe VI forced Edward to lift the sieges of Nantes and Rennes and concentrated on Vannes where he employed every possible method to breach the defences. Meanwhile, in late December, the French army trapped Edward in his siege lines before Vannes. However, before the fighting started, envoys of Pope Clement VI intervened negotiating a three-year truce that allowed both sides to maintain their positions in Brittany and declared the neutrality of Vannes. Edward sailed for England in February 1343.

In May 1345, John de Montfort escaped to England, swore homage to Edward, and returned to Brittany with another English army. He marched across Brittany in one week stopping just short of Rennes, when the Count of Blois captured Quimper. Montfort quickly returned and put Quimper under siege until Blois was able to relieve it. Montfort died on 26 September 1346 at Hennebont. Northampton took Roche-Derrien in November after a three-day siege, giving the English a foothold in Brittany. Early in 1346, Sir Thomas Dagworth met and defeated a French army near Ploërmel. In June 1347, after the Crécy Campaign, Charles returned to besiege the town of Roche-Derrien. He built a large siege camp and bombarded the town with nine catapults, one of which hurled 140kg (300lb) stones. The siege went on for three weeks before Dagworth managed to organize a relief force of fewer than a thousand men and launched a surprise attack on the French siege camp at night. Heavily outnumbered, Dagworth's force was near defeat when the garrison sallied from the town, struck the French from the rear, and put them to flight. The victory went to Sir Thomas, whose men captured Charles of Blois and sent him to the Tower of London. Meanwhile, in Flanders, the English siege of Calais ended one year after the victory at Crécy.

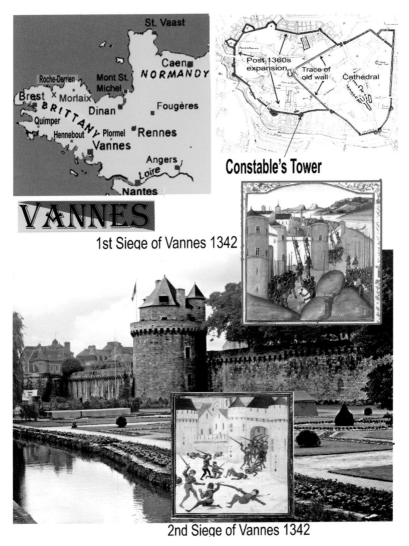

Map of Brittany. Photo: Constable Tower at Vannes, built after the 1360s. Plan of Vannes and medieval drawings of two sieges of Vannes in 1342. Painting of siege by Jean de Wavrin, a fifteenth-century Burgundian soldier, politician, and chronicler.

Solidor and Combourg. Top: Château Solidor built by John V, Duke of Brittany, between 1369 and 1382 to control the mouth of the Rance River by St. Malô. Bottom: The twelfth-century Château Combourg with inset showing Combourg after centuries of modification. It was owned by the du Guesclin family and was eventually bought by the writer René-Augustus de Chateaubriand.

One of the most interesting sieges took place early in the war at Réole, south-east of Bordeaux in Guyenne. France had ceded the town of Réole and its castle[26] to England in 1325 after a short war. In October of 1345, the Earl of Derby and Sir Walter Manny surrounded the town and launched daily assaults on it. According to Froissart, the English built two three-level belfries mounted on four large wheels with fireproof cover on the sides, a relatively standard procedure on most siege machines. Each belfry – claimed Froissart – included 300 shooting positions and held 100 archers, which is probably an exaggeration. The Englishmen filled in the 'dikes' in their path and hauled the belfries to the walls. Meanwhile, 200 men with pickaxes tried to undermine the walls. After one month, the burgers opened the gates and the French garrison took refuge in the castle that their captain, Sir Agot des Baux, had prepared for a siege with large quantities of food and wine. Derby laid siege to the castle, bombarding its walls day and night with his artillery. However, when the walls proved too strong, Derby called in his miners who, after eleven weeks of tunnelling, reached the base of the keep, but were unable to penetrate the hard rock. Sir Argot, realizing the end was near, accepted terms of surrender and the English allowed him and his men to leave for Toulouse. Derby continued to take castles and towns, culminating with the capture of Angoulême. He ended the campaign by wintering at Bordeaux.[27]

In 1345, Edward III landed at St. Vaast in Normandy and left a trail of devastation through one town after another between Barfleur and St-Lô, but he failed to take the citadel of Cherbourg. On 26 July, he came before Caen, a city of over 8,000 inhabitants and the second largest in Normandy. Its castle, one of the most formidable in Normandy, was connected to the walled Old Town. The New Town, the wealthiest part of the city, which was on the Île St. Jean and had no walls, was linked to the Old Town with a fortified bridge.

The castle of Caen, with curtain walls erected between 1060 and 1080, dates from the period of William the Conqueror who built a palace, a church, and a town on a low rocky limestone plateau commanding the lower Orne River Valley. He also built a dam to divert waters from the river and turn St. Jean into an island. Henry I built a large keep in the northern corner and an exchequer and other structures in William's palace area. This castle served as a residence and palace for the dukes of Normandy and construction continued on it until the end of the twelfth century. William and his successors used it as a second capital for Normandy. Under the first Plantagenets, the castle became mostly a residential and administrative centre losing its military role. When Edward III arrived in 1346, the old entrance on the north side had been reduced in size and major changes had taken place under Philippe Augustus who had taken Caen from King John of England in 1204 without a fight. Philippe created the citadel by building a curtain wall with four circular towers and a deep ditch around the keep. The enceinte was probably a wooden palisade at first.

It received eleven simple rectangular stone towers late in the twelfth century. Philippe added a round tower and two heavily fortified entrances: the Porte des Champs in the east and the southern entrance. In the fifteenth century, a second round tower designed for cannons was built in the south-east corner. In the first half of the fifteenth century, barbicans were placed in front of each of these gatehouses. Before Edward III landed in Normandy, the locals had built a wooden palisade along the river, which turned out to be ineffective against the English.

Raoul of Brienne, the Constable of France, had possibly up to 1,500 soldiers under his command, but his force was heavily outnumbered by Edward's contingent. The Constable thought to hold the town walls – claims Froissart – but the townspeople decided to meet the enemy in the field instead. Once they clapped eyes on the overwhelming English army, however, they fled back into the city. The Constable tried to hold a tower gate at the bridge, but it was too late as the Englishmen overwhelmed the defenders, slaughtered the hapless burghers, and captured the Constable and other French noblemen. Edward and his men pillaged Caen for five days before moving out. However, he failed to capture the castle, which was held by about 200 men-at-arms and 100 Genoese crossbowmen.

After the English departed in 1346, the people of Caen replaced the wooden palisades with stone walls and added another entrance on the south side of the wall, square shaped barbicans with round corner towers to the Porte des Champs, and a bridge leading to the main gate. They also cut a deep moat into the rock in front of the outer enclosure, which had over a dozen rectangular and round towers. The Old Town city walls connected to this enclosure, but the Porte des Champs and the northern part were outside city's enceinte. The new walls were up to 2m (6.6ft) thick and included thirty-two square and round flanking towers with artillery positions. At this time, the Leroy Tower was built on the left bank of the river and the Landais Tower on the right. A chain extended between them to bar the river to enemy ships. The Leroy Tower has three levels and battlements on the roof. An external staircase connected it to the city wall. Like the other towers, it was built of local Caen limestone. All this work took place between 1346 and 1363.

Edward moved on from Caen and eventually met and defeated the French army at Crécy on 26 August. Next, he put under siege the port of Calais, which was surrounded by a wall and a moat. Calais' plan was almost rectangular with two sides measuring over 1,000m (1,090 yds) and the other two over 300m (37 yds). The walls included several semicircular or rectangular towers and a large circular tower in the north-east corner. They were built by Count Philippe Hurepel, son of Philippe Augustus, who also erected a castle in the north-west part of the town in 1229. The castle was laid out in a square, about 100m by 100m (328ft by 328ft). It included thick curtain walls with six cylindrical towers, a large circular keep with a chemise, a gatehouse, and a wet moat.[28] When Edward III approached Calais the walls and the castle were about a century old, but there is no good account of their condition at the time. Both Peter Reid, author of *Medieval Warfare,* and Jim Bradbury, author of *The Medieval Siege*, claim that there was a single moat on the coast side and a double moat on the other sides. If the double moat was added after the construction of the walls in the thirteenth century, the defences probably were in good repair.[29] Dunes around the city and marshes beyond them presented difficult terrain for the attackers. Inside the walls, the 39m (128ft) high Tour du Guêt (Lookout Tower) built with Hurepel stood out in particular.

After the battle of Crécy, Edward III could have marched on Paris instead of Calais, as Alfred Burne observes in *The Crécy War*. However, this move would have put him at a disadvantage for several reasons. In the first place, the defences of Paris were still too formidable for an army without heavy siege equipment. After Crécy, Edward's army was deep in enemy territory and badly in need of replenishment. In the second place, Calais was a port close to home where he could expect support from his navy despite being challenged by the French fleet. Thus, during the first week of September, a victorious but tired English army marched north, looting and burning towns on its way. By the time the English army reached Calais, the French commander, Jean de Vienne, had prepared the city for a long siege. At the beginning of the siege, Edward ordered his carpenters to build bastides between the town and the river.[30] In addition, he set up a large town for his forces so they could to rest and carry out a normal routine behind the front lines. Finally, he surrounded Calais on all landward sides.

In October, while Edward was preparing the siege, King David II of Scotland – the ally of Philippe VI – invaded England. On 17 October 1346, an English army half the size of David's defeated and captured him at Neville's Cross. Now Edward had a free hand. As the siege dragged on, the English received reinforcements from the beaches west of the town, and evacuated some troops that had served their time. According to some sources, Edward's army grew from 10,000 to over 30,000 men. However, it may have not been possible to logistically maintain such a large force. The French expelled several hundred poor citizens from Calais in order to conserve their rations and Edward fed them and let them pass. Since the marshy ground precluded mining operations, Edward attacked in November after a convoy reached the French and once again in February, but both efforts failed. After two more supply convoys got through, Edward cleared the French from the sand spit north of the harbour and ordered his men to build a wooden fort dubbed Lancaster's Tower, which he garrisoned with archers. He also installed cannons and catapults to prevent additional French ships from reaching the beleaguered town. The siege continued into the summer when Jean de Vienne expelled several hundred more people – mostly elderly, sick, and children – from of the city. This time, Edward did not let them pass and forced them to stay between the lines until they died.

That summer, King Philippe assembled a new army and went on the march despite diversions from King Edward's Flemish allies. The French army failed to capture the heavily defended bridge over the Hem River west of Calais, and thus could not break the siege. On the first week of August 1347, Jean de Vienne surrendered notifying the defenders from the Tour de Guêt. Edward fed the burghers before he forced them to leave the city and Calais became English.

When the Black Death struck both England and France in 1348, a new truce was called and there was a several-year lull in the war until the epidemic ebbed. During this time, King Philippe VI died in 1350 and his son Jean succeeded him. Before long, the English launched a chevauchée, burning down hundreds of villages and towns. The next decisive action took place in 1356 during the Great Chevauchée of the Black Prince, which ended with the battle of Poitiers, when King Jean was captured.[31] The Dauphin,[32] the future Charles V, improved the defences of Paris while he put down the peasant revolts in northern France known as Jacqueries, and tried to control the free companies that had begun to ravage Burgundy, Languedoc, and other areas. Edward III led his last major incursion, driving on Reims only to find its defences too strong to storm. He had to settle for an unsuccessful siege while his raiders ranged as far as the outskirts of Paris.[33] After seven weeks, when foraging to support his army became increasingly difficult, Edward raised the siege and withdrew, leaving a path of destruction behind him. The two kings signed the Treaty of Brétigny in October 1360 ending the first phase of the war. Jean died in 1364. His successor, Charles V, 'the Wise', created a regular French army paid by the Crown, putting an end to the free companies. Jean de Vienne led the French navy's first assaults on the English coast while the king managed to recapture most of the territory lost to the English by the treaty. The Constable of France, Bertrand du Guesclin, recaptured the key port of La Rochelle and much of the land lost to the English by the treaty.

Once a mere fishing village, La Rochelle had become a seaport under Eleanor of Aquitaine in the twelfth century. At this time, the town acquired defensive walls and Henry II's Vauclair Castle, which had four large corner towers and high walls. Louis VIII took the port from the English in 1224, and the English reclaimed it with the Treaty of Brétigny in 1360. The seaward side of the port included three towers. The oldest, the Lantern Tower, which dated to the twelfth century, controlled shipping entering the port and served as a landmark for navigation.[34] Two towers were erected at the entrance to the port during the Hundred Years War. The St. Nicholas Tower was built between 1345 and 1376. It required wooden piles since it stood on marshy land. It was 36m (118ft) high and had four levels. It served as a luxurious residence with fireplaces, latrines and galleries in the walls. It was not yet completed in 1372 when Constable du

Guesclin pushed the English from the region, took the mayor of the town, and tricked the English commander into surrendering. Shortly after the fall of La Rochelle, Charles V ordered Vauclair Castle levelled, which made St. Nicholas Tower the dominant feature of La Rochelle. Between 1382 and 1390, the French built the Chain Tower across from the St. Nicholas Tower to form a gateway into the port, which was barred by a huge chain between the two towers.[35]

After his death in 1380, Charles V was succeeded by his son Charles VI, 'the Mad.' The new king outlived his English rival, Richard II, who had ascended to the throne in 1377, and matched his disastrous reign. The pace of the war slowed until the next century when Henry V of England decided to go after his weak rival.

Map of the Hundred Years War, fourteenth century.

Porte des Champs

Curtain Wall

Tour Leroy

Chateau

Old Town

Isle Saint Jean

Porte du Chateau

Orne

Chateau

English assault of 1346

Caen: Top left: Champs Gate. Top middle: South-east Curtain. Middle: Barbican of Porte du Chateau and Leroy Tower near river on town wall. Bottom left: Old sketch of the château. Bottom right: Illustration from Froissart's Chronicles *of the siege of Caen.*

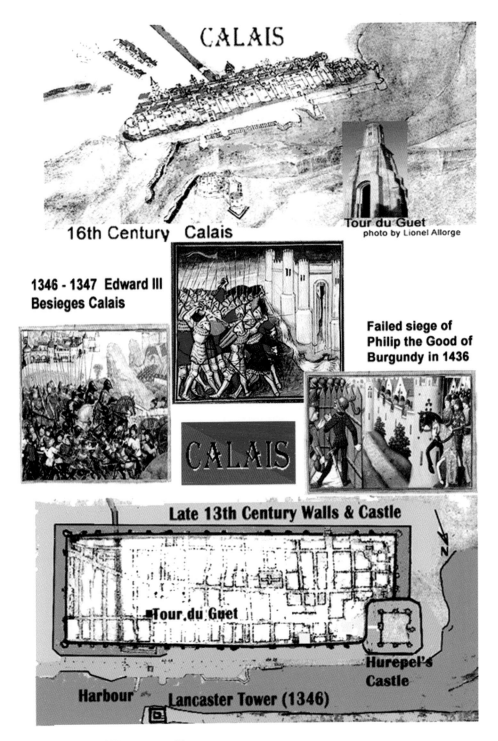

CALAIS

16th Century Calais

Tour du Guet
photo by Lionel Allorge

1346 - 1347 Edward III
Besieges Calais

Failed siege of
Philip the Good of
Burgundy in 1436

CALAIS

Late 13th Century Walls & Castle

N

Tour du Guet

Hurepel's
Castle

Harbour   Lancaster Tower (1346)

Calais in the twelfth century and later.

A. Lantern Tower   B. Chain Tower   C. St. Nicholas Tower

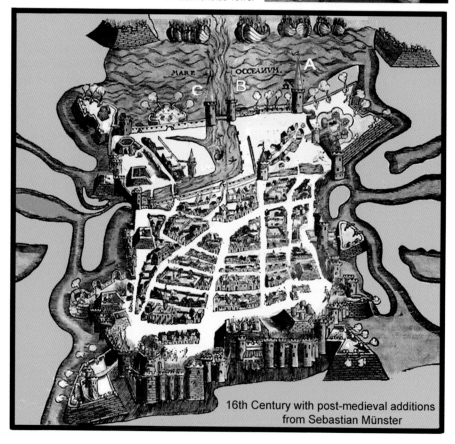

La Rochelle: Plan of La Rochelle and photographs of three surviving towers on the coastal side covering the harbour.

Vincennes

The future King Charles V ordered the Provost of Merchants, Étienne Marcel, to improve the defences of Paris while his father, King Jean, was an English hostage. However, in 1358, Marcel led a revolt closed the city to the outside world, broke into the Dauphin's palace and threatened Charles. This spurred him into finishing the work already begun at Vincennes outside Paris where he could be secure from another mob. He built the Bastille as a refuge from Paris and Vincennes as a second 'safe house' outside the city. A royal manor house, Vincennes began in the

Vincennes. Top: Two views of the château of Vincennes. Bottom: The outer walls and plan of the site. The 52m (170.5ft) high keep is supposed to be the tallest in Europe.

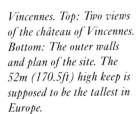

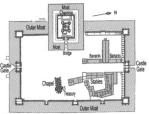

twelfth century as a hunting lodge. Philippe VI began the construction of a large donjon near the manor in 1337. Charles V completed the work of turning it into a fortress in 1380. Philippe VI had envisaged an independent citadel like the one of Aigues-Mortes, which explains why the new donjon is separate from the manor and has a large enclosing wall. Charles V was born at Vincennes the same year the work began. When he was crowned in 1364, the donjon had three levels. Work continued until it became six storeys and 52m (170.5ft) high in 1369. It acquired its own enceinte (or chemise) in 1373. The gatehouse included standard features such as drawbridges, portcullis, and machicoulis. A large rectangular enceinte 175m by 334m (190.5 yds by 364 yds) and 15m (49.2ft) high enclosed the old manor and connected to the smaller enceinte of the keep. Completed in 1380, it included four flanking towers at the corners and three gatehouses, each with about 42m (137.8ft) high and 3m (9.8ft) thick walls. The roofs of the towers accommodated mangonels and trebuchets. Two smaller flanking towers occupied a position on the east wall opposite the castle between the gate and corner towers. All the towers had both interior and grill covered exterior windows, a common feature in the fourteenth century, especially since the living quarters were on the lower stories and needed light. The 22m to 28m (72.1ft to 91.5ft) wide and 12m (39.4ft) deep moats around the donjon were filled with water from a nearby stream until the seventeenth century.

After the battle of Agincourt, the English occupied Paris and Vincennes and Henry V of England died at the castle in 1422. The French led by Joan of Arc briefly occupied the castle in 1430, but the English took it back and Henry VI resided there. In 1432, the French quietly took the donjon by escalade and soon a battle broke out. The entire fortress fell and held by the French until 1434 when the English recaptured it.

Phase Two of the War: 1369 to 1396

Bertrand du Guesclin led the French military to victories reclaiming lost lands from the 1370s to the 1390s. He was taken prisoner at the battle at Auray in 1364 by John Chandos' Anglo-Breton army[36] and was captured again in 1367 at the battle of Nájera in Iberia. When he became Constable of France, he conducted sieges against the English between 1370 and 1396, but he declined to meet them in the field. When the Bishop of Limoges opened his city to the French in 1370, John of Gaunt, Duke of Lancaster and brother of the Black Prince, came from Bordeaux to retaliate. After mining the walls, he took the city and sacked it. While the English launched several chevauchées in the 1370s, the French pressed forward with sieges in Gascony. By 1377, they were within 30km (20 miles) of

Bordeaux. In August 1373, John of Gaunt led one of the largest chevauchées from Calais into the heart of France a year after the loss of La Rochelle.[37] With only 9,000 mounted troops, he was unable to lay sieges, but he could and did plunder the countryside. His raids ended at Bordeaux in December when many of his men contracted the plague. After the deaths of Edward III in 1377 and of

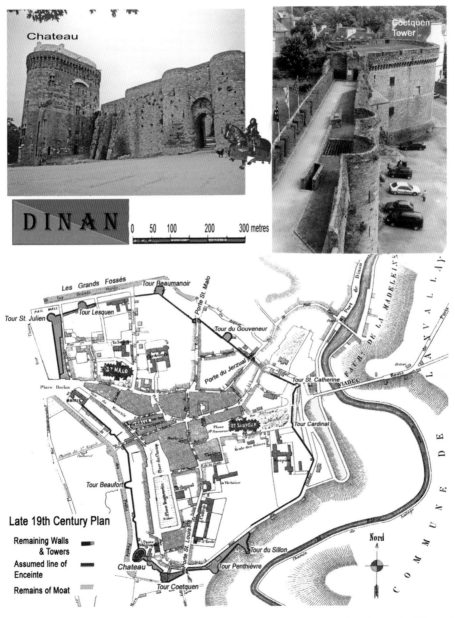

Dinan. Top left: View of the 34m (111.5ft) high Château Keep built in 1383. Top right: View of the wall walk and the Coelquen Tower with two intermediate towers with arrow loops.

Charles V and du Guesclin in 1380, the fighting died down thanks to truces and relatively incompetent kings in command.

When Jean IV de Montfort returned to Normandy in 1379, he set up his court at Dinan, Brittany, the site of a motte-and-bailey castle dating from the eleventh century that had stood on a promontory apart from the nearby settlement. In 1380, he contracted Étienne le Tur to build him a keep. Construction ended in 1393. The keep consists of two adjoining 34m (100.5ft) high round towers

Dinan. Top: Bridge over the Rance leading into the fortress of Dinan. Bottom: Plan and view of the keep.

Saumur: Several views of the Château of Saumur including a bartizan, bretèche over the entrance, and a view across the Loire. The painting often used to depict a typical French castle is Saumur in 1410. Built in the early thirteenth century, the castle was modified more than once. It was adapted for cannon and protection against artillery at the end of the Middle Ages.

connected with two flat walls forming a flattened oval plan. It has five levels (the fourth level is split into a fourth and fifth floor) and includes machicoulis on the third floor.

The enceinte of Dinan, which is one of the best preserved of the period in Brittany, originally stretched for 2.7km (1.7 miles) and included four massive gates and ten towers, some built in the fifteenth century and had arrow loops adapted for handguns and casemates for cannon. When it was built during the thirteenth century, it had smaller circular towers at intervals. The towers off the escarpment overlooking the Rance River Valley served only for observation. The Montforts increased the height of the walls and the increased the defences of the gates.

In the thirteenth century, Henry II's castle of Saumur on the Loire was rebuilt. Louis I of Anjou, the brother of King Charles V, converted into a luxurious château-palace after 1356. It has a trapezoidal plan with a 40m (131ft) long base and four 37m (121.4ft) high octagonal flanking corner towers connected by curtain walls. Despite a major war, the nobility could still afford to enjoy its luxuries.

Chapter Three

The End of the Age of Castles, Part II

The French Civil War

Control of the mentally impaired Charles VI of Valois (reigned 1380–1422) fell to his council and relatives who included his brother Louis II Duke of Orléans and his cousins the Dukes of Anjou, Berry, and Burgundy. His daughters were married to Richard II and Henry V of England and to Jean V Duke of Brittany. The father of Jean I of Burgundy controlled the crown until his death when Louis II of Orléans and some of his other relatives took the reins. Except for the Duke of Burgundy, these individuals strove to maintain the traditional feudal order despite the financial crisis engendered by the Hundred Years War.[1] After 1402, Louis also began a campaign to take Guyenne, capturing a number of fortified places until the English stopped him in 1407. Jean I 'the Fearless', Duke of Burgundy and Count of Artois, a populist supported by the bourgeoisie, gained power in 1404. Like the English, he was involved in the Flemish textile trade and wanted to establish in France a system that resembled the one found in England. During the schism in the church between 1378 and 1418, he supported the Pope in Rome while the Orleanists and the other members of the French royal family backed the Anti-Pope in Avignon. As divisions deepened, Jean arranged for the assassination of Louis of Orléans in November 1407 and entered Paris in early 1408. His actions initiated a civil war between the Burgundians supported by the Parisians and the Old Order represented by the Orleanists also known as the Armagnacs because they were backed by the count of Armagnac.

When Jean the Fearless left Paris in the summer of 1408, the Armagnacs seized control, even though support for the Burgundian was widespread in the city. When Jean marched back on Paris in November, the royal family and the opposition fled to the fortress of Tours where they set up court. After negotiations, the royal family returned to Paris in March 1409. Jean crushed the opposition while he controlled the king and the government in 1410. The Armagnacs planned to rescue the king and isolate Jean from his holdings in Flanders and other lands by marching into Northern France and taking the fortified town of Coucy,[2] which was loyal to their cause. More negotiations took place while both sides tried to court Henry IV of England.

In September 1411, the Earl of Arundel landed at Calais with 200 men-at-arms and 800 archers to support Jean the Fearless. Before additional troops could arrive, Jean moved against the Armagnacs who held fortified towns and castles on the Somme and Oise Rivers. In Paris, the Armagnacs attacked his loyalists and assaulted Saint Denis by draining the moat and bombarding the town with trebuchets as they pushed their mobile towers toward the walls.[3] The Burgundian garrison of Saint Denis held out until 14 October. Jean's army, reinforced with English troops, advanced on Paris and on 16 October took the walled town of Pontoise and its bridge over the Oise. On 22 October, he seized the fortified bridge at Melun and advanced on Paris where 3,000 Parisians joined him as he marched on the Louvre to put Charles VI under his 'protection'. The next month, he tried to dislodge the Armagnacs from the fortified bridge over the Seine at St. Cloud, which was defended by 1,500 men. Despite an aggressive assault and attacks with fire ships, the bridge held until a massive offensive drove the survivors from the bridge into the donjon.

The Burgundians and the Armagnacs tried to get the support of Henry IV of England. In April 1412, Henry sent an expedition to Lower Normandy to help the Armagnacs. Meanwhile, Jean, with the French king in tow, advanced on Bourges where the opposition held out under the Duke of Berry. Jean first attacked the fortified town of Dun-le-Rois, the last obstacle on the southern approach. In 1181, Philippe Augustus had authorized the expansion of the town beyond the Gallo-Roman fortifications and the creation of a new enceinte consisting of a stone wall with forty towers and a 10m (32.8ft) wide ditch. When it was finished, it followed the river on the west and north and reached the swamps on the east. A large circular donjon was built in 1188 with a 23m (75.4ft) diameter, 6m (19.7ft) thick, and 38m (124.6ft) high, dominated the ramparts on the south-east section, the most vulnerable side. On the first day, the Burgundians destroyed one tower and breached another one using a large bombard; on the next day, they breached the walls. The defenders surrendered on the ninth day, after the walls had taken a battering, but only on the condition that they could depart.

After taking Dun-le-Rois, Jean surrounded Bourges where the Duke of Berry had taken refuge. The large donjon of Bourges was 38m (125ft) high and 23m (75.4ft) in diameter with walls 6m (20ft) thick and a moat 7m (22.9ft) deep.[4] The city walls, also from the time of Philippe Augustus, had replaced the old Gallo-Roman walls in 1188.[5] They consisted of rubble with ashlar facings, included five gateways and forty towers, and came up to the Yèvre and Avron Rivers. A 10m (32.8ft) wide ditch ran in front of the enceinte. Two fortified bridges and water obstacles across the marshland on the west side completed the defences. The marshes prevented the complete encirclement of the city.

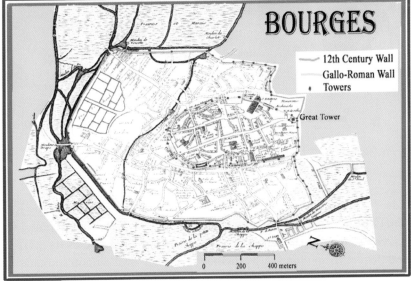

Top: Only the donjon of the twelfth-century castle of Châteaudun remains. Bottom: Eighteenth-century plan showing the location of the old Gallo-Roman walls and medieval walls of Bourges.

Map of the Hundred Years War, fifteenth century: Statue of Henry V.

The Duke of Berry refused to surrender to anyone other than the King or the Dauphin. Jean the Fearless put Bourges under siege on 11 June 1412. Weeks of bombardment devastated the city and the morale of its garrison. The defenders responded with crossbows and their own cannon and catapults on the walls forcing the besiegers to pull back their lines after taking heavy casualties. Foraging became difficult for the besiegers as their own logistical support proved to be lacking. In addition, the defenders constantly ambushed foraging parties. The Armagnacs sallied out of friendly towns and castles to attack supply convoys from Burgundy, which led to other smaller sieges. Besides a large number of desertions, disease raged in the Burgundian camp in July leaving 2,000 men dead. To avoid further losses, both sides opened negotiations and Bourges surrendered on 15 July 1412.

Meanwhile, Thomas Lancaster, the Duke of Clarence, led an English expedition to Normandy in July only to find that he no longer had an Armagnac ally. His mission changed as he now led a chevauchée to south to reclaim the lost lands in Guyenne the Armagnacs had promised in exchange for English support. He reached Bordeaux in time for winter. In Paris, Jean the Fearless encouraged a bloody uprising after meeting opposition from the government. When his own supporters turned against him, he left Paris to the Armagnacs and returned to Burgundy in August 1413.

Sources: Desmond Seward, *The Hundred Years War*, and Jonathan Sumption, *The Hundred Years War: Cursed Kings*.

The Hundred Years War Resumes: The Fifteenth Century

France began the new century with the incompetent Charles VI still in power. In England, Henry IV of Lancaster, who had deposed the Plantagenet Richard II, became enmeshed in the Welsh revolt led by Owain Glyndwr which broke out in 1400. Henry V, who succeeded him in 1413, had gained experience leading an army during the Welsh war. In 1415, after he supressed the revolt and England began to prosper again, Henry V saw an opportunity to secure and expand his French holdings while the Armagnacs with the Duke Jean the Fearless of Burgundy were engaged in a civil war leaving the mad King Charles VI caught between the two factions. Both sides appealed to Henry V. In April 1415, Henry began appropriating funds and assembling a force of about 12,000 men. In mid-August, his army sailed from England in 1,600 ships and landed unopposed near the port of Harfleur on the mouth of the Seine. Unlike Edward III, he did not aim simply to defeat France by destroying its economy and morale with chevauchées and to hold a few key fortresses. He actually intended to occupy and hold territory while taking advantage of the existing civil war.[6] When he landed in Normandy, his troops no longer came to plunder, but to conquer. He went to France armed with gunpowder artillery, including bombards, to break down the walls of strongholds.[7] The siege of Harfleur, which lasted from 18 August to 22 September, was first major encounter of this phase of the Hundred Years War.

Harfleur was a walled port city with three gates protected by three barbicans, twenty-six towers, additional earthworks and water-filled moats protecting the barbicans. The Lézarde River ran through the town to empty in the Seine estuary.

The French had dredged the river up to the city wall and created a harbour behind it for shipping, which made it the only port on the north side of the estuary. According to Alfred Burne, author of *The Agincourt War,* and other historians, the barbicans were made of wood and earth and should be called bulwarks. Recent excavations revealed that the city walls were 1.1m (3.6ft) to 2.2m (7.2ft) thick and about 2km (1.2 miles) long. Construction began in the thirteenth century and ended in the 1350s.[8] The base of the walls consisted of limestone blocks and sea pebbles bound with a light mortar. Most of the towers were round or U-shaped. However, excavations show that the tower in the north wall was polygonal on the outside and U-shaped on the inside and was covered with ashlars of white or yellow limestone and flint. The outer covering of the enceinte consisted of ashlars of grey and black flint held together with a light mortar. A water-filled moat surrounded the entire enceinte, except on the east side facing a ridge. It is believed that this section was dry but that a second ditch served as an additional obstacle. The English began mining operations at this point. The defenders flooded the low areas around the town. A ridge on the east and a plateau to the west overlooked the valley and Harfleur. The French garrison, reinforced with up to 700 men, had sufficient provisions, but the town had 5,000 to 8,000 residents.[9] Henry set up a camp on the plateau west of the town, about 200m (218 yards) from the city and blockaded the port. Meanwhile, his brother Thomas, Duke of Clarence, placed a camp on the ridge about 100m (109 yards) east of the town walls, but he came too late to block the arrival of reinforcements. The duke began mining operations, but French countermines defeated his efforts.[10] Henry set his cannons close to the walls behind protective earthworks.[11] The defenders fought back with their own artillery and the townspeople worked to repair damaged walls and towers at night. The unhealthy marshy environment around Harfleur caused disease that took a toll on both sides. The English diverted the river to cut the town's water supply. Although the French destroyed an English position during a successful sortie on 15 September, the English began to overwhelm their defensive bastions beyond the barbicans. Henry's bombards continued to inflict extensive damage. Finally, on 16 September they smashed the south-western barbican, the wooden barbicans, and at least two of the gates. On 17 September, after using fire arrows to set the south-western barbican on fire, the English stormed the position and doused the flames as the defenders retreated across the moat into the town. Finally, with no relief in sight and seeing their town and its walls badly battered, the French surrendered. According to Monstrelet, two well-defended towers on the side facing the sea held out for ten more days. Henry lost a quarter of his siege force. About three dozen were killed in battle, another 1,300 died from disease, and possibly up to 1,700 men had been sent home suffering from dysentery.

Henry V remained in the city for fifteen days. Since he needed to maintain Harfleur to support his invasion, he ordered the repair of the badly damaged fortifications, which lasted until 1416. Recent archaeological excavations have uncovered fallen masonry, which confirms the existence of a great moat to the west of the city attributable to this period of English occupation. Apparently, Henry's men dumped the soil excavated from the moat behind the city wall to reinforce its 1.5m (4.9ft) thickness.

Leaving a garrison of 300 men-at-arms and 900 archers at Harfleur, Henry V marched his army of 2,000 men-at-arm and 13,000 archers on Calais through Upper Normandy. He had not yet given up the practice of chevauchée. The French tried to block him from crossing the Somme by defending and/or destroying all bridges and fords as they massed their forces. Henry continued to move up river meeting light opposition, but failed to find an unprotected crossing. At one tributary, he bypassed a castle where the garrison was too small to interfere with his crossing and went on to find a ford the men of St. Quentin had failed to defend. He crossed the Somme and was heading for Calais when he was engaged by the French at the decisive battle of Agincourt on Saint Crispin's Day (25 October) where he crushed the largely Armagnac army of 12,000 to 36,000 men.[12] A few French men-at-arms and several hundred peasants from the nearby Agincourt Castle, from which the battle took its name, seized Henry V's baggage, causing the English to slaughter many of their prisoners in the belief that an attack was coming from their rear. The Count of Armagnac raced to Paris, seized Charles VI and the Dauphin, and tried to ward off the English with the remnants of his forces. Henry V resumed his ride to Calais and later returned to England.

During the summer of 1416, the French blockaded Harfleur until the Duke of Bedford won a decisive naval victory, which secured English domination of the Channel in 1417. Henry V and his brothers, the dukes of Clarence and Gloucester, returned to Normandy in July 1417 with about 10,000 soldiers to launch a campaign of conquest. After landing at the mouth of the Touques River without opposition, they quickly laid siege to the castle of Bonneville sur-Touques, which surrendered in four days after the governor, Jean d'Engennes, extracted the promise that the French royal garrison could depart unhinderd.[13] Other towns and castles followed suit and barely resisted. The next major objective was Caen, the second largest city in Normandy, where the situation had changed since the siege in 1346. Improvements to the walls of Caen, which were over 2m (6.6ft) thick, included twelve gates and thirty-two towers. According to various sources, the city had 8,000 to 40,000 inhabitants.[14] Guillaume de Montenay's garrison included 400 men-at-arms and 100 Genoese mercenaries. The city militia numbered about 2,000 men, 50 mounted crossbowmen and their valets, which totalled about 6,000 defenders.[15] Montenay ordered the destruction of two walled abbeys located on the east and west side of the city, but the abbots refused let the demolition proceed. When the English invested Caen on 16 August, they seized both abbeys whose curtain wall towers proved

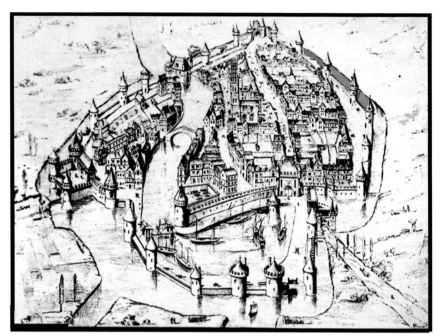

HARFLEUR   15TH CENTURY

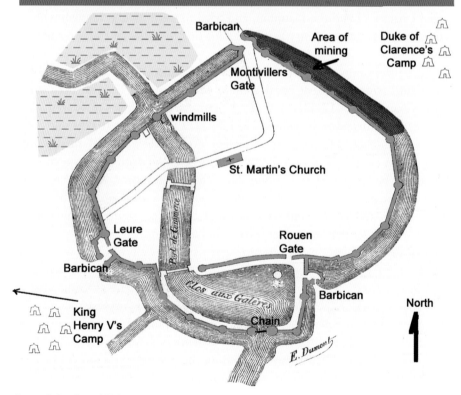

Barbican

Area of
mining

Duke of
Clarence's
Camp

Montivillers
Gate

windmills

St. Martin's Church

Port de Commerce

Leure
Gate

Rouen
Gate

Barbican

Clos aux Galères

Barbican

North

King
Henry V's
Camp

Chain

E. Dumont

Siege of Harfleur, 1415.

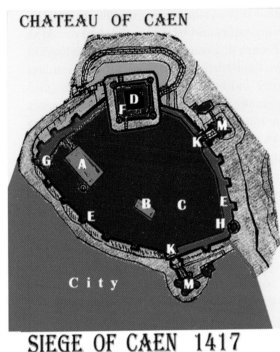

CHATEAU OF CAEN

A. **Palace area of William I and location of Exchequer of Henry I**
B. **St. George Church**
C. **Bourg created by William I an later added to Chateau**
D. **Keep of Henry I**
E. **Late 12th century rectangular towers of enceinte**
F. **Citadel of Philippe II with rectangular curtain wall with moat around the keep**
G **13th Century circular tower**
H **Early 15th century circular tower for cannons**
K **Gates of Philippe II and later modified***
M **Barbicans with cannon ports from first half of 15th Century**

***Southern gate destroyed and rebuilt in 19th century**

SIEGE OF CAEN 1417

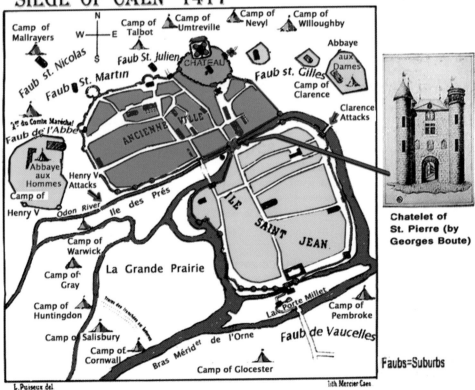

Chatelet of
St. Pierre (by
Georges Boute)

Faubs=Suburbs

Château of Caen and Siege of Caen, 1417.

excellent for mounting artillery. Abbot la Rue, who left an account of the siege, wrote that after several unsuccessful assaults and heavy losses, Henry tried to undermine the city walls while the French dug countermines. When the English tried to scale the walls with ladders, the French pelted them with large stones and doused them with scalding water and boiling oil.[16] However, the English artillery continued to wreak havoc among the defenders and opened breaches in the walls with bronze and marble roundshot. The English launched a major assault on 4 September and the Duke of Clarence's troops finally took the Châtelet of Saint Pierre breaking through the enceinte and driving the French into the castle. On 5 September, Henry started bombarding the castle. Angered by his losses, he allowed his men to butcher about 1,800 people including possibly 600 defenders. According to Livius, he spared priests, women, and children.[17] The moats were filled with the bodies of dead Englishmen killed by the bows, ballistas, and catapults of the defenders. Montenay, 100 townsmen, and the remains of his troops holed up in the castle where they held out for three more weeks and only surrendered when it became evident that no relief was forthcoming and on condition they could depart with their baggage.

Population: Big vs. Small

Where feudalism was the strongest, most small cities, towns, and villages were rather small, numbering no more than a few thousand people. Major cities possibly reached 10,000 or more inhabitants. After the eleventh century, as feudalism began to wane, towns and cities began to grow. Below are populations for some of the largest cities in France, England, and the Iberian and Italian Peninsulas at the time the Hundred Years War began.

Year	Paris	Naples	Milan Venice	Granada	Genoa	Bordeaux Orleans	London	Rouen	Rome
1200	110,000*	30,000	**	60,000	30,000	**	25,000	**	35,000
1330	150,000	60,000	100,000	150,000	100,000	***	35,000	35,000	***
1500	225,000	125,000	100,000	70,000	58,000	50,000	50,000	40,000	55,000

* In 1200, Palermo, Sicily was the largest city with 150,000.
** Fewer than 25,000.
*** Fewer than 30,000.

Although the numbers include women, children, and elderly, the populations of most of these cities were larger than the medieval armies found in Western Europe at the time. The ability to attack or besiege these cities was a difficult task as was the case with Rouen and Orleans with populations smaller than the rest. In most cases, it was preferable to avoid a siege.

The largest English and French cities with 35,000 or more in 1330 and 40,000 or more in 1500:

Year	Paris	Tours	London	Bordeaux	Lyons	Orleans	Marseilles	Rouen
1330	150,000	*	35,000	**	***	***	***	35,000
1500	225,000	60,000	50,000	50,000	50,000	50,000	45,000	40,000

*St Omer had 35,000 in 1330.
**Angers had 33,000 in 1330.
*** Fewer than 25,000 in 1330

In 1350, the population of the French lands totalled over 15,000,000 while England (including Wales) totalled 2,400,000, which did not include the French holdings. In 1400, the population of France dropped to 14,000,000, mainly due to the plague, while the population of England and Wales rose to 3,000,000. In 1450, at the end of the Hundred Years War, the French population was still at about 14,000,000 while the English and Welsh had steadily grown to 3,300,000. In Iberia, the population grew steadily from 5,000,000 in 1350 to 6,000,000 in 1400, and 7,000,000 in 1450. The population of Italian Peninsula in 1350 was 8,000,000 (down by 2,000,000 from 1300) and steadily increased to 10,500,000 in 1450. Thus, France had the largest population in Western Europe (and Europe) before and after the Hundred Years War. Italy with the second largest population in the West was divided into several countries and the Holy Roman Empire was on the verge of dismemberment.

Source: Inna Guzenfeld and Christine Bourgeois, 'Populations in Medieval Cities', posted by Bryn Mawr College. City data from the Bairoch database by Paul Bairoch, Jean Bateau and Pierre Chèvre, *La population des villes européenes de 800–1850* (published 1988).

Henry V swept through lower Normandy taking many towns and castles and encountering little resistance. Du Guesclin, the Constable of France, had ordered some garrisons to Paris and others to focus on Jean the Fearless since the civil war marked by numerous sieges raged on. French resistance began to collapse in Lower Normandy after the fall of Caen. Towns like Bayeux and Lisieux yielded without a fight in late September. In October 1417, the English laid siege to the fortified town of Argentan and its castle whose inhabitants, shaken by the fate of the people of Caen, agreed to surrender if relief did not arrive in a few days. More towns and castles surrendered to Henry V who left behind strong garrisons. When he reached Alençon on 15 October, he divided his forces between the town and the castle. The town was surrounded by deep moats and high walls with closely spaced towers. The castle had similar defences and stronger towers than those of the town. However, the defenders, like those of Argentan, agreed to surrender if they were not relieved soon. Most towns as far south as Le Mans gave in as well. At Falaise, the French improved the defences by placing guns and other engines at the gates, working on the defensive ditches, and creating water defences. The castle, located above the town, was well fortified. The siege began on 1 December. Even though the town's people wanted to surrender, the soldiers convinced them to resist. In January, as the severe winter dragged on and no relief force materialized, the town decided to submit. The castle continued to resist while Henry built siege engines, tried to exploit breaches to no avail, and his miners found the castle stood on solid rock. On 16 February 1418, with no relief force in sight, the castle garrison surrendered.

Meanwhile, in March 1418, the Duke of Gloucester was sent into the Cotentin where many towns like Vire and its castle and Carentan quickly capitulated, while others like St-Lô, Valognes, and Saint-Sauveur[18] gave in after the English prepared the siege and finished building siege engines. Finally, the duke reached Cherbourg, which had a 'marvellous great defence' according to Livius. The town occupied a low sandy plain surrounded by steep hills and divided by a small river. Its castle – report the chroniclers of the era – was an impressive stronghold located on the north side of the town, next to the harbour. It included a strong keep with four large towers.[19] One thousand defenders could and did endure a long siege inside its walls. The town wall, almost 2m (6.6ft) thick, was lapped by high flood tides that filled the deep ditches surrounding it. The commander at Cherbourg destroyed the bridges and burned the suburbs beyond the walls while strengthening his defences.

The English reached Cherbourg in mid-March 1418. The main body of Gloucester's army encamped on the flat land west of the town, but the shifting sands caused many difficulties. To counter them, the English gathered stones and brushwood from the hillside to build shelters, but no sooner did they erect then then the defenders destroyed them with their mangonels, flaming shot or 'tore it up with barbed claws flung out from the walls'.[20] When the English placed a siege engine close to the walls and built a bulwark to protect it, the defenders sent out a small force to set it on fire and damage it. The Englishmen also raised mounds to the height of the walls so they could storm the ramparts, but the French repelled the assault. The only weak spot was the northern wall facing the sea, but the English could not place their cannons on that side, even at low tide. Gloucester finally concluded that instead of storming the town he must starve it out. He blockaded the harbour with ships and fortified his siege lines with towers and ditches placing his encampment beyond the range of enemy artillery. With time on their hands, the English miners set to work, but they could not reach the walls because of the combination of unstable sand and dense rock.

The siege ended after five or six months in August or September, depending on the source. The garrison surrendered when it realized there was no hope of succour. The English suffered heavy losses. After the siege ended, a few thousand soldiers were sent to reinforce Henry V in his campaign against Rouen. The men left behind repaired the fortifications of Cherbourg, and left it with a garrison of 40 men-at-arms and 120 archers.

In March 1418, the Duke of Clarence crossed the Touques River, advanced towards the Seine, and isolated the port of Honfleur. Meanwhile, the Count of Harcourt left his wife to hold his family castle while he went to defend upper Normandy from the Duke of Burgundy. The lower courtyard of Harcourt Castle, which included a châtelet and six towers, was surrounded by a deep and wide moat that separated it from a smaller upper courtyard with several towers. Despite its formidable defences, the castle did not resist for long. It surrendered on 9 April after a fifteen-day siege and yielded the Harcourt family treasure. Clarence next moved on the Benedictine monastery of Bec. Like many abbeys, it had high walls allowing the French garrison to hold out until 4 May when the English agreed to allow the defenders to depart. The English left behind a garrison of twenty men-at-arms and sixty archers. On 12 May, Évreux capitulated after a four-day siege. On 18 August, 400 French troops re-entered the town but were driven out by a small English garrison. On 8 June, Clarence reached the recently fortified town of Louviers, defended by triple ditches and high walls. This did not prevent the English artillery from smashing the town and the sappers from mining the walls. During the siege, a stone from a catapult barely missed Henry V when it hit his royal pavilion. He took revenge when the town surrendered on 20 June by hanging eight French artillerymen. On 20 August 1418, 1,000 Burgundian troops of Jean the Fearless came to relieve Louviers but they were repelled by the 100-man English garrison.[21]

Meanwhile, the Earl of Warwick was given the mission of subduing other locations like Domfront, located high on a rock. The earl was afraid that his cannon could not reach it and that it was too high for scaling ladders – claimed Livius. He decided therefore to starve out the defenders and to prevent their escape by blocking all points of access with ditches. In the following weeks, the besieged raided Warwick's positions inflicting a great deal of damage. Finally, the English took the town on 29 June and the castle garrison capitulated on 22 July, but had to leave its artillery behind. Thus, most of Normandy fell like a house of cards with few long sieges except for Cherbourg and Domfront.

Henry V was already moving against Rouen in June. On 27 June 1418, a detachment reached Pont-de-l'Arche and its fortified bridge up the river from Rouen. This was the only crossing of the Seine above Rouen for many kilometres. The heavily-fortified town of Pont de l'Arche was located at the south end of the bridge. A square fort on a small island near the right (north) bank guarded the bridge. Known as Fort Limaie, it was built by Philippe Augustus on the ruins of an earlier stronghold built by Charles the Bald and consisted of a large round Philippine tower. In 1417, the French strengthened the site in view of the growing threat from the English.[22] In mid–July 1418, after the English launched a series of unsuccessful attacks on Pont-de-l'Arche, they decided to open a diversionary assault with about 5,000 men while another force led by John Cornwall crossed the river. On 14 July, Cornwall's group reached the northern side of the river. The Armagnac garrison of Pont-de-l'Arche received no help from the Burgundians stationed at Rouen, which exacerbated the friction among the French warring factions. On 20 July, the outnumbered Frenchmen surrendered Pont-de-l'Arche, but not without inflicting many casualties on the English forces. At the end of July, Henry V crossed the Seine and, after Rouen defiantly refused his demand to capitulate, he moved east of the city to complete its encirclement and prepare a new siege.

Rouen, which was considered second only to Paris at the time, had a high city wall that spanned about 8km (5 miles) built under Philippe Augustus after he had razed the previous walls. The eastern section of the walls had been repaired during the first decade of the fifteenth century. The section facing the river had several gates leading to quays; the landward side had five gates with flanking towers, a moat, and outworks. A deep moat protected the walls, which had sixty towers with three guns each. The walls were reinforced with earth piled up behind them. The defenders placed thousands of caltrops in front of the walls and dug pits. The castle of Bouvreuil – built on a hill of the same name by Philippe Augustus at the site of Gallo-Roman ruins – dominated Rouen from the north-west corner of the city wall.[23] A moat surrounded the castle's large donjon – known today as the Tower of Joan of Arc – which had walls about 4m (13ft) thick and was 30m (98.4ft) high with a circumference of 46m (151ft). It was connected to a wide dry moat that surrounded the courtyard in front of it. The curtain walls of the courtyard included round towers and a double-towered gatehouse with a drawbridge leading into the lower courtyard. East of the city, the abbey of St. Catherine on a steep dominant hill was referred to as St. Catherine's Castle due to its position and strong walls. The English tried to isolate it from the city and attacked it more than once. The captain of the garrison surrendered on 1 September when he became isolated from the rest of the city.

After the Burgundian takeover, probably about 2,000 soldiers in addition to the local militia defended Rouen with a fair number of artillery pieces.[24] In addition to cannons in the towers, the defenders pressed older weapons into service including ballista, mangonels and trebuchets. Henry V put up four camps around the city and linked them with trenches. During the siege, his force may have risen to about 45,000 men with reinforcements. He blockaded the river to prevent reinforcements and supplies from reaching the city. Although all relief attempts failed, the French continued to hurl stones and shoot arrows at the English and even sallied in groups of up to 1,000 men only to be driven back.

Henry continued to batter the walls and the gates with bombards and artillery and built fortifications in front of each of the gates to block them. By October, as they started to run out of food, the besieged resorted to eating dogs and rats. Disease and malnutrition started to take their toll, but the garrison stubbornly clung to the hope that relief would soon arrive. In mid-December, 12,000 non-combatants were forced out of the city, but Henry refused to let them pass through his siege lines and the defenders refused to let them back in. After 2,000 men launched a last breakout attempt, the garrison finally surrendered on 19 January 1419.

The fall of Rouen led to a general collapse of resistance in Normandy and adjacent regions as the main towns and castles submitted including Montivilliers, Dieppe, Arques, and Fécamp in Upper Normandy. Honfleur, Tancarville, Mantes, and Vernon also fell by the end of February 1419. Henry V remained in Rouen for two months and had the defences repaired. On 23 September 1419, the last resistance in Normandy ended at Château Gaillard. Only the bastion of Mont-Saint-Michel remained in the region under French control. Henry established his own garrisons and put English officials in charge of administration throughout Normandy. However, an advance on Paris and a siege were beyond his means. Except for raids in the direction of Paris, the furthest his troops went was Pontoise, which they took in July 1419.

Henry V Victorious and the French Resurgence

The civil war took its toll as the Burgundians usurped power from the Armagnacs. Like the war with England, most of the civil war involved sieges. On 3 September 1417, Jean the Fearless used his cannon to bring down the walls of Beauvais, which fell on 5 September. On 9 September, he took Pontoise. On 14 September, the townspeople of Meulan on the Seine opened the gates to him followed by Mantes and further down river, Vernon. The strong donjon at St. Cloud (a western suburb of Paris) withstood his assaults on 16 September, so he left it surrounded and advanced to the walls of Paris. On 29 September, he took Provins and moved on to Étampes. In mid-October, a short siege handed him Chartres. Bernard of Armagnac, the Constable of France, broke Jean's ring around Paris, but his siege of a Burgundian castle to the south failed. In November, Jean took Vendôme and went on to Chartres with the queen. On 10 January 1418, he formally took control of the government and the queen dismissed Bernard of Armagnac as constable. Jean had already ordered the removal of all Armagnac leaders from fortified towns. Meanwhile, Henry V continued the conquest of lower Normandy and moved on to Rouen in 1418, as Jean seized control of the French government and the civil war continued.

During the summer, the Dauphin, leader of the Armagnac faction, met with Jean the Fearless and agreed to further negotiations. The meeting took place on 10 September 1419 on the bridge of Montereau, but before the discussion could begin, one of the Dauphin's men cut down Jean, ending any chance of reconciliation. Jean's son, Philippe III 'the Good', took his place as Duke of Burgundy and contracted an alliance with Henry V on 19 December 1419. He mediated between Henry V and Charles VI who signed the Treaty of Troyes on 21 May 1420 making Henry V the heir and regent of Charles VI and declaring the Dauphin illegitimate.

Henry V consolidated his power in June by besieging and quickly taking the little town of Sens defended by its Roman walls. Later that month, Henry and Philippe III put Melun, an island fortress on a bend of the Seine, under siege with a force of 20,000 men. The garrison of the town numbered only 700 men. In June, while the siege continued, Henry and Philippe made a triumphant entry into Paris where the French government ratified the Treaty of Troyes. In the meantime, at Melun, Armagnac countermines intercepted the English tunnels beneath the moat, which did not prevent English cannon from blasting a breach in the walls. Melun finally capitulated on 18 November 1420.

In June 1421, Henry V launched another campaign. He returned from England, landing at Calais with 28,000 men (85 per cent archers) and advanced almost unopposed taking the fortified town of Dreux and retiring to Paris. Next, he placed Meaux under siege in October. The town had a castled called Marché built on a rock and held by 1,000 men. As often happened, disease struck his camp taking many men and incapacitating the king. The defenders repulsed an assault on the castle inflicting heavy losses on the English. Henry lost 4,000 more men to disease and could only maintain the siege with difficulty. Meaux surrendered on 9 March 1422, but its garrison moved into a fortified suburb where they held out until 10 May.[25] The 35-year-old Henry returned to Paris gravely ill and died on 31 August at Vincennes. He appointed John, Duke of Bedford,[26] as regent for his infant son Henry VI, the heir to the throne of England and France, and the Duke of Gloucester as his regent in England. Charles VI died on 21 October making the young Henry VI king of France.

The Dauphin's forces continued to resist even though they suffered a major setback at the battle of Verneuil in 1424. The English continued to campaign in a conflict that consisted of raids and sieges and few major field battles like Verneuil.[27] In July 1427, the Earl of Warwick led about 5,000 men in the siege of Montargis, south of Montereau, where his artillery damaged the approaches to the town. Two months later, the defenders broke many dikes and flooded the area, drowning many of the besiegers as a relief force of 1,600 men led by Jean de Dunois, the 'Bastard of Orleans', attacked the besiegers' camps. This was the first major victory for the Dauphin.

According to Monstrelet, in 1427 the French took the English-held little island of Tombelaine across from the fortified monastery of Mont-Saint-Michel. The English, on the other hand, forced the surrender of Pontorson in April,[28] but their position was vulnerable because of Mont-Saint-Michel.

The occupation of Normandy and other areas required garrisons, especially for castles, since the loss of any fortified site to a revolt or a French raiding force threatened potential havoc. Troops required money and feudal obligations were not sufficient. When Henry V put Englishmen in charge of each district, he had to provide funds from his government to maintain the occupation forces. The garrisons of some castles numbered only a few men while key fortified cities required hundreds. By 1420, Henry deployed 4,000 men on garrison duty or operations that included conducting sieges.

The Dauphin's forces remained active through 1428. As usual, everything revolved around taking one fortified site after another. In May, Étienne de Vignoles, 'La Hire',[29] led a French force against Le Mans[30] and drove the English into the one remaining tower where they held out for three days until Talbot at the head of a small force took the besiegers by surprise and drove the French off.[31] In 1428, Thomas Montague, Earl of Salisbury, sailed from Southampton for Harfleur and marched towards Paris with about 2,200 archers and 450 men-at-arms. He augmented his contingent with men drawn from some garrisons on the way so that he could launch an offensive to clear the Loire Valley in August. His first key objective was Orléans. He cleared all opposition, took Chartres, continued to the walled town of Janville, which he took by storm after a siege of only a few days, and proceeded to Orléans. By October, he had taken over forty towns. However, the great battles of Crécy, Poitiers, and Agincourt did not win the war for the English, but they greatly weakened the French army. In addition, these three encounters discouraged the French from engaging in major field battles. Orléans became the turning point of the war.

Orléans was well prepared for the English attack. Jean, Count Dunois, an effective commander, was in charge of its defence. The defenders had more artillery then the English, about seventy cannons many of which guns were small, but also some large ones that fired 90kg (200lb) balls. In 1418, the governor had added boulevards[32] to each of the five heavily defended gates. In 1425, he put a deep ditch around the town. Although most sources estimated the garrison at about 2,400 soldiers, one contemporary chronicler claimed that there were fewer than 1,000, most of whom were crossbowmen and archers. The citizenry of about 30,000 provided a militia of 3,000 men.

The original enceinte of Orléans was a Roman castrum that was extended to about 1.59km (1 mile). During the first quarter of the fourteenth century, a bourg on the west side of Orléans was enclosed, which added another 1km (0.6 miles), giving it a length of about 2.6km (1.6 miles). The massive walls, which included thirty towers and other defences, mounted cannons. The enceinte was in the shape of a wide and irregular horseshoe. The side that ran along the river was about 1km (0.6 miles) long.

The Earl of Salisbury first moved against the fortified towns on the Loire on either side of Orléans before he approached the city. First, he took the walled town of Meung and its bridge without encountering any resistance. Next, he crossed the Loire and headed for Beaugency where the defenders clung to its castle and bridge, which he approached from the south. The siege began on 20 September ended on 25 September 1428 with an assault on the castle from the north and the bridge from the south under the cover of an artillery bombardment. The garrison surrendered the next day. Afterward, he moved up river. On 2 October, Sir William de la Pole laid siege to Jargeau, located on the left bank, which only held for three days. Chateauneuf,[33] further up river, fell quickly. The only town in the area still in French hands was Châteaudun.[34] Orléans, on the north bank of the Loire, was isolated except for its heavily defended twelfth-century bridge over 350m (1,148ft) long and with nineteen stone arches. Bridge fortifications included Les Tourelles, a gatehouse of two large towers on the south end separated from the bank by a drawbridge and a boulevard beyond that.

The 4,000-man English contingent that came to lay siege to Orléans was smaller than the defending force because Suffolk had had to leave garrisons to occupy the newly captured towns. On 12 October, Salisbury joined Suffolk near the south end of the bridge and the siege was underway. The English bombarded the town and set miners to bring down the boulevard on the south end of the bridge. According to the *Chronique de Cousinot* composed by Guillaume Cousinot[35] in the fifteenth century, the English occupied the Convent of the Augustines, south of the boulevard, and turned it into a bastille. The French had just begun levelling the suburbs when the English showed up and demolition was not finished at the convent. According to recent research, the destruction took place mainly in November. After the English turned the convent into a bastide with deep moats and fences, they often emerged from it to skirmish in front of the boulevard. Their bombards and cannons fired day and night against the city walls and Les Tourelles. The Earl of Salisbury took up residence in this bastille and ordered his men to start excavating a mine in order to take the boulevard. On 21 October, the English assaulted the boulevard for four hours. The French discovered the English mine and began a countermine. At midday on 23 October, the earl launched a fierce assault against the boulevard at the end of the bridge of Orléans. According to Cousinot, English casualties were heavy. The French pushed the men on scaling ladders into the moat from which they could not escape and they were pelted with hot coals, lime, boiling oil, and scalding water provided by the women of Orléans. The English worked day and night to get a mine under the boulevard. Before they could set fire to the mine, the French burned the boulevard, fell back to Les Tourelles, and raised its drawbridge. After the bombardment badly damaged Les Tourelles, the defenders withdrew leaving a few men behind and destroyed the adjacent arches of the bridge.

On Sunday, 24 October, Salisbury launched an assault on Les Tourelles and his men took the position with scaling ladders in the early afternoon.[36] Each side lost a couple of hundred men in the encounter. In the evening, when Salisbury came to inspect the position and climbed one of its towers to observe the enemy, a French cannonball hit the structure, mortally wounding him. He died a week later. This was the high point of the English effort. They tried to surround the city with a series of bastilles, but all five were on the north-west side and a sixth on the riverbank a good distance east of the town. Another was on an island and two on the south bank including the one at the Convent of the Augustines. According to Cousinot, the English built thirteen bastilles during November and the city was isolated by December. By this time, Lord Talbot had taken command of the English troops, but he failed to stop French reinforcements. The chain of bastilles did not cover the north-east side of Orléans so that if a French force could penetrate the English lines north of the Loire or reach Châteaudun, it could advance from there and reach this unblocked area. The French launched a couple of unsuccessful

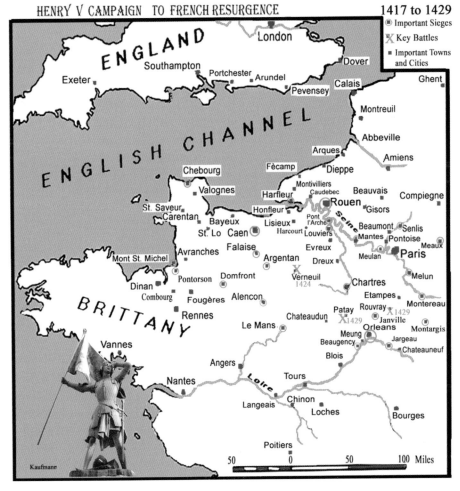

Map of Northern France showing key cities and towns from 1400 to 1429. Statue of Joan of Arc.

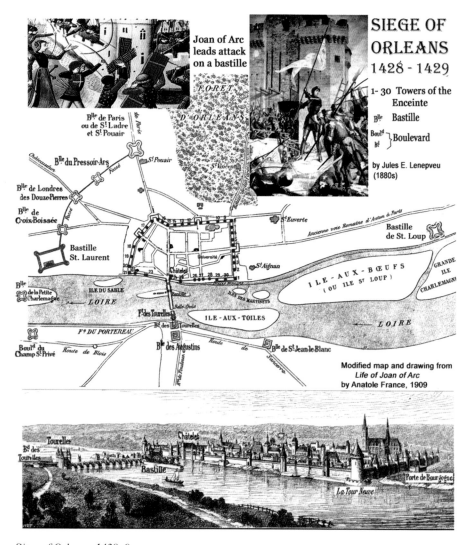

Siege of Orleans, 1428–9.

sorties to deter the English construction efforts. In early December, the English unsuccessfully assaulted a French boulevard built near the north end of the bridge. On 23 December, two large French cannons named 'Montargis' and 'Rifflart' inflicted damage on the English position south of the city. In January 1429, English attacks on the north bank against the western sections of the French defences failed. Additional attacks also failed. The English faced difficulties in their siege positions during the winter. On 12 February, a large supply convoy carrying salted fish escorted by 1,000 archers and 1,200 Burgundian foot soldiers led by John Falstolf was intercepted by the Count of Clermont coming from Blois and Count

ORLEANS 1428-1429

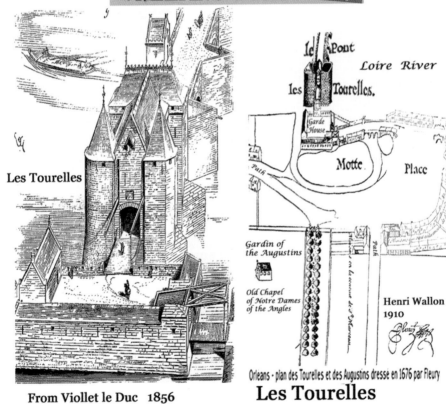

Les Tourelles

Loire River

le Pont

les Tourelles.

Garde House

Motte

Place

Path

Park

Gardin of
the Augustins

Old Chapel
of Notre Dames
of the Angles

Henri Wallon
1910

Orleans - plan des Tourelles et des Augustins dresse en 1676 par Fleury

Les Tourelles

From Viollet le Duc 1856

Siege of Orleans and Les Tourelles.

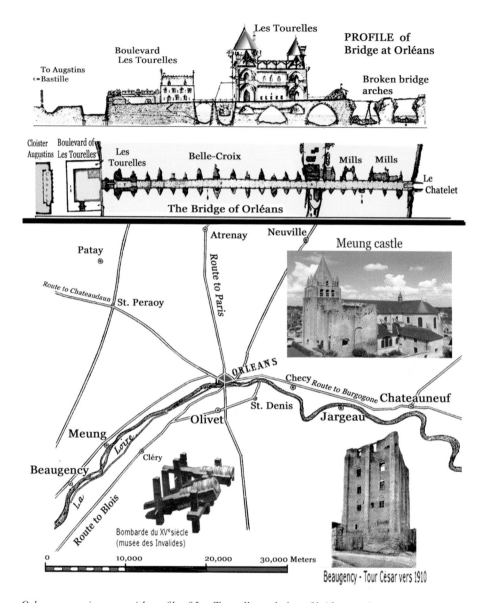

Orleans campaign map with profile of Les Tourrelles and plan of bridge crossing.

de Dunois from Orléans near the town of Rouvray. The English formed a laager (circled the wagons) and, despite enemy cannon and determined assaults, they beat off the French and continued to the siege lines. The encounter went down into history as the 'Battle of the Herrings' due to the cargo.

Meanwhile, Joan of Arc reached the Château Chinon and met with the Dauphin who dreaded another defeat, but allowed her to lead an army to relieve Orléans. She got there on 28 April and entered the city the next day. On 4 May, she led a supply convoy through the English line of bastilles. Next, she joined Dunois in an attack that overran the English bastille of Saint Loup, killing 140 defenders. The French crossed to the south bank and captured two additional bastilles. On 7 May, Joan crossed the river and joined in the assault on Les Tourelles held by 500 archers and men-at-arms under William Glasdale. Although she was wounded in the morning attack, Joan led the evening assault that finally stormed Les Tourelles, killing 300 Englishmen and capturing most of the rest. According to H. Poulain, author of *Prise des Tourelles par Jeanne d'Arc*, the defenders tried to lower the drawbridge, but the locals moved a barge with flammables beneath it to prevent it from coming all the way down and set it on fire. Glasdale and several other men drowned trying to escape. This battle put an end to the siege since Suffolk dismantled the bastilles and lifted the siege on 8 May. Although the English retreated, they still held the nearby towns. Nonetheless, the war had finally turned in favour of the French thanks to one great siege rather than a field battle. The siege of Orléans proved to be a mistake for the English who had been unable to completely isolate the city and had lacked the manpower to achieve a victory.

Conquest by Cannon

Orléans was not the first battle or siege where cannons had a role, but after the English defeat, gunpowder weapons proved to be a major element in most important engagements. It also had a truly crushing effect on stone fortifications. On 11 June, Joan led French troops out of Orléans against the fortified town of Jargeau. The Duke of Suffolk, William de la Pole, at the head of a force of 700 men faced 3,000 French troops. Both sides had artillery. The town had an enceinte with five towers, three fortified gates, and a fortified bridge. When the French attacked a suburb outside the enceinte, the English left the security of their walls to engage them. Joan rallied the French who were retreating and drove the English back. A day and night-long bombardment followed. The French artillery included a huge bombard named 'Bergère' which brought down a large tower. On 12 June, Joan led troops carrying ladders into the moat where one of the rocks thrown from the wall struck her on the head, but she was undeterred. Suffolk, unable to hold the walls, pulled back to the bridge, but he was captured and up to 500 of his soldiers were killed in the two-day battle. Supposedly, prisoners were executed and the town was badly damaged, probably from the bombardment.[37] When word spread of the victory, other towns quickly surrendered and Meung and Beaugency fell a few days later. On 15 June, Joan moved west against Meung while the Duke of Alençon launched a sudden attack and took the fortified bridge. The English held the town and the castle, a large thirteenth-century rectangular structure with four corner towers, located just outside the town walls. On 16 June, the French moved against Beaugency, but the English withdrew inside the town walls and to the 36m (118ft) high, six-level, square keep from the twelfth century, garrisoned by about 600 men. The French artillery fired at the town walls and the keep all night and the next day from positions across the river. The English agreed to surrender if they could leave and promised not to take up arms against the French for ten days. On 18 June, resistance ended at Meung and the French moved on the fortified town of Janville. On the same day, Joan and La Hire led the French army to its first victory after the siege of Orléans in a major field battle at Patay defeating 5,000 Englishmen with only 1,500 men of the army's vanguard. The townspeople of Janville barred the fleeing English from their town and opened it to Joan.

Between 26 June and 17 July, as Joan led the Dauphin from the Loire to Reims to be crowned king, many towns and cities opened their gates to them since there were no English garrisons in most cases. On 29 June, Joan's army prepared to put Auxerre under siege, but the townspeople paid to prevent an assault. On 5 July, the French army reached Troyes where a population less sympathetic to the Dauphin stood firm. The fortified city was defended by up to 600 English and Burgundian troops. After several days of futile negotiations, when the townspeople saw Joan prepare her artillery and troops to attack the city, they surrendered on 11 July. The city of Châlons-en-Champagne welcomed the arrival of the French army. Joan triumphantly reached her main objective, the friendly city of Reims, on 16 July.

The English were ready and waiting behind the fortifications of Paris having reinforced the gates by placing boulevards in front of them to protect them from cannon. The moats and other obstacles around the city were improved and artillery and a large supply of cannonballs were emplaced. Meanwhile, after Charles VII was crowned, more towns went over to him including Laon, Soissons, Provins, Senlis, and Compiègne among others. Joan reached Saint Denis on 26 August. After days of probing the defences, she directed her efforts at the north-western gate of St. Honoré on the right bank of the Seine. Like the other city gates, it had a large gatehouse with the typical array of defensive features like gunports. The water-filled moat was about 3m (9.8ft) deep. The French forces were not large enough to encircle the city and face the 3,000 English defenders. The assault began at mid-morning on 8 September with an artillery bombardment while the French tried to fill in the moat with fascines and other materials. The 8m (26ft) high and 3m (9.8ft) thick walls and the 15m (49ft) high towers held out rather well. The French troops advanced across the moat with scaling ladders. The attack lasted about five hours. The defenders put up a vigorous defence that drove the French back after Joan was wounded and the cannons and guns on the ramparts inflicted many casualties. Joan was prepared to renew the assault the next day, but the king called it off and left for Sens, according to Monstrelet.[38]

In 1430, Philippe the Good, Duke of Burgundy, laid siege to Compiègne after he forced the surrender of the castle of Choisy-sur-Oise and demolished it. Compiègne had a single bridge across the Oise. A boulevard on the right bank had been added to the bridge defences. It was surrounded by a wet moat fed by the Oise and walls with over forty towers and several gates.[39] Philippe erected a fort or bulwark within bowshot of the defences of Compiègne and dug a deep ditch to allow his men to move back and forth to the front protected from enemy cannon fire. Philippe used several cannons and five large bombards to breach the walls. In March, Joan of Arc came to support the defenders. On 23 May, during a raid in which she had to retreat to the town, she was captured as the gates closed in front of her. Philippe's artillery continued to batter the gates with huge stones and destroyed some mills. Several deep mines advanced towards the walls with little success. Philippe had to send troops to defend the castle and town of Namur threatened by the Bishop of Liège. After two months, the boulevard in front of the bridge fell in a surprise night attack. Many of the defenders drowned trying to escape across the river. The Burgundians turned the captured artillery against the town. However, Philippe had to leave Compiègne to take possession of the Duchy of Brabant whose duke had just died. He left John of Luxembourg in charge of the siege. As the winter progressed, supplies and rations dwindled inside the city walls. To counter the numerous sallies by the garrison, John built a large fort close to the gate on the south side leading to the castle of Pierrefonds. In the spring of 1431, word came that a relief force of 4,000 was on the way and John decided to intercept it. While he was away with the bulk of his troops, the besieged stormed the fort blocking the southern gate. Finally, the Burgundians decamped, lifting the siege and leaving behind a large number of cannons for the French. In this siege, it appears that cannon matched cannon.

As the war continued with many more sieges, gunpowder artillery gained increasing importance in warfare. The English attacked the tidal island fortress of Mont-Saint-Michel from a nearby islet. Between 1415 and 1420, Abbot Robert Jolivet built a wall with impressive gates around the town, which had expanded below the monastery.[40] Shortly before that, work began on a châtelet at the entrance to the monastery and the barbican in front of the châtelet blocking the long winding stairway from the town below. In 1434, the English took the village at the base of the hill and tried to reach the entrance to the abbey above the village, but they were repelled by 119 Norman soldiers who drove them back across the sand flats and captured their cannons.[41]

In 1434, Jean Bureau, a French artillery expert, joined Charles VII. In September 1435, the Duke of Bedford, the best English commander, died. Worse for the English, in 1435 the Treaty of Arras brought peace between Burgundy and Charles VII. In April 1436, Duke Philippe, who now sided with Charles VII, put Calais under siege only to be driven back by a counter-attack in August. That year, Charles VII occupied Paris.

The situation deteriorated for the English as they attempted to hold every fortified town against superior numbers. John Talbot – released from captivity in 1436 – recaptured Harfleur from the French in 1440. The next year, Jean Bureau's artillery brought about the fall of Pontoise in a siege that lasted from June to the end of October. In 1443, the French took the port of Dieppe, which put them back on the Channel. In 1444, the Truce of Tours was signed between

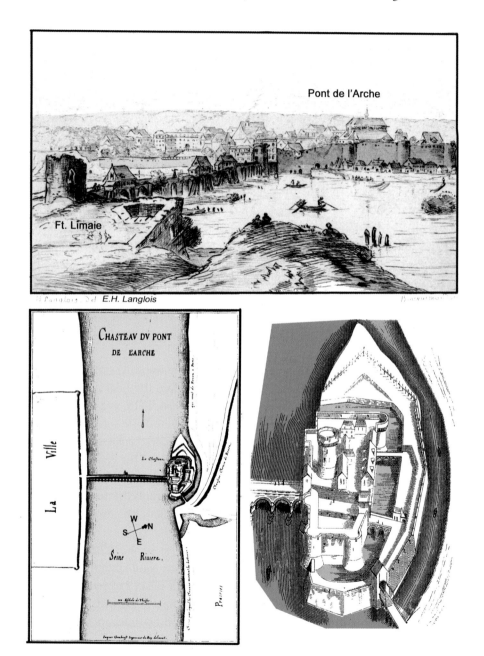

Pont de l'Arche. Top: Old drawing of Pont de l'Arche showing Fort Limaie on right bank of Seine, and walled town on left bank. Bottom: Plan showing Château of Fort Limaie.

Chateau of Philippe Augustus

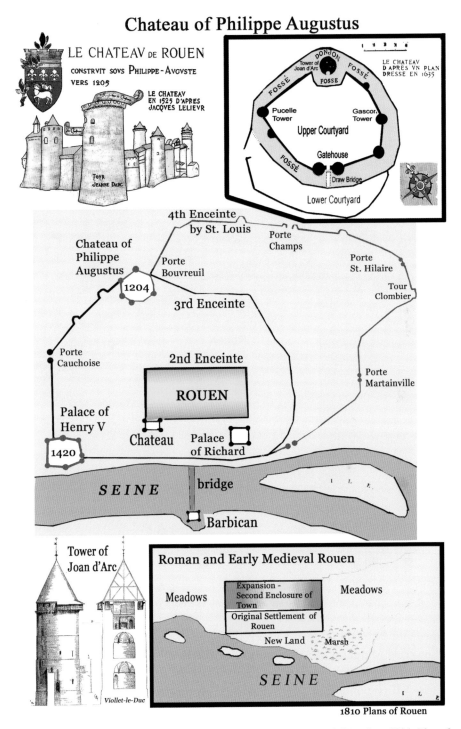

LE CHATEAV DE ROUEN

CONSTRVIT SOVS PHILIPPE-AVGVSTE
VERS 1205

LE CHATEAV
EN 1525 D'APRES
JACQVES LELIEVR

TOVR
JEANNE DARC

LE CHATEAV
D APRÈS VN PLAN
DRESSE EN 1635

DONJON
Tower of
Joan d'Arc   FOSSÉ
FOSSÉ   FOSSÉ

Pucelle
Tower   Gascon
Tower

Upper Courtyard

Gatehouse

Draw Bridge

Lower Courtyard

4th Enceinte
by St. Louis

Chateau of
Philippe
Augustus

Porte
Champs

Porte
Bouvreuil

Porte
St. Hilaire

Tour
Clombier

1204

3rd Enceinte

Porte
Cauchoise

2nd Enceinte

ROUEN

Porte
Martainville

Palace of
Henry V

1420

Chateau   Palace
of Richard

SEINE   bridge

I L E

Barbican

Tower of
Joan d'Arc

Roman and Early Medieval Rouen

Meadows

Expansion -
Second Enclosure of
Town

Meadows

Original Settlement of
Rouen

New Land   Marsh

SEINE

I L E

Viollet-le-Duc

1810 Plans of Rouen

Rouen: Drawing and plan of Chateau of Philippe Augustus built on a hill in about 1204. Plan of defences of Rouen showing original settlement, 2nd enclosure from Roman times, 3rd and 4th enclosures with a drawing of the Joan of Arc Tower, the only remaining part of Château of Philippe Augustus.

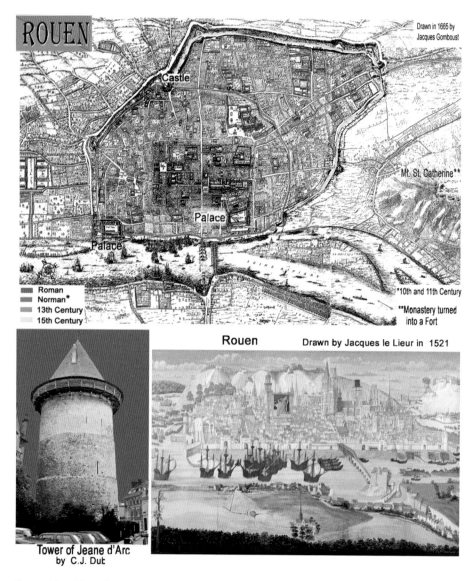

Rouen. Top: Plan of Rouen showing the defences and location of fort on Mt. St. Catherine. Bottom: Photo of Joan of Arc Tower by C.J. Dub and painting of Rouen from 1521.

France and England. Henry VI secretly agreed to yield Maine to Charles VII and married Margaret of Anjou, a niece of Charles VII, the next year. The truce was broken in March 1449 when English troops attacked and took Fougères. Charles VII responded by taking Pont-de-l'Arche on 15 May and launching an invasion of Normandy in July. In August, several fortified sites fell to the French including Verneuil, Lisieux, Mortain, Vernon, Évreux, Louviers, and Harcourt. In September, Roche-Guyon, Fécamp, St-Lô, Alençon, Argentan and Gisors fell to the French who recaptured Fougères and put Rouen under siege in October.

BATTLE OF FORMIGNY

Fougères and Formigny: Top: Monument to French victory at Formigny in Normandy. Below: Plan of Fougères.

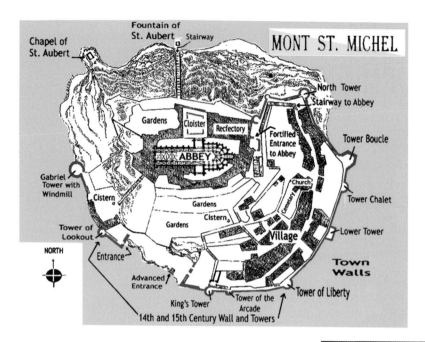

Mont-Saint-Michel. Top: Plan of Mont-Saint-Michel: Below: Model showing the site before it was fortified.

MONT SAINT-MICHEL

Mont-Saint-Michel. Lower left: Fortified entrance to the abbey showing the barbican and châtelet behind it at the entrance to the abbey. Lower right: The isle at low tide viewed from Avranches.

Rouen surrendered in November. Château-Gaillard came under siege between the end of September and late November. The French besieged Harfleur in early December 1449 and its defenders gave up on New Year's Day 1450. Honfleur was next, falling in mid-January 1450. On 15 April, the decisive English defeat on the battlefield of Formigny led to the rapid collapse of resistance in Normandy.[42] The French took Avranches and Bayeux in May as the Bretons drove the English off

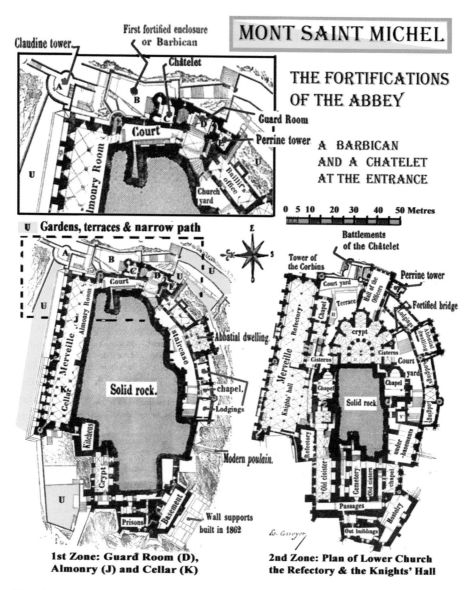

Claudine tower.

First fortified enclosure
or Barbican

Châtelet

MONT SAINT MICHEL

THE FORTIFICATIONS
OF THE ABBEY

Guard Room

Perrine tower

A BARBICAN
AND A CHATELET
AT THE ENTRANCE

0 5 10   20   30   40   50 Metres

Gardens, terraces & narrow path

Battlements
of the Châtelet

Tower of
the Corbins

Perrine tower

Fortified bridge

Abbatial dwelling.

chapel.

Lodgings

Solid rock.

Modern *poulain.*

Wall supports
built in 1862

Solid rock

**1st Zone: Guard Room (D),
Almonry (J) and Cellar (K)**

**2nd Zone: Plan of Lower Church
the Refectory & the Knights' Hall**

*Mont-Saint-Michel: Plans of two levels of the Abbey with detail on its fortifications. Drawings
from Edouard Corroyer in* Descriptive Guide of Mont Saint-Michel.

the island of Tombelaine, removing the threat to Mont-Saint-Michel. Caen was
the next to come under siege in June 1450. It was bombarded by Jean Bureau
for three weeks before the English surrendered. In July, Falaise endured a siege
of two weeks before the French allowed the garrison to leave. Domfront fell on
2 August. Cherbourg had resisted fiercely since 6 July, but the garrison capitulated
in August. This removed the English from Normandy after about sixty sieges in a
campaign that had begun in 1449.

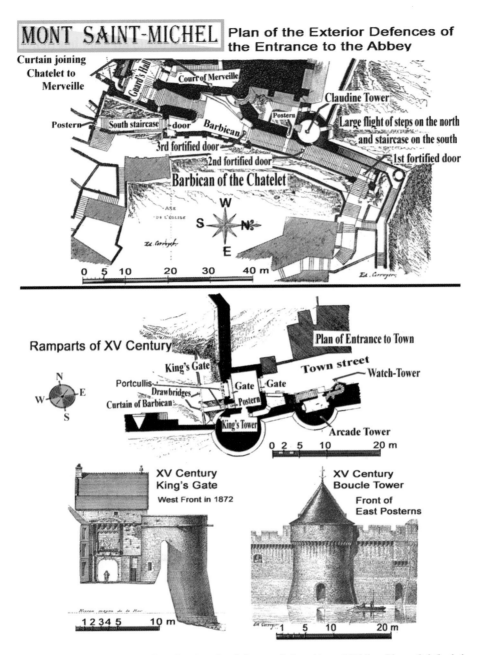

Mont-Saint-Michel. Top: Plan showing the defences of the abbey. Middle: Plan of defended entrance to the town walls below the abbey at King's Gate. Bottom: Profiles of King's Gate and Boucle Tower. Drawings from Edouard Corroyer in Descriptive Guide of Mont Saint-Michel.

After that, the campaigning shifted to the south-west as Count Dunois and the artillery of the Bureau brothers took Bordeaux on 30 June 1451. However, John Talbot easily reoccupied Bordeaux the next year. In 1453, Jean Bureau put

Castillon under siege and Talbot tried to lift it. On 17 July, a battle involving the large-scale use of gunpowder weapons ensued outside the French camp. Talbot lost his life and the English forces were routed.[43] No further major engagements followed and Bordeaux capitulated in October as the French cleaned up and the war ended. Thus, the great war that revolved around many sieges, few major battlefield engagements, and began with a major siege in Normandy concluded in an attempt to lift a siege at the appropriately named town of Castillon-la-Bataille. The English now only held the port of Calais in France.

From Medieval to Renaissance Warfare

From the beginning of the Hundred Years War until the Italian Wars of the century that followed warfare changed greatly in the number of battles and sieges and size of armies. Armies after the Hundred Years War were more professional and much larger. As can be seen by the chart below, the Hundred Years War involved many more sieges than battles. This changed when that war ended.

Sieges of the Hundred Years War			
Era of French King	Castles, Fortresses	Towns, Bastides, Cities	Total
Philip VI Feb. 1328 – Aug. 1350	15	40	55
Jean II Aug. 1350 – Apr. 1364	9	20	29
Charles V Apr. 1364 – Sep. 1380	27	74	101
Charles VI Sep. 1380 – Oct. 1422	35	68	103
Charles VII Oct. 1422 – Oct. 1453	49	96	145
TOTALS	135	298	433

The numbers come from a listing of recorded sieges that may have ranged from small to large in scale. There may have been more than the above number. In some cases a siege of a town and castle were combined.

Major Battles of the Hundred Years War: Saint Omer (1340), Champtoceaux (1341), Morlaix (1342), Auberoche (1345), St. Pol (1346), Blanchetaque (1346), **Crécy (1346)**, La Roche-Derrien (1347), Ardres (1351), Mauron (1352), Comborn (1353), Montmuran (1354), **Poitiers (1356)**, Cocherel (1364), Auray (1364), **Najera (1367)**, Montiel (1369), Pontvallain (1370), Chieset (1372), Roosebeke (1382), **Agincourt (1415)**, Fresnay (1420), Bauge (1421), Cravant (1423), La Brossinière (1423), **Verneuil (1424)**, St. James (1426), Herrings (1429), Jargeau (1429), Meung-sur-Loire (1429), Beaugency (1429), **Patay (1429)**, Gerbevoy (1435), **Formigny (1450)**,

Castillon (1453). Although this may not be an exhaustive list of battles, it represents most of them. A total of thirty-five battles, some large and some small.[44] The battles of Jargeau, Meung-sur-Loire, and Beaugency mainly involved engaging troops in castles, fortified towns, and at fortified bridges. At least eight battles were significant (**in bold print**), while of the major included Caen (1346), Calais (1346–7), Harfleur (1415), Rouen (1418–19), Orleans (1428–9), Rouen (1449), and Castillon (1453). The siege of Castillon was included with the last major battle.

The Hundred Years War revolved heavily around sieges of fortified sites with only a few important battles. By contrast, the Wars of Roses in England (1455–85) involved almost twenty battles in thirty years. The siege of Harlech Castle, which lasted from 1461 to 1468, was the longest in English history, but it was not decisive. Although there were few sieges during this war, they were significant because most fortified sites surrendered after the defenders army was defeated on the battlefield.

By comparison, the Italian Wars between 1494 and 1530 involved many more major battles (with forces in the tens of thousands instead of thousands) than the Hundred Years War and several sieges. The French invasion between 1494 and 1504 comprised four major battles. The War of the League of Cambrai (1508–16) consisted of nine major battles (including one in Britain and one in France) that included the siege at Padua in 1509, the Papal army attack and capture of the citadel of Mirandola in 1511, the French assault on the fortress of Ravenna in 1512, the capture of Milan by Swiss mercenaries, and the siege involving these same Swiss troops at Novara in 1513. The wars in the peninsula that lasted from 1521 to 1530 numbered about six significant battles that included the siege and battle of Pavia in 1525, the attack and sack of Rome in 1527, and the siege of Florence from 1529 to 1530. Most of the other battles and sieges of the Italian Wars were on a larger scale than those of the Hundred Years War.

Sources: Eggenberger, *Dictionary of Battles*; Dupuy and Dupuy, *Encyclopedia of Military History*; Wikipédia L'encyclopédie libre, *Liste des sièges de la guerre de Cent Ans* https://fr.wikipedia.org/wiki/Liste_des_si%C3%A8ges_de_la_guerre_de_Cent_Ans

Chapter Four

The Fringes

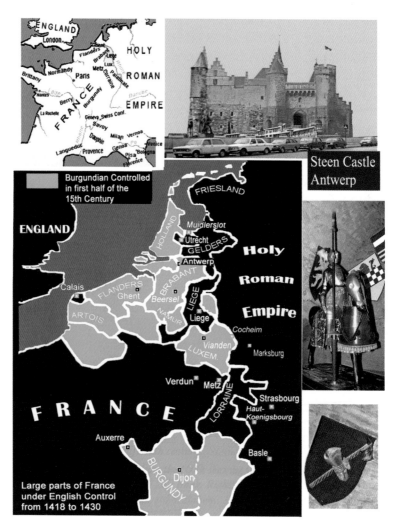

Map of the Low Countries, Burgundy and Lorraine in the fifteenth century. Top right: Photo of Steen (Stone) Castle in Antwerp on the Scheldt, built in the early thirteenth century. Emperor Charles V renovated it in 1520 with sandstone that is lighter in colour than the original Tournai limestone. It is the oldest stone building in the city. In the 1540s, it was turned into a prison for the next three centuries, its only other claim to fame. It was partially destroyed to widen the harbour. Right centre: Full suit of armour on display at Bouillon. Full suits of plate armour replaced mail in the Late Middle Ages.

Border Lands

The lands between France and the Holy Roman Empire, which had once been part of the Western Roman Empire, were a bone of contention during most of the Late Middle Ages. They included the modern-day Low Countries of Belgium and The Netherlands, parts of Burgundy, and the territories of modern-day Alsace and Lorraine located between France and the Rhine River. Even though the Low Countries fell under the control of the newly formed Holy Roman Empire of the ninth century, a count who was a vassal of the French king ruled most of Flanders. By the thirteenth century, the modern day Low Countries, which included the counties of Flanders (eastern Flanders), Namur, Loon (Looz), Holland/Zeeland and Guelders[1] and the duchies of Brabant and Limburg, became secular principalities in the Empire. The Empire exerted more control over the Duchy of Luxembourg. In the fourteenth century, several cantons of the future Switzerland became autonomous. After the battle of Sempach in 1386, they achieved de facto independence, but *de jure* independence was not recognized until 1648.

The areas in contention between the French, the Burgundians and the Holy Roman Empire included a region known as Lotharingia, which became a duchy when the Frankish Empire broke up in the tenth century.[2] Lower Lotharingia included the Low Countries and Upper Lotharingia comprised Lorraine.[3] West of the Rhine, Suebia formed modern Alsace. From the Middle Ages to the twentieth century, the entire region, which is home to Germanic (including Dutch and Flemish) and Latin (including French and Walloon) groups, has been a cause of conflict between the English, the French and the Germans.

Castles of the Fringe West of the Rhine

Today, the castle of Bouillon stands in the province of Luxembourg of Belgium on the rocky spur of a peninsula formed by a loop of the Semois River above the town of the same name. First mentioned in a manuscript of 988, the stronghold may have been centuries older. It controlled a passage through the Ardennes running north–south between Upper and Lower Lotharingia. Godfrey of Bouillon, the fifth and last duke of the House of Ardennes, sold the castle and his duchy, which was part of the Holy Roman Empire, to the Bishop of Liège to finance his participation in the First Crusade in 1096.[4] The bishops controlled the castle until 1483, when the Le Marck family took it from them.

The present castle is not Godfrey's since little of it remains, except possibly for the underground chambers. His eleventh-century castle most likely consisted mainly of wooden components although there may have been a stone keep according to some sources. Much of the present-day castle dates from the Hundred Years War and includes numerous modifications by Vauban who turned it into a cannon-bearing fortress in the seventeenth century. A drawbridge gave access to a barbican-like structure over a deep cut from a Vauban-type defensive position. A second drawbridge allowed access from the barbican to a large tower that served as a gatehouse where passage was blocked by an iron portcullis. Both drawbridges were converted to stone after the Middle Ages. A third drawbridge spans a water-filled moat. Beyond it lies the courtyard at the end of which is located Godfrey's subterranean room cut into the rock at the site of the original keep. Here also is the Vauban-era Austrian Tower and the so-called Clock Tower that the Bishop of Liège, George of Austria, had rebuilt and changed into a caponier in the early 1550s. At the far end of this section, there is a structure called Godfrey's Easy Chair, a double observation post cut into the rock that predates the Clock Tower and nearby walls. From here, one can observe the road from Liège. Much of the castle shows the work of Vauban, which turned it into a post-Medieval fortress. According to local lore, a deep cellar at this far end of the castle might have been an oubliette. Near the entrance by the chapel, behind the guardhouse and third drawbridge, there is a cistern fed by a natural spring and a 50m (164ft) deep well that could support a garrison of 300 men. The castle, which stretches for about 170m (558ft) along the top of the spur and averages about 18m (59ft) in width, stands over 73m (239ft) above the river.

Bouillon Castle went through several sieges, which are recounted in Marcel Leroy's *Bouillon et son château dans l'histoire*. The 1141 siege took place at a time when the Duchy of Bouillon faced many difficulties. Raynaldus de Bar surprised the garrison and seized the castle, property of Abron II, Prince-Bishop of Liège at the time. The bishop sought the help of Henry IV 'the Blind', Count of Namur and Luxembourg, and dispatched a strong army to take back the castle. The siege lasted for weeks, but the garrison's food supply did not run low. Abron, inspired by the example of Godfrey of Bouillon at Jerusalem a century earlier, led a religious procession from Liège and paraded it in front of the castle. In the meantime, his troops captured a tower on a crest from which they could fire projectiles against the castle's stone keep. Raynaldus capitulated and pleaded for God's forgiveness. Over a hundred years later, in 1267 the governor of Bouillon, Gerard de Jambe, revolted against the Prince-Bishop Henri de Gueldre, who took it back. In 1287, the Count of Luxembourg quietly positioned his army to take the castle. However, he managed to capture the castellan, Jean of Flanders, who was on hunting expedition, and seized the castle without a fight. In 1378, Pope Urban VI appointed Arnold de Horne, Bishop of Utrecht, to the Bishopric of Liège where a faction supported by the Anti-Pope Clement VII picked Persan de Rochefort for the same position. Persan seized the castle by force of arms, but Arnold struck back, levelled the town, and took control of Liège in 1379. John III of Bavaria succeeded Arnold as Prince-Bishop of Liège at the age of 15 in 1389. However, before long, he earned the enmity of the burghers of Liège because of his dictatorial ways. The irate burghers drove him from the city, picked a new bishop, and took Bouillon in 1407. John asked his brother-in-law, John the

Fearless of Burgundy, to help him and his army of mercenaries. In 1408, he took back his duchy and the castle. He attacked Liège with the Burgundian army that same year and reassumed the title of Prince-Bishop until the pope forced him to give it up in 1418.[5]

In 1482, the La Marck family, backed by Charles VIII of France, assumed the title to the duchy. Duke Robert I died taking part in a siege elsewhere in 1489 and his son Robert II replaced him. In 1495, the duchy and castle fell to an army from Luxembourg, which was defeated the next year by Robert who took back his castle. In 1521, Robert II managed to muster an army of 5,000 men and declared war on Holy Roman Emperor Charles V. He was routed and the forces of the Empire took his castle. The emperor ordered the moat filled and some of the castles defences destroyed. In 1552, the French helped Robert IV de La Marck take back Bouillon. Robert, who only had a small force, tricked the garrison into believing that his army was much larger than it was and the castle surrendered without a fight. The history of the castle of Bouillon during the Middle Ages and later demonstrates how many castles, even those in strategic positions, went through many sieges now considered little more than historic trivia since they seldom played an important role in the great scheme of things.

Gravensteen Castle, known as the Castle of the Counts, located in Ghent at the confluence of the Lieve and Lys Rivers, held a key position in this lowland region. The present structure dates mainly form the twelfth and fourteenth centuries and underwent restoration in the late nineteenth century. In the tenth century, Arnulf I, Count of Flanders, fortified a high sand dune on the location of the future castle with wooden buildings. In the eleventh century, the large central wooden building was replaced with a stone one. This fortified residence had walls whose thickness ranged from 1.65m to 2.2m (5.2ft to 7.2ft) and consisted of three levels. In the twelfth century, a motte and bailey with a moat appeared on the site. The earth from the excavation of the moat formed a mound around the main building turning its ground floor into a cellar and its upper floor (the second storey) into the ground floor. In 1180, the first two levels of the original structure became the cellars of a new keep. Other buildings were later added on this motte as well as curtain walls with a stone gatehouse. After Count Philip of Flanders returned from a crusade in 1179, he made these additions to the complex in the 1180s before he departed on another crusade in 1190. Some of the castle's features are the result of observations he made during his first crusade. He commemorated his adventure with a cross cut above the main entrance.[6] The keep is 35m by 12m (115ft by 39ft) and 30m (98ft) high. Count Philip added two new levels to the two original ones of the old structure. The older walls and a tower are now located below today's castle. There is a building with a pair of flanking towers against the keep. Its ground floor may have been for the castellan and the upper level held a chapel and a residence. The kitchens were located on the narrow side of the keep. The residence of the count stands across from the keep against the outer walls.

Post-medieval Bouillon. Most of the medieval remains of the castle were modified in the Renaissance. Top: View from the Austrian Tower across upper section. Bottom left: View of the Austrian Tower inside the upper courtyard. Bottom right: View of the Austrian Tower from the entrance to the upper courtyard. Plan of castle.

The surrounding curtain wall – sometimes called a chemise – with twenty-four turrets on its buttresses, form an oval with a maximum diameter of 85m (279ft). One turret, covered and enclosed, is larger than the others are. It served as a watchtower known as the 'tub' because of its shape. Each of these semicircular turrets is open in the rear and has a lower level on the wall walk with loopholes and an upper level with battlements. Each turret includes machicoulis. Except in the 'tub', wooden floors were installed in the turrets in times of emergency. The walls and buildings are mainly built with limestone and bricks of various colours.

Gravensteen underwent a major siege in 1128 in an attempt to drive out the Normans. In the fourteenth century, the burghers of the town besieged the castle when the French took control of Flanders in 1302. The local aldermen took refuge there after they tried to raise taxes and the burghers revolted. The mob put the wooden components to the torch, forcing the occupants to surrender. At the beginning of the Hundred Years War in 1338, Louis of Nevers, Count of Flanders, fled to the castle as well when the locals rose against him. The guilds were incensed with him for not siding and promoting good relations with England so they could continue importing English wool for the weaving industry. Led by Jacques van Artevelde,[7] the burghers breached the wall of the castle. Louis fled to France and died in the battle of Crécy in 1346. His son, Louis II, moved his residence out of the castle to a safer location. Even though repairs took place in the fourteenth century, the Counts of Flanders did not use Gravensteen as their main residence. In time, the castle became an administrative centre and an infamous prison.

Other important castles in this region seldom affected the course of history. One of the better-known castles in the Netherlands is Muiderslot ('slot' means 'castle'). Unlike the Bouillon and Gravensteen, it looks like the stereotypical castle with an almost square shape (32m x 35m [105ft x 115ft]), four round corner towers with conical roofs, a gatehouse with a drawbridge, and a wide wet moat around it. Its brick walls are 1.5m (5ft) thick.

In 1280, Floris V,[8] Count of Holland, built this brick castle in the middle of the Vecht River near the confluence with the Zuider Zee south-east of Amsterdam to control the trade route to Utrecht. It is possible that he actually purchased a pre-existing stronghold. His castle had brick walls and towers and, according to local historians, wooden interior buildings. In 1296, Floris was kidnapped by conspirators during a hunting trip, imprisoned in his castle for five days, and stabbed to death when he tried to escape. The three noblemen who kidnapped him had a trial resulting in one execution, and the two sent into exile. Willem van Mechelen, archbishop of Utrecht, captured the castle in 1297 after a siege and, according to legend, he razed it to the ground in 1300, but local historians now believe that he may not have destroyed it. However, after 1300, it faded from the annals of history for almost a century. In 1370, Albert I, Duke of Bavaria and Count of Holland and Zeeland, built a new castle or rebuilt the old one. The construction took about fifteen years. The Duke of Burgundy took Holland in the next century. The son of Philip the Good, Charles the Bold, who broke relations with his father between 1463 and 1465, lived in the castle until he succeeded to his father.

Gravensteen Castle at Ghent. Top: Châtelet at entrance. Middle: Bartizans along the walls and the Count's residence with the keep to the right. Bottom: Plan.

Muiderslot experienced major sieges in the sixteenth century. In 1505, the Duke of Gelderland (Guelder) took the castle when he revolted against Burgundy. However, he had to surrender it when he signed a treaty in 1508. The next siege came in 1576 when the castle was in Spanish hands. From 1280 until the end of the eighteenth century, the governors of the castle were also Bailiffs of Naarden and Gooiland and Sheriffs of Muiden. The garrison varied from ten to thirty men since it is a relatively small castle. The southern tower housed the quarters for the garrison. It includes two living levels and a roofed room with the battlements above them. A type of oubliette or dungeon was added below the ground floor during the fourteenth century reconstruction. It was accessed from the upper level of the western tower rather than the ground floor. The garrison commander ran the castle from the gatehouse, which had bretèche that covered the entrance. By 1500, the castle had become obsolete since it could not resist artillery. Muiderslot's greatest claim to fame, besides tourism, is its many appearances in films.

Another castle whose main claim to fame comes from its use in modern films is Doornenburg, a unique Dutch brick stronghold located in Gelderland.[9] Like many castles, Doornenburg saw little to no action of interest during the Middle Ages. A fortified manor, which had existed on the site since the ninth century, was turned into a castle in the Late Middle Ages. A rectangular keep surrounded by a wet moat is linked by a bridge to the fifteenth century rectangular bailey, which includes a gatehouse, a couple of corner towers, and corner bartizans (échauguettes). A wet moat surrounded the bailey. The castle acquired a farm after the Renaissance. The castle was restored just in time for the Germans to turn it into a headquarters in 1941. It was destroyed by Allied bombing in 1945 and was restored to its fifteenth-century splendour after the war.

The red-brick castle of Beersel, located in the Flemish Brabant,[10] saw action more than once. It was built during the first decade of the fourteenth century in the lowlands on marshy ground, barely 43m (141ft) above sea level. It has a large moat fed by a tributary of the Senne River. Its oval enceinte with high brick walls has three large horseshoe-shaped towers connected to each other by a wall walk. The main defensive tower on the north side includes the entrance with a drawbridge and portcullis. The tower on the opposite side served as the residence of the governor of the castle. The western tower is slightly smaller. All three towers were three storeys high. Men in the guardroom on the first floor of the north tower controlled the drawbridge and portcullis below. The top floors of the towers served as armouries and gave access to the battlements. The lower floors served as dungeons or prisons. Some were adapted for small cannon at the end of the Middle Ages. A couple of small sally ports opened into the moat. The towers had small windows (now enlarged) opening into the courtyard. Along the walls of the courtyard, other buildings, probably wooden, served as kitchens and other facilities. Today's castle is largely a reconstruction.

'tHvys te Mvyden.

Muiderslot Castle, located near Amsterdam, is laid out in the manner of what many would consider
a typical castle with four round corner towers, a gatehouse and wet moat in a rectangular shape with
a courtyard and buildings along the walls.

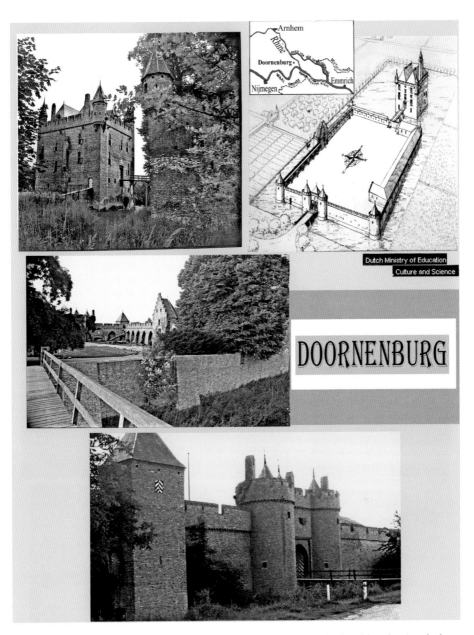

Doornenburg Castle. Top: Photo of the keep and the rear wall of the bailey. Plan showing the large bailey and the keep. Middle: View of interior of the bailey from the bridge leading into the keep. Bottom: Gatehouse at the entrance to the bailey.

Jan II, Duke of Brabant,[11] gave permission to Godfrey of Hellebeek to build Beersel Castle as an outpost to protect the southern approaches to Brussels. At the time, Jan II was concerned about the encroachment of France and the pro-French count of South Holland in the Brabant. While the Hundred Years War raged, the

Beersel Castle located just south of Brussels. Top: View of interior and side of tower with number 1617 on it. Other views of the castle and its three towers.

Brabant was engaged in its own war of succession with its neighbours and in the mid-1350s, the castle was damaged during regional fighting and repaired later. In the 1470s, Beersel became involved in a major dispute and revolt resulting from the marriage of Mary of Burgundy to the future Holy Roman Emperor Maximillian. Her father, Charles the Bold, had aligned himself with the French and fought against the Swiss. The people of the Netherlands, which included Belgium at the time, finally revolted, but Jan III van Witthem, governor of the castle, remained loyal to Emperor Maximillian.[12] In November 1488, supporters of the revolt from Brussels unsuccessfully besieged the castle. They returned in April 1489, this time supported by French artillery, and after a brief siege breached the walls and stormed the castle. The victors destroyed the gate tower and southern tower, set fire to the wooden structures, and plundered the castle. Maximillian's soldiers recaptured Beersel and forced the people of Brussels to rebuild it between 1491 and 1508. The castle remained occupied until the late eighteenth century. It is not clear when the stepped style was added to the towers and whether the battlements of the walls on the western sides were covered.[13] The gate tower has a large number '1617' engraved on it and the other towers include turrets overlooking the courtyard. However, it is not possible to tell how many of the changes took place during the reconstruction of the castle.

Vianden, one of the largest castles in Western Europe, is located in northern Luxembourg. It occupied the site of a former Roman castellum on a rocky promontory at an elevation of 310m (1,017ft), about 100m (328ft) above the town and the Our River. Most of it was built during the High Middle Ages in Romanesque style. However, in the Late Middle Ages the style switched to Gothic, mainly in the interior spaces. During the ninth and tenth centuries, a wall encircled the site and a large hall on the west side. Major construction took place in 1100. The first structures of the medieval castle included a square keep and a few smaller buildings. Later, a large square structure was erected on the west central side and the old hall was converted into a palace (the Knight's Hall). The keep was replaced with a newer 'residence tower' (see plan). A two-floor octagonal chapel was added on the south side. Both the chapel and palace walls were higher than the older structures. Between the thirteenth and fifteenth century, many of the structures were connected to each other forming a massive castle. A tower on the north side and three on the north-east side along the new palace provided additional protection. During the first half of the thirteenth century, Henry I, Earl of Vianden, launched a new construction phase. He connected the palace to the chapel with the so-called Byzantine Gallery. High Gothic gables and high roofs replaced much of the earlier Romanesque superstructures of the palace and chapel. The residential tower was enlarged, the lower baily was extended along the south-west side, and two entrances were added. New walls were erected along the path on the west side that led to the castle and the forecourt or bailey on the south side below. With the gateway of the bailey, this resulted in the addition of two gateways. The bailey on the east side of the castle has another gate that leads to the main entrance of the castle. Beyond that, a gate opens into another bailey that occupies the northern and eastern area just below the castle walls. The castle without the baileys is 90m to 100m (295ft to 328ft) long and about 30m (98ft)at its widest point.

The town wall was enlarged at the end of the thirteenth century. It covered 1.5km (0.9 miles) and had two gates, two circular towers, and sixteen open-backed towers. These walls connected to the southern end and to the western side of the outer walls of the castle.

The dynasty of the Counts of Vianden ended after 1417 and their holdings passed to the count of Nassau did not use Vianden as a residence. During the Dutch revolt against Philip II of Spain in the sixteenth century, the Count of Nassau took part in the fighting against the king. In retaliation, Philip confiscated his castle and gave it to the governor of Luxembourg. The only significant action the castle engaged in was in November 1944 when thirty men of the militia successfully held the castle against an assault by a company of German SS soldiers, but they had to abandon it later during the battle of the Bulge.

Castles abound near the Rhine. Cochem Castle in the Palatinate (Rheinland-Pfalz) stands on a hill over 100m (328ft) above the Moselle, appearing like a castle out of a fairy tale. The original stronghold built in the eleventh century, consisted of a square keep 5.2m by 5.2m (17ft x 17ft) and walls up to 3.7m (12ft) thick. It was erected by Ezzo, founder of the Ezzonid dynasty, whose members served as counts of the Palatinate in the Holy Roman Empire. As in many German castles, the square Bergfried (keep) stands in the centre surrounded by other structures. The counts of the Palatinate built and owned Cochem until 1151 when Emperor Conrad III took it from them. In 1294, the Empire gave it to Balduin, Archbishop of Trier. In the early fourteenth century, Balduin enlarged the castle and connected it to the town with massive walls and Gothic architecture replaced Romanesque. The castle served as a toll station, like several other Rhine castles. A chain was used to block passage on the river. Cochem Castle suffered much damage during the Thirty Years War (1618–48) and Louis XIV's French troops in 1689 caused great destruction to the site. Reconstruction of the castle began in 1871.

Castles also dot the landscape of the Vosges in Alsace. One of the largest is Haut-Koenigsbourg on a rocky spur of the Vosges. From its mountaintop perch on the Stophanberch (Staufenberg) near Sélestat, the castle overlooks the Alsatian plain by the Rhine. The major trade routes were within its view and reach. Haut-Koenigsbourg was first mentioned in the twelfth century. It was built or expanded by a brother of the Hohenstaufen Holy Roman Emperor. Early in the next century, it was taken over by the dukes of Lorraine; in 1454, it was occupied by Elector Palatine Frederick I. In 1462, when the castle became a haven for robber knights, a coalition of the cities of Strasbourg, Basel, and Colmar sent a force of 500 men armed with cannon to clear them out. The attackers burned the castle down, leaving only the stone shell. In 1479, Emperor Frederick III

Vianden Castle in Luxembourg is one of Europe's largest. Top left: View of north-west side of castle and its entrances. Right: Entrance to the Byzantine Gallery. Middle: Plan and view of the main gate. Bottom: Plan showing town and model showing Vianden in the eleventh century.

gave the ruins to the Counts of Thierstein who rebuilt it in a manner adapted to artillery. Swedish troops destroyed it during the Thirty Years War in 1633 and reconstruction took place many years later.

Haut-Koenigsbourg stands at an elevation of 755m (2,476ft) and stretches from west to east over two high points of the mountain. A road winds up to the castle making it difficult to assault. Due to the amount of reconstruction, the castle is

COCHEM

B = Bergfried
C = Chapel
E = Entrance
F = Stonghold
    and buildings
S = Squires quarters
W = Well

North

Mosel River

Cochem Castle on the Mosel. Top: View of the Bergfried and surrounding buildings of the stronghold with plan. Middle: painting of view across the Mosel. Bottom: View of Cochem overlooking the town and river.

mostly built with local pink or reddish sandstone fashioned into facing ashlars – some of which are rusticated – and coarse rubble. The donjon at the east end of the high castle towers 60m (195ft) above the defences. It is located almost in the centre of the entire stronghold, which had acquired an eastward-extending advanced position in the Late Middle Ages. Some of the walls built before the medieval reconstruction still remain and their bricked-up windows can be seen. The outer wall served as a shield from artillery. Beyond it, there is a heavily-defended entrance leading into the lower courtyard, which connects to the advanced work to the east. The lower courtyard used to house the stables, a tower with a windmill for the bakery, a forge and other facilities. It leads up to the high castle with the donjon with access through an entrance with a well-defended drawbridge. On the south side beyond this entrance, a tower houses a 61m (200ft) deep well. The high castle consists of the donjon and other structures that have undergone changes from the end of the Middle Ages to the nineteenth century. It includes an inner courtyard surrounded by the four-story main building with a kitchen on the bottom floor. The third floor gives access to the donjon. The upper floors hold the chapel and the residence. On the west side of the main building, one can find a garden, a large courtyard, the Great Bulwark, which was added in the Renaissance, and a pair of rounded towers designed for artillery. The battlements include machicoulis that are now roofed. The entrances have bretèches, heavy doors, and portcullis. The distance from the Great Bulwark and the end of the High Castle is about 100m (328ft) and another 40m (131ft) across the lower courtyard. The entire fortress is about 270m (885ft) long and about 40m (131ft) wide. Some of its walls are up to 9m (29.5ft) thick. Kaiser Wilhelm II restored it to its Thirty Years War appearance.

Many castles are located along both sides of the Rhine and occupy sites formerly used by the Romans since this area once was on the frontier of the Western Roman Empire. Some of the better-known castles include Drachenfels near Bonn, Burg Eltz, Marksburg, Rheinfels, and Pfalz near Koblenz. Drachenfels or 'Dragon's Rock' stands on a 321m (1,053ft) high hill. It was built by Archbishop Arnold I of Cologne in the mid-twelfth century to defend the city from the south. It was abandoned after the Thirty Years War and only the ruins of the Bergfried and some walls are left today. Burg Eltz is further up the Rhine Valley on a crag 70m (230ft) above a bend in a tributary of the Moselle River. It was also built in the twelfth century for the counts of Eltz. It includes eight residential towers, some up to 40m (131ft) high. Its main claim to fame is that it is one of the few Rhine castles to have escaped the devastation of war.

Marksburg Castle, which overlooks the Rhine from its right bank, consists of several groups of buildings around an early twelfth-century Bergfried built by the Eppstein family[14] to defend the town of Braubach. Count Eberhard II of Katzenelnbogen bought the Romanesque-style castle in 1283 and his successors added the Gothic section of the castle. The 40m (131ft) high Bergfried stands in the middle of a triangular courtyard surrounded by three wings of residential structures. This mostly thirteen-century Romanesque castle also served as a palace with Gothic-style additions. The present curtain wall with round towers for cannons dates from the fifteenth century and bastions were added later. Like Eltz, it is intact. A short distance the south, overlooking the Rhine, stands Gutenfels Castle built in 1220, a square structure with sides about 2.5m (8.3ft) and a Bergfried with a rectangular courtyard. It looms over a smaller structure

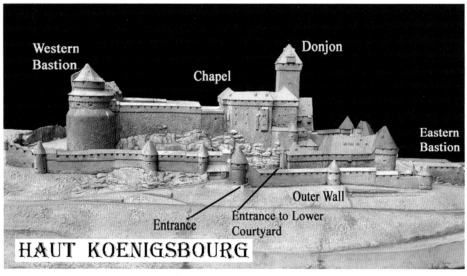

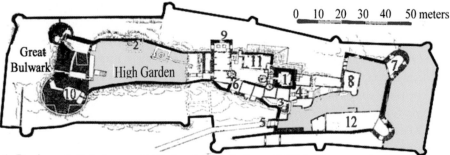

1. Donjon   2. Bakehouse   3. Well   4. Drawbridge   5. Main Entrance   6. Chapel
7. Mill   8. Forge   9. Cisterns   10. Great Tower   11. Kitchen   12. Stables

Haut-Koenigsbourg in Alsace. Top: Model of the castle with all its additions. Middle: Plan. Bottom: Left: view at point #4 on plan looking west into entrance of castles main buildings. Right: View looking east toward chapel (#6) and donjon (#1).

in the middle of the river known as the Pflazgrafenstein built by King Ludwig of Bavaria in 1327. A pentagonal tower in the centre of the Pflaz served as a toll station that worked in tandem with Gutenfels Castle to control the river traffic. A hexagonal enclosure was added to the Pflaz shortly after it was built. After the sixteenth century, corner towers and a bastion completed the defences of the island stronghold. Further up the river, on the right bank, are the ruins of Rheinfels, once the strongest and most massive fortress on the Rhine. Built by the counts of Katzenelnbogen in the mid-thirteenth century, this rectangular castle includes a Bergfried and it could accommodate 4,000 people. In 1255, it resisted an army of the Rhenish League. The counts built another castle across from it on the left bank of the Rhine in the fourteenth century to bolster their control of the river traffic. The castle resisted a major French offensive that took all the other Rhineland castles in the late seventeenth century. Further up the river there were other castles including the Burg Maus on the right bank begun by Archbishop Bohemond II, the Elector of Trier, in 1356 and finished thirty years later.[15] It was built to protect Trier from the Counts of Katzenlnbogen who had owned Burg Rheinfels, and to allow Trier to collect tolls on the Rhine. It included two residential buildings overlooked by a round Bergfried. The 'Robber Barons' used most of these castles to control river trade in the High Middle Ages. Over a dozen castles overlook the Rhine between Bonn and Mainz. Some were updated up to and during the Vauban era and were turned into true fortresses.

Grandson Castle stands above the shores of Lake Neuchatel. The first castle, which was built during the eleventh century on the site of a Roman fortified settlement, was owned by the Grandson family. In the thirteenth century, it was rebuilt by Otto I of Grandson, a friend of Prince Edward of England with whom he participated in the Crusades and the conquest of Wales in 1283. The family was also close to the Savoys one of whose architects – Master James of Savoy (James of St. George) – worked for the English king. Grandson Castle became the property of Jacques of Savoy, an ally of Charles the Bold of Burgundy, at the end of the fifteenth century. After the Swiss Confederation seized it in 1475, Charles the Bold retook it with a large army equipped with cannons in February 1476. Charles executed the 400-man garrison when it surrendered after a ten-day siege. The Swiss Confederation relief force of about 18,000 men arrived too late to save the garrison, but defeated the Burgundian army of about 20,000 at the battle of Grandson in March.[16] Next, the Swiss army turned against the castle in a frenzied assault that brought the quick surrender of its Burgundian garrison.

Today's castle consists of the thirteenth century building modified in the fifteenth century by the Chalons-Orange family. The castles' irregular rectangular trace is almost 61m (200ft) long and is curved on the west end. Initially built around a square keep, today Grandson Castle has five towers (two semicircular and three circular) linked by high curtain walls with covered battlements. The towers lack battlements and machicoulis. The enceinte encloses several buildings:

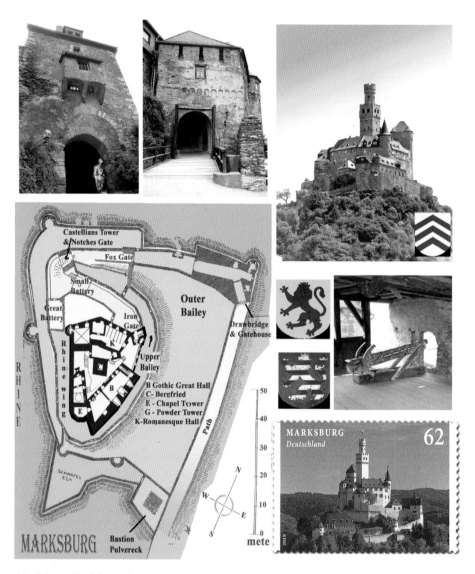

Marksburg: Top left to right: Notches Gate (Arrow Slit Tower) with knight in suit of full plate armour, gatehouse and site of drawbridge of entrance, view of Marksburg with coat of arms of the Eppsteins in the corner. Middle: Coat of arms of Katzenelnbogens and below it coast of arms of the Landgraves of Hesse. View of castle battery position with a mounted small-bore breech-loaded veuglaire in its firing position.

the modern chapel, the knight's hall above it in the south-west corner and the lord's residence. A larger and older building stands in the south central section between the two southern towers and another structure along the eastern wall. A small courtyard occupies the north-western section. A châtelet, attached to an outer wall that encircles the castle, protects the entrance on the west end. On the south side, toward the lake, the outer wall encloses another courtyard. When it was built in 1450, this wall had two corner towers, one of which was the

Rhine castles: Top: One of many castles dominating the Rhine. Middle: Pflaz Castle in the middle of the Rhine took on the shape of a ship. Bottom left: Residential section of Maus Castle with Bergfried overlooking it. Bottom right: Eltz Castle.

detached Bourgogne Tower located closer to the shore to protect the port. Only the Bourgogne Tower survives today. The castle once had a moat, barbican, and drawbridge, which are now gone.

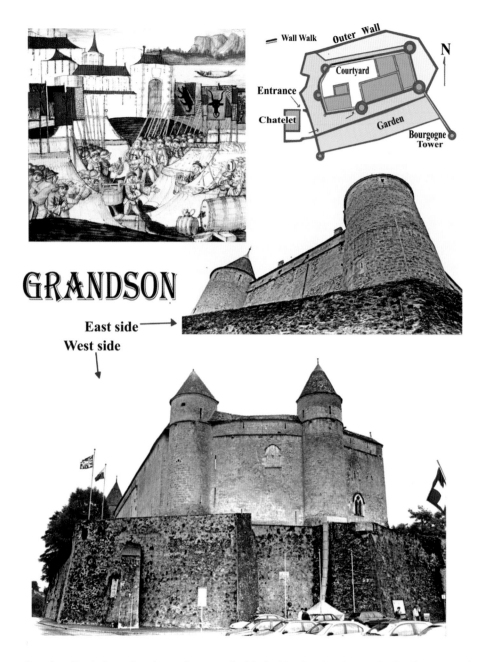

Grandson Castle located at the south-west end of Lake Neuchâtel in Switzerland. Illustration of the battle at Grandson. Middle: Photo of towers on east side. Bottom: Photo showing outer wall and two towers on inner wall on the west side.

Further to the south, the northern route around Lake Leman (Lake Geneva) from Geneva leading through Lausanne to Montreux remains one of the best routes from southern Switzerland to Italy (Savoy). At the end of the lake, near

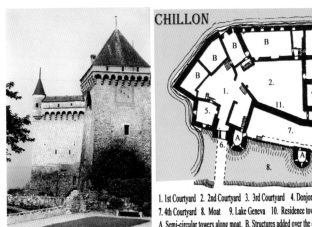

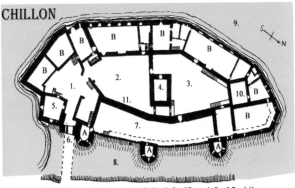

1. 1st Courtyard 2. 2nd Courtyard 3. 3rd Courtyard 4. Donjon 5. Guard Tower 6. Gate & Drawbridge
7. 4th Courtyard 8. Moat 9. Lake Geneva 10. Residence tower 11. Interior Walls
A. Semi-circular towers along moat. B. Structures added over the centuries to serve various purposes from quarters to prisons.

Chillon Castle on Lake Geneva. Top: Photo of south side showing entrance (#6) and Guard Tower (#5) with donjon (#4) in background. Bottom: Plan and another view of Guard Tower (#5).

Montreux, stands the splendid castle of Chillon, which used to guard a narrow defile between the lake and the mountains. Beyond it, Aigle Castle covers the route into the Saint-Maurice pass and the Upper Rhône Valley. Chillon sits on a rocky island once occupied by the Romans. Sometime after the construction of the first enclosure, the stronghold was greatly expanded until the thirteenth century. Chillon Castle was the property of the Bishops of Sion as a fief from the

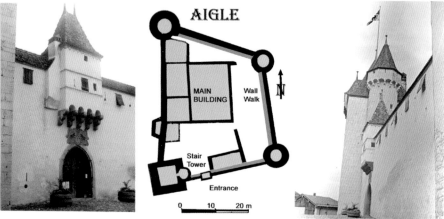

Aigle Castle in Switzerland. Top: View of east side and west side of castle. Bottom: Plan and two views of entrance on south side.

Count of Savoy beginning in the twelfth century. In the thirteenth century, the Counts of Savoy used the castle as a summer home. The castle served as a toll station. In 1536, the Bernese took possession of it after a three-week siege.

The island was separated from the mainland by a narrow strip of water that served as a moat, which had to be widened in the 1200s. The height of three semicircular towers adjacent to the moat, also built at that time, was increased in the next two centuries. At the entrance, a large square tower served as a guard post. The main gate is located between it and one of the semicircular towers. The castle has four courtyards. The tall eleventh-century keep near the centre had a drawbridge on its first storey. All the towers, except the keep, have machicoulis and roofs. A second wall runs behind the walls with the towers creating a fourth courtyard. The oval shaped castle is about 100m by 50m (328ft by 164ft). Chillon owes its fame mostly to Lord Byron's poem about a monk imprisoned there in 1530.

In 1179, the canton of Vaud was ruled by vassals of the Savoys who built the first castle in the town of Aigle in the thirteenth century to defend against French and Swiss incursions. Later in that century, they rebuilt it with a donjon and a curtain wall. In the last half of the fourteen century, the castle came to the Compey family through marriage. After 1450, the Compeys added a large donjon to the south corner. During the conflict with Burgundy in the later part of the century, Jean II of Compey and the Savoy family allied themselves with Charles the Bold against the Swiss Confederation. When a Swiss army led by Bernese troops surrounded the castle, Jean fled the castle during a truce. After the siege ended, the castle was set on fire. Meanwhile, the Swiss defeated Charles at Grandson and Morat in 1476,[17] which led to Bernese control of the region. Aigle Castle was rebuilt. The present tall, square donjon replaced a round tower. The massive curtain wall and its three drum towers with a bretèche over the entrance and on the tower over the entrance present a formidable obstacle. The round stair tower attached to the donjon was crowned with machicoulis. A wall walk served three sides and accessed the covered battlements of the curtains.

Crossroads

The region referred to as Burgundy, located between France and the Holy Roman Empire, is the gateway to the Italian and Iberian peninsulas. It fell under Lothair's control when the Frankish Empire was divided after the death of Louis the Pious. By the late ninth century, it consisted of three parts: the Duchy of Burgundy, the Kingdom of Upper Burgundy, and the Kingdom of Lower Burgundy. The Duchy of Burgundy remained independent until the end of the Middle Ages when it became a permanent part of France. Upper Burgundy largely fell under the domination of the Holy Roman Empire except for the area west of the Jura, known as the County (Comté) late in the Middle Ages, which was controlled by the Duke of Burgundy. The remaining part of Upper Burgundy eventually became the western Swiss cantons where the castles of Grandson, Chillon, and Aigle are found. Lower Burgundy occupied much of modern south-eastern France on the Lower Rhône. Its history involves the struggle between Catalan, Burgundian, and German magnates vying for control of its parts. Here are found the cities of Arles, Avignon, Valence, Grenoble, Lyons, Marseille, and Nice.

Rudolph II of Upper Burgundy took Lower Burgundy from Hugh of Arles in exchange for dropping his claim to an Italian throne. In 933, Rudolf melded the two parts into the Kingdom of Arelat. In 1032, when his grandson, Rudolph III, died without issue, the kingdom became part of the Holy Roman Empire by treaty. During the next three centuries, the kingdom split into sections that included Provence (the southern part), the Free County of Burgundy (west of the Juras), Dauphiné, Savoy and present-day western Switzerland. The latter became a duchy held by the Zahringen family for the Empire until it passed to the Hapsburgs. The Swiss inhabitants broke away at the end of the Middle Ages. In 1190, the Hohenstaufen family took over the Free County for the Empire. The Duke of Burgundy took the Free County (Comté) in the Late Middle Ages. The Dauphiné was controlled by a vassal of the Empire, who gave it to the king of France in 1349 in exchange for settling his debts. In 1246, the Anjou family took over the larger territory of Provence, which became part of France in 1484 together with most of the other sections of Burgundy except for the Swiss sections and Savoy.

The entire region was a fringe area that included many important fortifications along the Rhône, the Mediterranean, and the mountain passes.

Intimidate, Protect, or Impress?

In general, castles were designed to fulfil the following functions: to intimidate the enemy, to protect territory, and/or to project social status. Their physical locations often achieved all three objectives even if the structure was not very strong. In the Late Middle Ages and after, kings and noblemen converted their castles into palaces, which decreased their ability to protect a position. In France, the military castle is called château-fort while the term château generally refers to a palatial residence like many of the famous châteaux of the Loire that served little to no military purpose. In urban areas, the town walls afforded protection to the burghers whereas the castle served not only to protect the ruling family but also to affirm its social standing and its dominance over the urban population. Religious sites also acquired fortifications mainly to protect the clergy but also to deter would-be plunderers.

The castles of the 'Robber Barons' along the Rhine are classic examples of the triple role of the castle. More than three dozen castles were built along the Rhine between Bonn and Mainz to control river trade, which had been critical for millennia. Marksburg Castle on the heights of the east bank overlooking the river is typical of these German strongholds. Built by the Eppstein family in 1100, it is the only medieval Rhine castle to survive relatively intact. It began as a 40m (131ft) high freestanding Bergfried, which looked like a keep but whose main role was defensive rather than residential. The stronghold expanded in 1117 to protect the nearby town. Walls, additional buildings, and a great hall in the Romanesque style were built around the square bergfried, which ended up standing in the middle of a triangular courtyard. In 1283 Count Eberhard II of Katzenelnbogen took possession of the Romanesque castle and strengthened the stronghold adding a Gothic great hall on the east side. The Landgraves[18] of Hesse acquired Marksburg Castle in 1479 and held it until the end of the eighteen century. A curtain wall with round towers was added in the fifteenth century. The Landgrave mounted six cannons in two batteries. Much later, bastions were added to the outer defences. The remaining castles on Rhine, mostly in ruins today, also dominated river traffic. The advent of cannon strengthened their control over the Rhine.

The coastal road that links the Italian Peninsula to Roman Transalpine Gaul[19] has been for millennia an important trade route that passes through ports along the seashore. The mountains overlooking the coast provide excellent positions from which fortifications can control the coastal road and the coast. Around 970, Count Conrad I of Ventimiglia built the castle of Roquebrune to protect the area around Cap–Martin from Saracen raiders. The Ventimiglian counts were vassals of Genoa and the castle was transferred to Genoa in 1115, but the fief of Roquebrune was sold to Charles of Anjou, Count of Provence. In 1273, Genoa's enemies marched on the castle and the castellan gave it up without a fight. In 1289, the Genoese regained possession of the castle when they gave the Count of Provence the kingship of Sicily in exchange for it. Between 1157 and 1395, the Republic of Genoa selected the castellans who served in a military and a political capacity. In time of war, the normal castle garrison of six crossbowmen and one sergeant received reinforcements. In 1355, Charles I of Monaco bought the territory of Roquebrune from Genoa.[20] The castle was involved in several sieges including one that lasted about two weeks in 1458 that ended when the enemy leader, Honoré Lascaris Count of Tende, was wounded in the leg by a crossbow bolt.

Originally, a curtain wall with six gates surrounded the village and the castle, which stands 300m (984ft) above the village. The thick-walled stone keep, the oldest in France, includes the entrance since the remainder of the castle was built behind it. Today, it is accessed by a stone bridge since the drawbridge no longer exists. A bretèche protects the doorway. The entrance led to the Great Hall whose vaulted roof collapsed after a fire in 1506. A new roof was destroyed in another fire caused by an artillery bombardment in 1597 and it was not replaced. The guardroom occupied the level above the Great Hall.[21] Above the guardroom was the archers' room above which there was a common room, a kitchen, an armoury and the castellan's quarters with access to the wall walk. Above these rooms there is a terrace accessed from the wall walk. In the fifteenth century, wide artillery crenels were added to the donjon. From the sea or the coast road, this small castle seems quite imposing.

Tarascon Castle, which is said to resemble the famous Bastille of Paris, occupied a dominant position along the east bank of the Rhône along with other castles. Located between Avignon and Arles, Tarascon faces Beaucaire Castle on the heights of the west bank. Louis II of Anjou, Count of Provence, started the construction of the present castle in 1400, which he intended to serve as a palace. This Gothic structure replaced a thirteenth-century stronghold. It passed to King Louis XI in 1481.

The main structure is 48m (157ft) high and includes four levels. It is connected to a lower court where food storage and quarters are lined up along the west side of the curtain wall. Three towers and an entrance gate guard the east side. The complex is surrounded by a moat on three sides and the Rhône on the fourth. A drawbridge was once part of the bridge that spans the moat at the entrance and gives access to a 'U'-shaped ramp that leads to the lower court and to a bridge, which enters the castle through the bottom of the donjon and used to have a drawbridge and portcullis. In addition to the donjon, four corner towers surround the interior courtyard surrounded by several chambers, a great hall, a chapel, and a kitchen. On the second and third floors above the chapel are the king's chamber and private chapel. The Artillery Tower mounted cannon that could dominate the Rhône, but the castle served no major military role. It became a prison from the seventeenth and the nineteenth centuries.

Further up the Rhône stand the remains of Mornas Castle. Its position on a 137m (445ft) rocky spur overlooking the east bank of the Rhône and a medieval village gives it an imposing aspect. It belonged to the Counts of Toulouse who had to contend with the claims of the Archbishop of Arles. Count Raymond VI of Toulouse was forced to surrender it to the church in 1209 when he was accused of helping the Cathars. The castle continued to change hands until the Hundred Years War when it served as protection from roving bands of mercenaries that ravaged the region. The castle played a role in the French religious wars of the 1500s, before it fell into oblivion. The present restoration only hints at the splendour and might of Mornas at the height of its glory.

Other castles, mostly situated in the mountains, stand out in south-west France. Among them is the castle of Foix, built in the tenth century on the ruins of a Benedictine Monastery on top of a rocky spur that dominates the surrounding valley. Its two square towers were built first, the four-level North Tower in the twelfth century, and then the three-level centre tower later in that century.[22] The 42m (138ft) high, five-level round tower was not erected until the fifteenth century. The castle was owned by the Counts of Foix who preferred to reside in the town after the thirteenth century. Simon de Montfort captured the town, but not the castle, during the Albigensian crusade and laid siege to it twice in 1211 and 1212. King Philippe III captured it half a century later. The castle fell again in 1486 due to treachery. In the next century, it served as a key position for the region in the war between the Catholics and Huguenots.

ROQUBRUNE

Roqubrune Castle: Top: View of castle from below. Keep is on far left and cannon ports can be seen that were added later to the upper levels. Middle: Plan showing location of the Great Room and the section were there were rooms with several levels. Bottom: View of the keep with the bretèche which covers the entrance which is masked by trees in the photo.

Château Tarascon built between 1401 and 1449 on the site of a destroyed castle, it had curtains 48m (157ft) high. Top left: View from across the Rhône. Top right: View of Château Beaucaire from Tarascon (B) on west bank from Clock Tower of Tarascon. Middle: Plan of Tarascon – E Entrance, 1. Entrance Court, 2. Keep, 3. Clock Tower, 4. Tower with stairs to allure, 5. Entrance Court, 6. South-west Tower, 7. Chapel Tower, 8. Artillery Tower, 9. Food storage and living quarters. Bottom left: View of east side of castle showing moat that once held water and bridge leading into entrance. Bottom right: View from Artillery Tower looking down at Entrance Courtyard (5) and the bridge leading into the keep (1).

Bonaguil Castle, also in south-western France, stands at Fumel several kilometres west of Cahors. A knight of the Fumel family built a small pentagonal donjon sometime after the 1250s.[23] The family allied itself with the English during the Hundred Years War, which led to the partial destruction of the keep

CHATEAU MORNAS

Château Mornas located several kilometres from Orange. Top: View of walls on south side where approach was made from a twelfth-century church. Middle left: View from cliff side looking at restored walls. Photo by Yodie on Wikipedia Commons. Middle light: View of tower by entrance (in 1980s) showing addition of gun ports. The small inset photo from Wikipedia Commons shows the restored entrance in about 2008. Bottom: General view of the ruins in 1980s before restoration, with the Rhône in background.

and additional damage to the castle as it changed hands during the conflict. In the 1430s, Château Bonaguil passed through marriage to the Roquefeuils, a prominent family in Languedoc. During the next decade, the castle underwent a period of extensive modification and expansion that lasted until the end of the century. A large round tower 35m (115ft) high was added at this time. The keep is 60m (197ft) high. A barbican and two round towers were added on the south side for protection against artillery. The barbican and a new outer wall of about 350m (1,148ft) in length served as a redoubt. The second line of defence was behind a wide dry moat partitioned into sections. A drawbridge gave access to the interior line of high walls, the towers and the donjon. Those high walls, which made escalade almost impossible, were vulnerable to cannons, which led to the construction of the outer line of defences called the fausse-braye. Cannon were mounted on the keep and other locations including the barbican and a boulevard of the outer line of defences. Over a hundred embrasures were adapted for gunpowder weapons. In 1563, the castle was captured in the Wars of Religion.

Pierrefonds is another impressive French castle with a limited military history. Located near Compiègne, it began as a simple donjon in the twelfth century. During the Hundred Years War, Louis, Duke of Orléans and Valois and the brother of King Charles VI, turned the site into a large quadrangular castle with eight towers and high curtain walls. Construction began in the 1390s and ended in 1407. In November 1407, Louis was assassinated by followers of John the Fearless, Duke of Burgundy, during their struggle for control over the mad Charles VI. In 1420, Pierrefonds was put under siege by the English and its garrison surrendered when it ran out of supplies. The castle changed hands several times until 1616 when it fell after a six-day siege during which artillery brought down some of its towers. It was dismantled on the orders of Cardinal Richelieu. Napoleon III asked Eugène Viollet-de-Duc to restore it as an imperial residence. Viollet-de-Duc's reconstructions, however, are often based on the idealized Romantic vision of castles rather than on objective reality.

This five-sided castle has high curtain walls connected to eight towers most of which are D-shaped or round. The square donjon and Great Hall stand inside the walls. The castle, which served mainly as a palace, included everything a monarch would need but had no viable defences within the curtain walls. Its machicolated battlements, roofs, other superstructures, and interior decors are attributed to Viollet-le-Duc. Pierrefonds was a testament to the power of the Duke of Orléans, but played a very minor role during the age of castles.

As in France, in England nobles converted into many old castles into sumptuous residences or built new ones designed for comfort rather than effective defence at the beginning of the Renaissance.[24] Bodiam, one of the last castles to be built in England, is the embodiment of the fourteenth-century medieval castle. Its owner, Edward Dalyngrigge, was one of Edward III's knights who made his fortune during the Hundred Years War by serving in the notorious free companies of

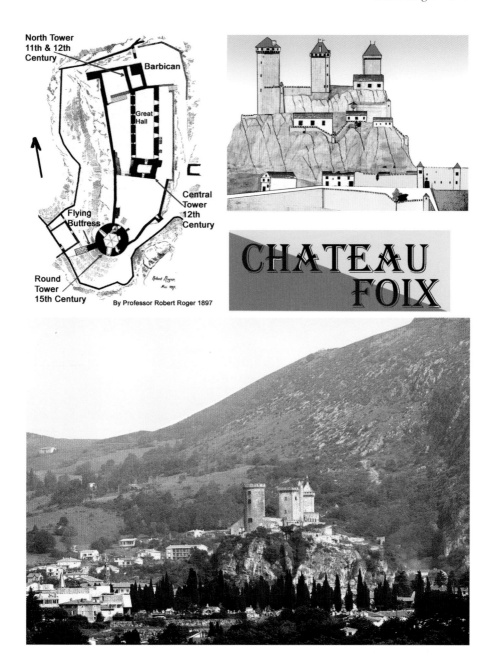

Château de Foix. Top: Plan of castle drawn by Professor Robert Roger in 1897 and side view of castle. Bottom: Photo of Foix.

mercenaries. He received permission to build his castle from Richard II because of French raids. However, Bodiam Castle was too far from the coast to be of value against enemy marauders. Its construction began in 1386 and ended before 1392. In 1470, the castle passed through marriage into the ownership of Sir

A. Outer
    Drawbridge
B. 2nd
    Drawbridge
C. Main Gate
D Staircase
    to Donjon
E. Donjon
F. Entrance
    through moat
G. H. Gates
    in moat
I. Square Tower &
    staircase

BONAGUIL

from E.E. Viollet-le-Duc

J. Tower w/internal
    spiral stairs
K. Small Drawbridge
L Round Tower
M. Advanced Work
    Platform
N. Moat
O. Outwork (Barbican)
P. Apartments
    or Barracks
R. Stables
S. Outwork

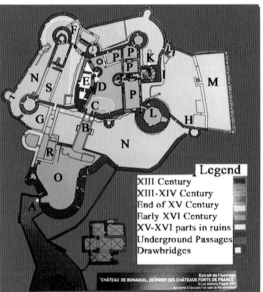

Legend
XIII Century
XIII-XIV Century
End of XV Century
Early XVI Century
XV-XVI parts in ruins
Underground Passages
Drawbridges

Château de Bonaguil. Drawing by Viollet-le-Duc and plan from display at the castle. The external wall (M and S) of 350m (1,148ft) length was a late addition. It was lower and backed by earth and had about 100 embrasures for artillery. The towers were adapted for heavy artillery. A barbican or advanced work (R and O) added with towers designed for arquebuses.

Thomas Lewknor, who supported the Lancastrians during the Wars of the Roses (1455–85). When Richard III took power in 1483, he accused Lewknor of treason and ordered a siege of the castle later that year. However, there are no records of

Château de Bonaguil and Pierrefonds: Top: Bonaguil with large round tower is on the left and flagpole on the top of the donjon. Built on a bluff dominating a defile in the Dordogne in the mid-thirteenth century, it was captured several times in the Hundred Years War and burned and abandoned. The walls were heightened and the keep rebuilt after the war to resist artillery. Bottom: Pierrefonds drawing. This fourteenth-century castle was restored by Violet-le-Duc under Napoleon III.

CHATEAU PIERREFONDS

NE Tower

FB

Moat

Courtyard

Chapel

Donjon

FB

FB

Entrance

A

North

Entrance

Château de Pierrefonds: Photos are two views of the entrance which is located on the south side (the location of the drawbridge can be seen in the top photo). E.E. Violet-le-Duc drawings – Top shows details of his reconstruction of the north-eats tower which may have been a result of his imagination. Below: plan showing the towers and donjon with layout designed to serve as a palace for Napoleon III. FB = Fausse-braye A = Inner Gate Entrance.

an actual siege. Lewknor appears to have surrendered without a fight. He was released by Henry VII in 1485. Bodiam Castle was partially dismantled during the Civil War of the seventeenth century.

Bodiam Castle originally had more extensive water defences than today's impressive moat, which is fed by springs, some of which are within the castle, making it difficult for an attacker to drain it. The moat is up to 2.5m (8.2ft) deep.

BODIAM

Archaeological Journal (1905)

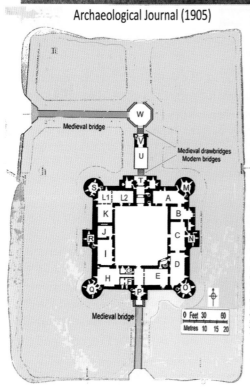

Bodiam Castle. Plan from the Archaeological Journal *(1905): Sections of wall that no longer stand are included: A. Household apartments, B. Chapel, C. Chamber, D. Great chamber, E. Lord's hall, F. Buttery, G. Pantry, H. Kitchen, I. Retainer's hall, J. Retainer's kitchen, K. Possible ante-room, L1. Possible service rooms, L2. Possible stables, M. North-east tower, N. East tower, O. south-east tower, P. Postern tower, Q. South-east tower, R. West tower, S. North-east tower (and prison), T. Gatehouse (with guard rooms to left and right), U. Inner causeway (man-made islet). V. Outer Barbican, W. Stone pier leading to outer causeway.*

South of the moat, there is an area of marshland. The rectangular castle is about 45.7m (150ft) by 41.2m (135ft). It includes a gatehouse consisting of two towers, four drum towers at the corners, two square towers, and a square postern tower. The drum towers are 8.85m (29ft) in diameter and 18.3m (60ft) high. The walls are about 2m (6.6ft) thick and rise to a height of 12.5m (41ft) above the moat. The entrance gate and postern have machicoulis, portcullises (three in the entrance gatehouse) and murder holes to shoot at attackers that made it past the first portcullis. The towers are mostly three storeys high and contained rooms for the family and servants. Buildings along all four walls included apartments, halls and various types of service rooms leaving a large rectangular courtyard in the centre of the castle. Over two dozen garderobes in the castle walls emptied into the moat.

One interesting feature of the castle is the approach to the main gate, which is connected by a drawbridge to a man-made islet at the end of which there once was a barbican. The islet connects to an octagonal-shaped pier with another drawbridge. From this pier, a wooden causeway crossed the moat at a right angle to the front of the castle exposing people crossing to missile fire from the castle battlements.

Castles like Bodiam, Pierrefonds, Castelnaud, Bonaguil, or La Mota were not built on the fringes of the old Western Roman Empire. Instead, they appeared near the end of the era of castle building when castles received with minor and major conversions to adapt to gunpowder warfare. They were equipped with positions for handguns and cannons and even included fausses-brayes and boulevards while maintaining the profile of a medieval castle.

Armies and Warfare in the Late Middle Ages and After

Most medieval battles involved small numbers of troops. Only eight major battles were fought during the 110 years of the Hundred Years War. That is an average of one every thirteen years. The most famous English victories were at Crécy in 1346 (9,000 English vs. 30,000 French), Poitiers in 1356 (6,000 English vs. 20,000 French), Agincourt in 1415 (5,700 English vs. 25,000 French), and Verneuil in 1424 (9,000 English vs. 15,000 French). The decisive siege at Orléans was conducted by 4,500 English troops against 5,000 French reinforced by 4,000 additional men during the siege. The decisive French victories took place at Formigny in 1450 (4,000 English vs. 8,000 French) and Castillon in 1453 (5,000 English vs. 8,000 French).[25] In England, this long war was followed by the Wars of the Roses (1455–85) that spanned thirty years with eleven major battles or an average of one every two and a half years. Six of these battles were fought in 1460 and 1461. The number of troops involved is not large with as few as 2,000 vs. 3,000 at St. Albans in

1460 rising to 20,000 vs. 16,000 at Towton in 1461. At Bosworth in 1485, the numbers were 12,000, vs. 10,000.

Sieges played a much smaller role in this war and most English castles had not kept up with improvements during the era of the Hundred Years War. One of the few sieges of this civil war started in November 1455 and lasted about two months at Powderham Castle, a short distance from Exeter, and involved two rival families. The castle was little more than a hall and residence with six towers built in the 1390s. In 1460, during the siege of Roxburgh Castle near the border, King James II of Scotland was killed when a bombard exploded. The Scots stormed and demolished the castle, which was the last English stronghold in Scotland. In 1462, several castles on the Scottish border like Dunstanburgh and Bamburgh fell to the Yorkists after a siege, but Edward did not allow an assault because he wanted them intact. These two castles were in turn used by the Yorkists to blockade Alnwick, but that siege, which lasted from December 1462 until January 1463, was raised when Warwick appeared with a relief army. A full siege of Bamburgh finally took place in 1464, but it did not last long because bombards brought down the walls and the defenders of the heavily-damaged castle surrendered as the Yorkist troops began the assault. The Tower of London faced a siege at least twice. In 1460, it held out for two weeks against the Yorkists who entered the city and bombarded its walls. After the battle of Northampton where the Yorkists captured Henry VI, they stepped up the siege, forcing the defenders to surrender on 19 July. In 1471, while Henry VI was a prisoner in the Tower of London, the Lancastrians attacked the city in May. They only took part of the fortified London Bridge before being held in check. Two days later, they tried again and crossed the Thames to the north, but they were still blocked on London Bridge. They took a city gate, but they were routed by troops who sortied from the Tower. Edward sent troops from the north and forced the rebels to withdraw.[26] The siege of Harlech Castle in Wales was longest of the war. It lasted from 1461 to 1468 when the Lancastrians surrendered.[27]

On the Continent, the war between Burgundy and the Swiss from 1474 to 1477 resulted in two major battles in the same year. At Grandson in 1476, 20,000 Burgundians met defeat when facing 18,000 Swiss in front of the castle of Grandson, which played no significant role. Soon after, a Burgundian force of similar size met the Swiss at Morat and was again defeated. The size of armies engaged in battles was increasing while, like in England, major battles took place more often and sieges seem to have become less important than smashing the enemy in the field.

After the end of the Hundred Years War, many castles were converted into forts and fortresses and their role in warfare changed. In the 1490s, the French king invaded Italy, smashing one castle after the other with his artillery until he took Naples. The next century began with both the French and Spanish engaged in warfare in Italy. The armies of 1503 were not extremely large with 6,000 Spanish vs. 10,000 French at Cerignola, but the number rose to 15,000 Spanish vs. 23,000 French/Italian at Garigliano the same year. In 1515, France returned to Italy with an army of 32,500 French/Venetians and defeated the once invincible Swiss at Marignano who had 22,000 men. In 1524, the fortified city of Pavia played an important role when Francis I laid siege to it without success. Early in 1525, a relief force of 23,000 Spanish/German/Italian defeated the 22,000-man French army.[28]

Early in the sixteenth century, warfare changed as the numbers of men with hand-held firearms increased and the numbers of archers diminished. Phalanxes of Swiss pikemen and even German Landsknechts had dominated the battlefield in the later part of the fifteenth century and reduced the effectiveness of cavalry. In the next century, due to the large-scale use of firearms, pikemen began to serve in mixed formations to protect the men with handguns. Cannons were used both in siege warfare and on battlefields. Forts and fortresses replaced castles. The new designs required larger garrisons and the besiegers needed larger armies to be successful. In addition, iron shot replaced stone shot and cannons increased their firepower. Strongholds now required lower and thicker walls to resist bombardment than they had in the fifteenth century.

Chapter Five

The Renaissance

End of an Era

Significant changes in fortifications began to appear in the fifteenth century as artillery evolved from noise-makers firing stone projectiles that shattered when they struck most walls to more effective, better-designed bronze or iron guns that used iron balls to smash stone walls. Gunpowder weapons were first mounted on castle walls during the 1300s, but even in the early 1400s fortifications were only able to accommodate handguns and small cannons because they did not have the space necessary for large artillery pieces and their recoil. In the latter half of the fourteenth century, new styles of loopholes were developed for small gunpowder weapons. The most common were the oillet, a circular opening with a vision slit[1] and the letterbox, a splayed rectangular embrasure that gave a wider horizontal field of fire. However, minor modifications could not prevent the extensive damage inflicted by iron roundshot on masonry walls. By the mid-fifteenth century, many castles underwent major modifications and acquired new features that altered their configuration. In most cases, they ceased to serve as residences of noble lords and became the types of forts and fortresses most commonly associated with the Renaissance and later periods.

The early modifications consisted of cutting down towers to the level of the walls to facilitate mounting and moving cannons and to present a smaller profile. Thin walls were often reinforced with additional masonry, but this procedure did not turn out to be as successful as backing them with earth. A better solution was to replace high, usually thin-walled, medieval towers with squat, thick-walled artillery towers called bastions. Most medieval towers are not solid and contain rooms on different levels. Bastions, on the other hand, are lower and are usually either solid or include thick-walled, single-level gun casemates capable of resisting artillery. Medieval fortifications that could not be modified had to be rebuilt or replaced. The fausse-braye was an expedient that consisted of an exterior position or even a concentric wall of earth or masonry much lower in height than the castle's curtain, designed to protect itself and the walls and towers behind it from artillery fire.

In the late fourteenth century, round and curved surfaces to deflect cannon shot began to appear. Sassocorvaro Castle, built in the 1470s, is one of the first examples of this style. Although Italy a backwater when it came to fortifications during the Middle Ages, but in the transition period Italian engineers and architects led the way with drastic changes to city walls, modifications of castles, and the emergence of the Renaissance fort/fortress. With the *trace italienne*, also known as the bastioned front and star fort, initiated a new age. The new types of fortifications began to appear throughout Italy and even in the Mediterranean possessions of the Republic of Venice and spread across Europe.[2]

Italy Transitions into the Renaissance

During the High Middle Ages, the Italian Peninsula was a collection of contending republics and principalities, many of which were run by powerful dynastic families. In 1309, the Popes moved to Avignon supposedly because Rome was too turbulent for their safety. This led to the Papal Schism, which lasted from 1378 until 1418 and generated serious regional struggles. Throughout the Hundred Years War and the Schism, organized companies of mercenaries from far and wide plagued Italy. One of these companies, John Hawkwood's Free Company, came from France to take part in the various conflicts like the war between Pisa and Florence and the conflict between the Pope and Milan. The ruling families included the Viscontis of Milan who tied to subjugate Northern Italy in fourteenth and fifteenth centuries, the Scalas (Scaligeri) who exercised control over Verona in the thirteenth and fourteenth centuries, and the Malatestas of Rimini who tried to dominate cities such as Imola, Cesena, Ravenna and San Marino in the Romagna and the Marches. Some of these dynasties lost power by the sixteenth century while others like the Dorias and Estes in Genoa and Ferrara respectively, continued hold sway. In the 1450s, the Sforzas, descended from the condottiere Muzio Attendolo, nicknamed Sforza, replaced the Viscontis in Milan. The Medicis, a banking family, in the meantime, rose to prominence in the Republic of Florence. Even the Spanish Borgia family led by Pope Alexander VI made their mark on the peninsula during a critical time at the end of the fifteenth century.

According to the historian George Procter, when the condottieri ravaged Italy during the High Middle Ages, even the simple walls offered relative protection.

> Italy was filled with petty village fortresses or castles, in which, on the approach of danger, the inhabitants secured themselves. Behind their ramparts the peasantry might defy the assaults of an unwieldy cavalry, and oppose a desperate and successfully resistance to the most merciless of enemies, who were unassisted by battering machines or cannon.[3]

Procter points out that during this period gunpowder weapons were still too crude, inaccurate and difficult to transport to have much impact and sieges continued to follow traditional patterns. One of the more interesting ones was conducted by Giovanni Visconti, Archbishop of Milan who tried to forge an alliance of cities in Tuscany to weaken Florence in 1355. The local Ghibellines joined him in a surprise attack on Pistoia held by a small force of Florentines. As the neighbouring walled villages held out, Visconti lifted the siege and turned his 8,000-man force on the small town of Scarperia, which was held by a 500-man Medici garrison. When Visconti built various siege engines such as moveable assault towers and battering rams, the defenders sortied and set them on fire. At least three times the defenders repelled the enemy who tried to take the walls by escalade. The demoralized Milanese army was forced to lift the siege and retreat to Bologna.[4]

Genoa and Venice became major naval powers and expanded beyond the peninsula as Milan, Florence, and the Papal States continued to try to expand their dominance as the new era began. Thus, when the French king invaded the peninsula in 1494 the main Italian states were Genoa, Venice, Milan, the Papal States, and the Kingdom of Naples.

Two castles of this transitional phase in the Kingdom of Naples are of particular interest. In 1495, the French king tried to force their submission with cannons. First, Castel dell'Ovo (Egg Castle) located on an island, now part of a peninsula, is the oldest fortification in Naples with a history that reaches back to the Roman Era. In the fifth century, the last Latin emperor of the Western Roman Empire, Romulus Augustulus, deposed in 476, went into exile and lived in the castle. Saracen raiders demolished the Roman fortifications and the Normans built a new castle on the site in the twelfth century. Later, the construction of Castel Nuovo diminished its importance when the Norman ruler moved his court there and used Ovo as a treasury and a prison. Notable prisoners included Conrad V, King of Jerusalem, in 1268 before his execution and in 1381, Joanna I, Queen of Naples. During the next century, the kingdom was ruled by Aragon and the changes made during this period are reflected in its present appearance. This almost rectangular castle 200m by 45m (656ft by 148ft) seems impregnable, but it proved vulnerable when sappers mined one of its supposedly inaccessible seaside walls. Not much could be done to modernize this castle.

In 1278 or 1279, Charles I of Anjou (ruled Naples from 1266 to 1285) commissioned two of his French architects to design and build Castel Nuovo because he wanted a more spacious castle than the Norman-built Castel dell'Ovo. He forced the people of the Neapolitan Kingdom to provide the resources and labour so that it was completed by 1282. The plan of the new castle was supposedly based on Angers, but it was not identical. It had a square layout with four 33.5m (110ft) high round towers with a diameter of 18.75m (61.5ft). A sluice located at the nearby Tower of San Vincenzo[5] (demolished in 1742) allowed seawater to fill the deep moat. Charles died before the work was completed. During the first half of the fourteenth century, King Robert 'the Wise' turned Castel Nuovo into a cultural centre frequented by such Renaissance luminaries as Petrarch. Charles' successors turned the castle into a place of intrigue, murder and a veritable fortress. According to legend, men were thrown to their death into the moat where a crocodile was kept. During that same century, Robert's daughter, Joanna I, contracted a second marriage with the son of the King of Hungary. When Robert died she became Queen. In 1345, her husband begged the Pope to make him king, but he was strangled before his request could be granted. While the outraged citizens besieged the castle, King Louis of Hungary came to avenge his son's death. After he sacked the city, the mob turned against him, forcing him to retreat leaving a garrison to hold the castle. After a long siege, the Neapolitans took the castle in September 1348. Joanna (reigned 1342–82) was restored to power, but her cousins subjected her to more sieges because she supported the anti-Pope and they did not. After she eventually surrendered, she was imprisoned in Castel dell'Ovo and was rescued a few days later by a fleet from Provence.

In February 1391, a three-year siege ended when King Charles VI of France took Castel Nuovo. Eight years later, King Ladislaus of Naples (reigned 1386–1414) recovered it. After a turbulent reign, his sister and successor, Joanna II (reigned 1414–35), left the castle to Alfonso I (Alfonso V of Aragon). The Aragonese occupied the castle in 1442. Later Alfonso took refuge in the castle when he was attacked by Duke Francesco Sforza, the founder of the Sforza dynasty of Milan, whose fiefs in the Kingdom of Naples he had confiscated.

Alfonso's renovations at Castel Nuovo included an outer line of fortifications – probably a fausse-braye – to resist artillery.[6] He also placed the white marble triumphal arch between the entrance towers to commemorate his takeover. In February 1495, Charles VIII of France advanced down the Italian Peninsula with a professional army armed with state-of-the-art castle-busting artillery. Except for the heaviest pieces, the cannons were mounted on wheeled carriages that increased their manoeuvrability and regulated their elevation. Many of the castles on Charles' route on the west coast of the peninsula surrendered without a fight when his army appeared. Although by this time, Italy had a wealth of architects and engineers who dabbled in new designs, few Italian castles had been modified. King Ferdinand II (reigned 1495–6) sought refuge in Castel dell'Ovo before he sailed away as Charles VIII took the city eleven days later. On 22 February, the French began bombarding Castel Nuovo. Their guns fired over 300 rounds in three hours.[7] Soon the garrison ceased resisting as its Spanish and Swiss troops began fighting each other. On 6 March, the defenders surrendered. Charles found the castle well stocked and resupplied his army before he headed back north. Ferdinand II returned in July to take back Naples. The French garrison of Castel Nuovo put up a stronger defence than the previous defenders and repelled numerous assaults. Ferdinand put Castel Nuovo under siege only to be harassed by the French cannons. In September, the plucky garrison sortied under the cover of its own artillery, but this effort and a naval landing late in the month failed. In late November, the Neapolitans tried to take the castle by escalade, but the defenders pushed back their scaling ladders. On 27 November, an explosive mine devised by Francesco di Giorgio Martini, a Sienese architect, brought down a section of the barbican, killing many of the French soldiers on the parapet and littering the ground with dismembered bodies. The Aragonese troops rushed in

NAPLES

Sketch by Wanda Ostrowska   **Castel Nuovo**

Castel Nuovo

Castel Dell'Ovo, Naples

(Sketch by Wojciech Ostrowski)

Naples. Plan, drawing and photos of Castel Nuovo. Bottom right: Photo shows entrance of Castel Nuovo with the Triumphal Arch between the two towers of the gatehouse. Bottom left: Drawing of Castel dell'Ovo. Middle left: Section of the sixteenth-century city plan of Naples from Braun and Hogenberg's city plans. The location of the two castles is pointed out and some of the sixteenth-century city walls with bastions can be seen. Drawings of Castel Nuovo and Castle Dell'Ovo from Medieval Fortress.

and forced the garrison back. After a couple of days, the Saint Vincent Tower fell, but the castle did not surrender until 8 December. The French defenders were allowed to leave Naples.

Under Louis XII (reigned 1498–1515), the French returned in October 1501 and seized Castel Nuovo. On 12 June, their erstwhile Spanish ally, Gonzalo de Córdoba took the Saint Vincent Tower, bombarded the fortress, sprung a mine under the seaward bastion, and stormed the castle. Castel dell'Ovo continued

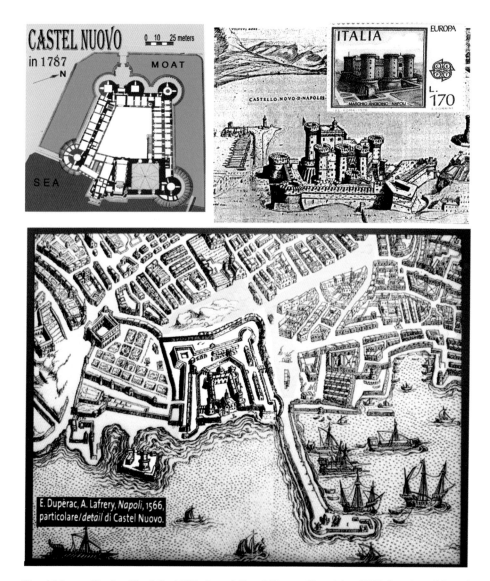

Castel Nuovo, Naples. Top left: 1787 plan of Castel Nuovo. Top right: 1540 drawing of Castel Nuovo by Francisco de Hollanda. Bottom: 1566 drawing of Castel Nuovo by Étienne Dupérac and Antonio Lafreri. Note the difference in shape of the two sea-side bastions of the outer wall.

to hold out and Gonzalo de Córdoba left some troops behind to besiege it. On 4 July, the Spanish took the causeway and on 11 July, they set off a mine that brought down part of a wall and forced the garrison to surrender.

Naples had a third castle named Sant'Elmo[8] located on the hill of St. Erasmus and built by Robert of Anjou in 1329. Soon after its completion, in 1348, it was put

Naples: Top: Etching by Baratta and Perrey in 1680 showing part of Castel Nuovo and Castel Sant'Elmo and photo of Castel Sant' Elmo. Left centre and bottom: Castel dell'Ovo with Mount Vesuvius in the background. Right centre and bottom: Castel Nuovo. Photos by Pierre Etcheto.

unsuccessfully under siege by Louis, King of Hungary. In the sixteenth century, Spain's viceroys renovated and modernized the fortresses and walls of Naples. Much of the work was done by Don Pedro de Toledo, appointed viceroy in 1532.

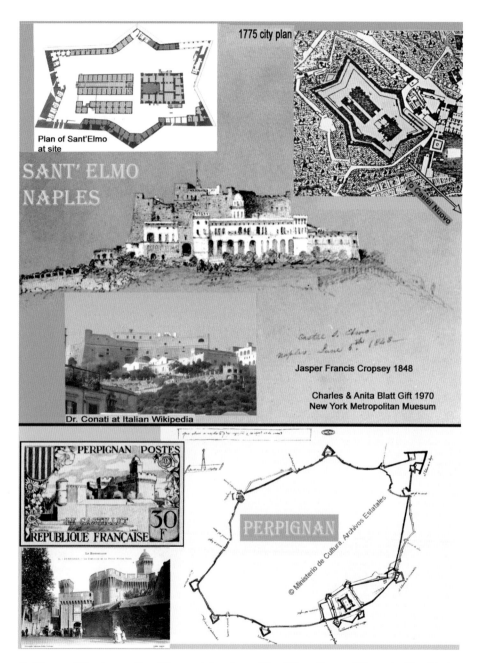

St Elmo and Perpignan: Top: Plans and drawings of Sant'Elmo Fort on hill overlooking Naples. Bottom: Plan of Perpignan showing the sixteenth-century city walls and pictures of the castillet built in the 1360s.

He built a modern fort with the *trace italienne* around the old castle on the hill, which became known as Castel Sant'Elmo. The Spanish military engineer, Pedro Luis Escrivá of Valencia, began to work on a star-shaped fort with six points and massive walls in 1537. His design includes a large powder magazine, warehouses, underground prison cells, a church and a massive cistern.[9] The fort is more than twice as large as Castel Nuovo and its garrison numbered up to 3,000 men. The remains of the older castle, destroyed in an earthquake in 1456, are on the parade ground. This fortress became the new centre of the Naples' defensive system.

Don Pedro's other major modifications involved making Castel Nuovo resistant to artillery. No major changes were made to the castle's exterior, which retained its five large drum towers. Don Pedro added an outer wall with new bastions that gave the fortress an inner and outer moat as depicted in Francisco de Hollanda's 1540 drawing.[10] The residential section of the castle faced the sea and the rooms for the court were in the central building to avoid direct exposure to siege guns. The Viceroys exercised Spain's control of Naples from the castle. In 1555, the year before his abdication, Emperor Charles V (King Charles I of Spain[11]) visited the castle.

Italian Renaissance Architects and Military Engineers

By the fifteenth century, Italian engineering was back in a position of leadership since the fall of the Western Roman Empire. It virtually jumped from the age of the castrum to the age of the Renaissance rocca (fortress). Following a long transition phase, the *trace italienne* launched a new era in military architecture.[12] Leon Battista Alberti, who described his views on the most effective types of fortification in the mid-1440s, is often credited with the invention of these new concepts. In his opinion, the walls should form uneven lines, like the teeth of a saw. Historian Jeremy Black defines *trace italienne* as a system based on thicker and lower walls with 'bastions, generally quadrilateral, angles, and at regular intervals along all walls . . . to provide gun platforms . . . [and] effective flanking fire'. The walls – Leon Battista Alberti wrote – should be broken 'here and there into angles or bastions jutting out at certain distances' since this would prevent the enemy from reaching them 'between two angles jutting out, without exposing themselves to very great danger; nor can their military engines attack the heads of those angles with any hopes of success'.[13] According to most historians, the bastions of this new system were angled rather than round. Thus, this *trace italienne* as interpreted by some to include circular towers that allowed flanking fires, but Battista and others initially went with round bastions.[14]

Other Italian architects/engineers who led the way included many 'Renaissance Men' such as Leonardo da Vinci (1452–1519) and Michelangelo (1475–1564) who were involved in military architecture as well as in other arts. Leonardo, who became Cesare Borgia's engineer in 1502, concluded that elliptical surfaces deflected iron shot and proposed a fortress with three tiers of casemates that included vents to remove the smoke from cannon. By the mid-sixteenth century, round towers became ubiquitous in new fortifications because they deflected roundshot. However, they left dead space near the base of the curtains and bastions not covered by flanking fire from adjacent bastions. Curved surfaces became widespread even on ramparts. North of the Alps in the Holy Roman Empire, Albrecht Dürer, in a book on fortifications in published in the mid-1520s, called for the use of round bastions and gun towers (rondel) with several tiers of guns, ideas similar to those proposed in Italy. A few fortresses based on his design began to appear north of the Alps. Similar gun towers also appeared in the Italian Peninsula.

One of the early leaders in the field was the artist and architect Francesco di Giorgio Martini (1439–1501) whose designs represent a transition from medieval defences in the Italian Peninsula. In a treatise on fortifications, he explained that the main function of the ditch was to force enemy miners to dig deep, to form the main obstacle against attacking infantry, and to shield the lower part of the walls from cannon fire. He recommended ditches 24m (80ft) to 30m (98ft) wide and 12m (40ft) to 15m (50ft) deep. He also included other requirements for fortifications. It was important – he pointed out – to provide for the garrison's needs by including a well, a mill, machinery for making gunpowder and an oven for baking bread. For the defence of the site, he recommended the equivalent of a keep, which had to be taller and stronger than the other towers to give the commander a view of the entire area. The other towers had to be of equal height, attached to the main wall, and arranged so that none could allow entry without the consent of the others. The outer wall had to be high but avoid exposure so that two-thirds of it was to include a scarp that did not rise above the level of the moat. The ideal fort – he advised – was as small as possible with loopholes closely spaced. A ravelin (rivellino) should be placed in front of each gate and the entranceway should be indirect and have covered passages. Ravelins appeared in northern Italy during the fifteenth century. Francesco Sforza, for instance, had a pentagonal one built in front of the entrance of the castle of Milan in 1452. Other ravelins were in the form of a semicircle, which gave rise to the term demi-lune and later became synonymous with ravelins of all shapes.[15] Leon Battista Alberti also mentioned ravelins at this time when he suggested the use of triangular projections in front of the exposed section of a wall, with one angle facing the enemy.[16] The Venetians followed di Giorgio Martini's advice and built the first triangular ravelins in 1482. Beyond the moat, he suggested an extensive glacis (ciglio) to give the defenders a clear field of fire over a large area, denying the enemy cover. Apparently, the glacis, a well-known feature, did not become practical until after 1460 and it was not until early in the next century that a gentle slope was included to create an esplanade (a large area for a clear field of fire in fortifications).[17] Di Giorgio Martini also suggested circular towers (actually early bastions) and the line of the wall as defence against gunpowder weapons because it 'least receives, and best resists any shock'. Since long walls were a problem, he recommended angular shapes like quadrangles, octagons, or pentagons for the enceinte, with towers located at every angle to defend each section of wall. He was a strong advocate of caponiers or casemates placed in the moat to protect its floor and the lower walls of the fort.[18] Many of these features appeared in fortifications during and after his time. Rounded towers became popular until they were replaced by angled bastions. Di Giorgio Martini's innovative designs continued to include machicoulis even though the *trace italienne* made them obsolete. In 1480, Di Giorgio Martini was contracted by the condottiere Federico di Montefeltro to design a palace and fortifications at Urbino, where, according to Quentin Hughes, he began applying his methods. His treatise became the first important work on fortifications for the modern era.[19] He finished the fortress of Mondavio in 1492, before he worked for the King of Naples. He also took part in the siege of Castel Nuovo in November 1495 and dug the gunpowder mine that exploded below it.[20] He is credited with designs of over a hundred forts and he worked with his associates on modifying the defences of several cities including Rome and Naples. In the mid-sixteenth century, however, many of the new forts still included a keep, which was not always centrally located.

Francesco di Giorgio Martini also designed siege engines. He studied the works of Mariano di Jacopo (1382–1453) of Siena, known as Taccola (the Jackdaw). Taccola was also an artist and an engineer who wrote treatises about siege weapons, which influenced Leonardo da Vinci. Hughes points out that one of Leonardo da Vinci's most important contributions before the end of the fifteenth century was showing that the ravelin not only protected gates but also other parts of the curtain. Meanwhile, the most prominent Italian family of architects and engineers, the da Sangallos, led the way. Francesco Giamberti da Sangallo the Elder (1405–80) has been credited with the design of triangular forts, which inspired the builders of the transitional fort of Sarzanello. This fort stands on a hill overlooking the town of Saranza, on a site that had been occupied by a High Middle Ages castle that had been renovated in the early 1400s. Although Francesco is mistakenly credited with the design of Sarzanello, the actual construction of the present fort did not take place until the 1490s under the Medicis who contracted Francesco di Giovanni known as Francione and Luca del Caprina for the project.[21] The fort had three drum towers barely rising above its moat, which concealed from below (in the location of the present adjacent parking lot, a point from which the enemy would have to launch an assault). The ravelin, which protected the entrance, was built soon in the early 1500s.

The Sangallo family included Giuliano da Sangallo (1445–1516), who continued his father's triangular designs, and his brother Antonio da Sangallo the Elder (1455–1534). Giuliano worked for Lorenzo de' Medici (1449–92), the ruler of Florence. One of his forts, begun in 1509, was used by the Florentines to hold Pisa in submission. Antonio added triangular bastions to Castel Sant'Angelo in Rome.

Map of Renaissance Italy. Insert: Photo of San Michel Tower designed by Michelangelo and completed by Giovanni Lippi when he died. The tower, near the mouth of the Tiber on the left bank, served as a lookout post on the coast built in response to Turkish raiders seeking slaves.

Earlier, Pope Alexander VI (the second Borgia pope) had contracted Giuliano to work on the defences of Rome where he had built the polygonal tower bastion on the medieval curtain wall of Castel Sant'Angelo. Giuliano also built the fortress/palace at Civita Castellana in Viterbo, which served as the northern bastion of the Papal States. His nephew, Antonio da Sangallo the Younger (1484–1546), completed the work at Civita Castellana in 1503 and began the construction of Fortezza Bassa in Florence in 1534, Fort Michelangelo in the harbour of Civitavecchia in 1507, and the city walls after 1515 where he used the *trace italienne*.

After Emperor Charles V's German mercenaries sacked Rome in 1527,[22] Pope Paul III (reigned 1534–49) called upon Antonio da Sangallo the Younger to update the defences of the Vatican and to fortify its Belvedere Palace. Antonio designed and built the Sangallo Bastion near the Adreatino Gate of Rome between 1537 and 1540. This position included some of the key features associated with bastions of the *trace italienne*: bombproof shelters for the gunners on the upper level, gun casemates below that flanked the walls, a magazine, and a cavalier, i.e. an emplacement for guns that rose above the position. It could accommodate sixteen heavy guns and eight lighter cannon. It also had a well in a lower chamber leading to positions for making countermine galleries. The cost was so great that further plans for similar additions to Rome's walls could not be carried out. As a matter of fact, by the end of the sixteenth century, no major city could afford a complete set of encircling bastioned walls. Even the small Siena, which tried to invest in new fortifications to defend itself against Florence, had to abandon the effort due to their high cost.

One of the lesser-known Italian engineers of this period was Baccio Pontelli (1450–92) who is better known for his design of the Sistine Chapel and who built the castle of Pope Julian in Ostia[23] (completed in 1486) around an older tower from 1424. This castle, which shows many transitional features, is triangular with corner bastions one of which is polygonal and two are semicircular to cover the curtains between them. A fifteenth-century keep, which stands in the centre of the stronghold, includes an underground chamber that used to lead to the Tiber until the river changed course after a flood in the 1550s. The river had also provided water for the moat around the tower. Although the design included cannon ports, the castle still had machicoulis that were vulnerable to artillery.

Leonardo da Vinci worked for Ludovico Maria Sforza, Duke of Milan, from 1483 to 1499. Cesare Borgia brought him to Rocca Sforzesca at Imola, to the south-east of Bologna, in 1502 to repair and strengthen the fortress he had battered into submission with his artillery in 1499. The Republic of Florence employed Leonardo from 1502 to 1504. Leonardo inspected the fortress of La Verruca, located about 5km (3.1 miles) from Pisa, and proposed changes to make it impregnable in 1503. The stronghold was eventually rebuilt by Antonio Sangallo in 1509. Leonardo also improved the fortifications of Piombino in 1504.[24] He worked for Francis I of France In 1515. In addition to being an artist, Michelangelo Buonarotti (1475–1564) was a military advisor to Florence in 1529. In 1547, he worked on new defences for the Vatican.

Like Leonardo da Vinci and Michelangelo, Donato Bramante (1444–1514) is better known for his non-military works. One of his major military contributions was at the port of Civitavecchia and its fortress, which he began in 1508. One of his students, Antonio da Sangallo the Younger, continued the work when Donato died in 1514 and finished the enceinte of the four-bastioned fort in 1535.

Siena. Top: Drawing of the siege of 1555. Drawing of Fortress Santa Barbara built after the siege on north side of city (all the drawings are looking to the south) from Mathus Merian, 1640s. Middle: Pietro Bertelli drawing from Theatrum Urbium Italicarum *of 1599. Bottom: 1572 drawing from Braun and Hogenberg. Inset: Photo of walls of Siena by Pierre Etcheto.*

The Castle was built between 1483 and 1487 by Cardinal Giuliano della Rovere to guard the mouth of the Tiber. The imposing staircase, with its frescoes thought to be by the Baldassarre Peruzzi school, was added between 1503 and 1513.

Pope Julius II's castle built between 1483 and 1487. In a triangular pattern, it includes two artillery towers (bastions) and a tall keep in an angular bastion. It also has machicoulis, gun ports and an escape tunnel to the Tiber.

Michelangelo, after whom the fortress is named, completed the maschio, an octagonal keep between two of the corner towers, in 1557.

Francesco Laparelli da Cortona (1521–70), one of Michelangelo's assistants, worked on the defences of Rome for Pope Pius IV (reigned 1559–65). He

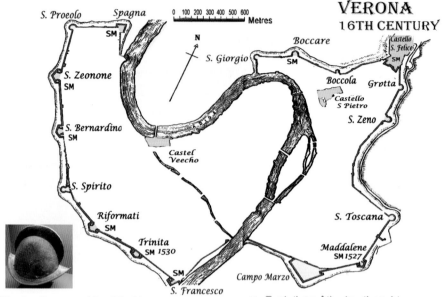

The bastions are identified by an SM (two with a date) if modified or rebuilt by Sanmicheli. Others were built before him, except Camp Marzo which dates from the end of the 16th century.

Evolution of the bastioned trace from F. Taylor's *The Art of War in Italy*

1485 -1559 Michele Sanmicheli, Venetian architect

Rome and Verona: Top: Map showing the modernized sixteenth-century fortifications of Verona. Bottom: Map showing location of Leone City, a district on the left bank of the Tiber where the Vatican is located. The wall and Castel Sant'Angelo are included. The inset is a drawing of Castel Sant'Angelo with late medieval defences highlighted in brown.

completed the defences of Castel Sant' Angelo between 1561 and 1565 by adding
an outer ring of three large bastions and two semi-bastions. During the same
period, he worked on the 3km (1.9 miles) long enceinte of the Vatican and the
defences for a new suburb known as Borgo or Leonine City. While he worked
on this project, the Pope sent him to inspect and direct work at other sites in
the Papal States, including the port of Civitavecchia. The Pope also planned to
replace the Aurelian Wall, but abandoned the undertaking when it proved to be
too expensive. In the summer of 1565, the great siege of Malta ended with the
defeat of the Turks, but the defences were badly damaged. The Pope dispatched
Laparelli to rebuild the fortifications of Valletta in Malta. Laparelli ran out the
funds before he could complete the mission, but at the end of the year, Pius IV
died and his successor, Pius V, was able to finance the project thanks to diplomacy.
The expensive plans for new walls of Rome, however, were abandoned.[25]

Many Italian artists and architects wrote treatises on fortress building during
the Renaissance.[26] Niccolò Machiavelli (1469–1527), dabbled in military matters
and published his *Art of War* in 1520. Although he opined that it was better to
depend on an effective citizen army rather than on fortresses, he dedicated some
of his writing to the importance of good fortifications. He devoted one chapter to
the topic the value of the ditch and thick walls.[27] Other notable Italian engineers
and architects of the sixteenth century include Jacomo Castriotto (1520–63),[28]
Girolamo Maggi (1523–72), Francesco de Marchi (1504–76) and the Dominican
friar, Giovanni Giocondo (1433–1515), who is thought to have invented the angled
bastion even though there are none on the walls of Treviso, which he built.[29] Other
writers did not mention the angled bastion until the 1530s. The Italian bastioned
system became popular as Italian theories, which emphasized geometrical designs,
were gradually adopted and governed military architecture for centuries to come.

Braye, Fausse-braye and Boulevards

Thick earthen banks were an early countermeasure against cannon fire. Piled
behind the castle curtains, they served to absorb shocks. However, once the
masonry was breached, excessive pressure from the earthen berm pushed
the wall outward, forcing debris and soil to pour out, giving the enemy a
form of ramp into the breach.[30] This procedure made the traditional method
of sealing breaches by creating defensive positions behind a breach more
difficult, if not impossible. Before the advent of the cannon, in some castles
the braye was an advance position that served against mining or sneak attacks.
It was a low defensive work in the form of a palisade or earthen wall placed
in front of the wall and moat. It served as a protected walkway that could be
patrolled. Sometimes, lookout towers were placed at intervals to protect the
sentinels.

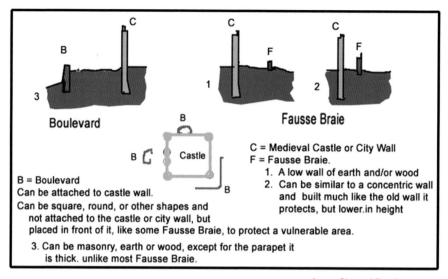

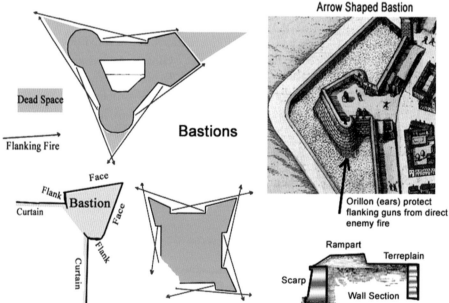

Boulevard, fausse-braye, bastions: Top: Fausse-braye and boulevard. The boulevard walls are backed by earth below the rampart. The fausse-braye, an earlier design, may be more like a traditional wall in which case some do not even consider it a fausse-braye. More often the fausse-braye is usually an earth and timber structure. Bottom: The coverage of flanking fires with dead zones for both round and triangular bastions is shown.

The fausse-braye, which evolved into the boulevard to counter the first gunpowder weapons, is similar to the braye, but stronger. It usually consisted of a wider rampart, which could be a small advanced position covering a weak point or a low wall surrounding all or most of the enceinte. The fausse-braye also had positions for cannons. Unlike the braye, it was actually defended to fulfil its function of protecting the walls from artillery and it often became a permanent masonry position.

In the fifteenth century and later, the fausse-braye became vulnerable when heavy artillery appeared[31] because it was just as weak as the high walls of a castle. The remedy was the boulevard (from the Dutch for bulwark) which replaced the fausse-braye and barbicans and was often similar to the castle or city walls it protected. The boulevard began as an elevated earthen position of similar height to the fausse-braye it supplanted, but it was also a low position designed to protect the older walls behind it from bombardment. It was grass covered to hold the earth in place. Eventually, it evolved into a permanent earthwork faced with stone or thick masonry with its own protective ditch and artillery positions on its ramparts. The boulevard encircled the fortification or covered weak points, often in front of gates. Boulevards went out of use by the end of the fifteenth century.

Many historians of military architecture do not distinguish the fausse-braye from the boulevard and often avoid using the terms. Boulevards that encircled older fortifications are often labelled as concentric walls. This does not make the distinction between actual concentric medieval walls like those of Carcassonne from the outer wall of the castle of La Mota, which may be considered a fausse-braye because it is too high and too narrow to be a boulevard.

Italian Wars in the Age of Machiavelli

The Italian Peninsula was not a peaceful and serene region before Charles VIII of France invaded it in 1494. Subsequently, it became a major battleground between the French and Germans, especially in the north. In October 1494, Charles supported by Milan, engaged a combined Papal and Neapolitan army near Bologna. Next, he defeated a Florentine army and proceeded south, alarming the Pope. Prospero and Gabrizio Colonna, two condottieri, betrayed the Pope and took Ostia in December as Charles marched into Rome. In February 1495, when the French took Naples, concerned Italian states formed the League of Venice. The French retreated from Naples in May, engaged in a battle at Fornovo di Taro near Parma in July, and retreated to Asti. In September, the French abandoned the city of Novara where the League had put them under siege, and retreated to France. Eventually, Spanish general Gonzalo Fernández de Córdoba drove the French from their castles in Naples.

In 1496, Holy Roman Emperor Maximilian I sent an army to intervene in a war between Pisa and Florence and, with Genoa and Venice, he sided with Pisa. He also strengthened Venice in accordance with their anti-French alliance. Florence, in the meantime, allied itself with France. In 1498, Louis XII of France concluded a treaty with the Germans and with the Spanish shortly afterward. In September 1499, he sparked the Second Italian War by wresting Milan from the Sforzas. In 1502, as part of his plan to take Naples, he joined the Florentines in a siege of Pisa. The French artillery opened a breach in the walls, but the defenders drove the attackers back ending the siege after only a couple of weeks. Louis signed a treaty with Spain agreeing to divide the Kingdom of Naples. Together, they took Naples in 1502 before they turned against each other, which led to the defeat of the French at the battle of Garigliano in December 1503 and loss Naples for France.

The Third Italian War began in 1508 after Pope Julius II tried to counter the expansion of Venice with an alliance that initially included Genoa and later, Maximilian I. Venice contested Louis XII's hold on Milan. In December 1508, the Papacy, France, the Holy Roman Empire, Spain, and Ferrara formed the League of Cambrai to fight against Venice. After defeating the Venetian army at Agnadello in May 1509, the Imperial forces went on to besiege Padua without success. Maximillian's defeated army departed ending the League of Cambrai. In February 1510, the Pope changed sides and hired Swiss troops to fight the French while he created the Holy League with Venice. Initially, the French pushed back the Holy League, but the Holy Roman Empire, England and Spain joined the league in 1511. Finally, in April 1512, Gaston de Foix crushed the Spanish army at the battle of Ravenna. When Gaston was killed during the battle, the French withdrew from Italy and Milan fell to the Swiss. Pedro Navarro, the brilliant military engineer of Ferdinand II, the 'Catholic', of Aragon, was captured during this battle. When Ferdinand refused to pay his ransom, Pedro entered the service of France a few years later. In 1513, Louis XII tried to recapture Milan again, but he met defeat at the battle of Novara in June. Maximillian defeated the Venetians that year and pushed on towards Venice, only to be forced back once more. Pope Julius II died in February 1513 and Louis XII in January 1515. His successor, Francis I of Valois, continued the war, which ended in 1516 with France and Venice in control of Northern Italy.

When the Third Italian War began in 1521, Pope Leo X, who had supported Francis I in the election for emperor in 1519 and feared retribution from Charles V, made peace with the emperor leaving France surrounded by Hapsburgs and with few allies. Even Henry VIII of England sided with the Pope. Charles V took Milan and restored the Sforzas in 1522. Francis led the French army into Lombardy and was defeated and captured at Pavia in 1525.

Florence – photos by Martyn Gregg.

Francis contracted an alliance with the Turks who defeated Charles' allies in Hungary the next year. Francis cried peace in January 1526, giving up his claims to Milan.

The War of the League of Cognac began after Francis' release in 1526. The Pope created the League with the Francis, Henry VIII of England,

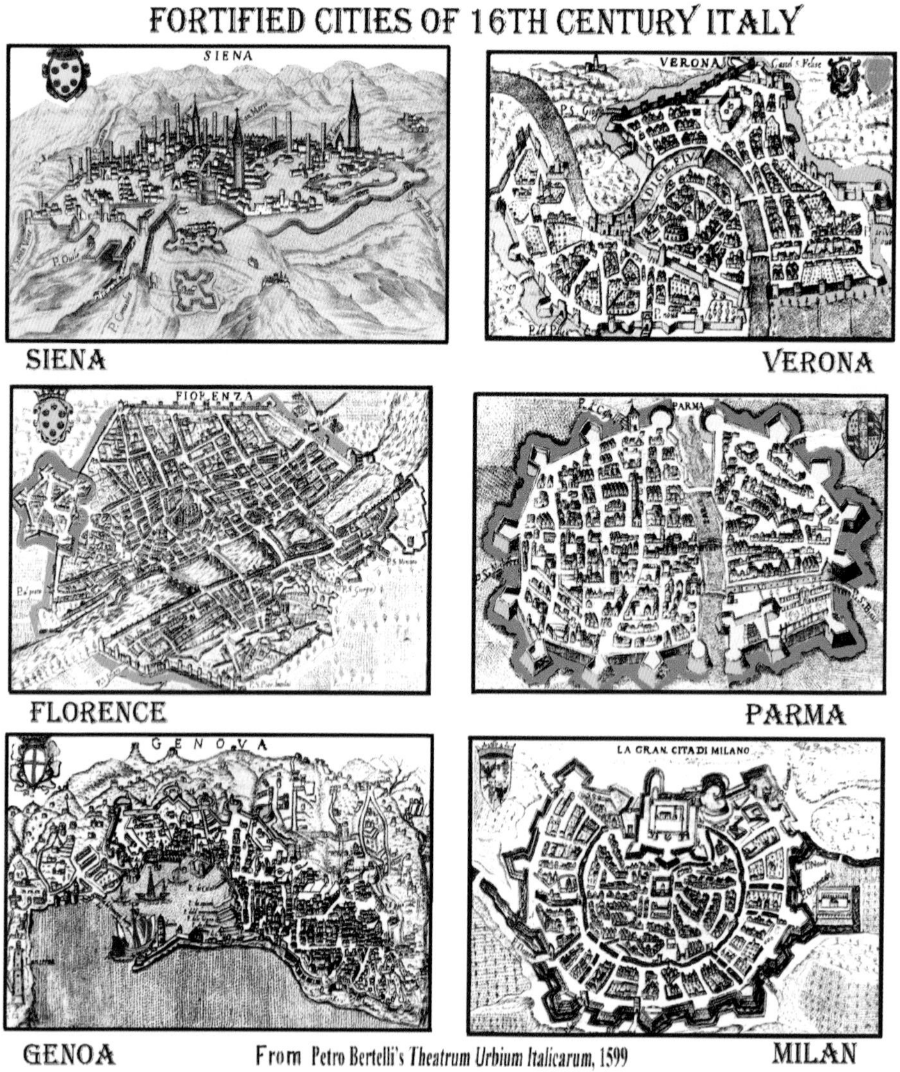
FORTIFIED CITIES OF 16TH CENTURY ITALY
SIENA
VERONA
SIENA
VERONA
FIORENZA
PARMA
FLORENCE
PARMA
GENOVA
LA GRAN CITA DI MILANO
GENOA
From Petro Bertelli's Theatrum Urbium Italicarum, 1599
MILAN

Fortified cities of Italy: Examples of several cities heavily fortified in the sixteenth century.

Venice, Florence, and Milan. After two sieges of Milan failed, the League began to break up. Charles' Imperial army took Florence and sacked Rome in 1527. The French put Naples under siege with the help of the Genoese fleet in 1528, but lifted it several months later, in August. Venice made peace with Charles and Florence was returned to the Medici family.

Francis I and Charles V confronted each other again in 1536. While the Empire engaged Islamic pirates in the Mediterranean, the French seized Turin in 1536. Charles invaded France and was repelled at Marseille in

Milan's Castello Sforzesco. A woodcut by Sebastian Munster from Cosmographia Universalis, *1550.*

September. The fighting spread to Flanders until an armistice was concluded in June 1538. As a result, the French kept some of the lands they had taken in northern Italy.

In 1542, Francis I and his Turkish ally declared war on the Holy Roman Empire. The Turkish admiral Barbarossa captured Nice in August 1543, but his siege of the fortress failed. The main French objective of the war was Milan. In 1544, Francis and Charles supported different factions in Florence and the Imperial forces were victorious. Francis, in the meantime, had to contend with an invasion of his kingdom by Henry VIII and Charles V. Since the emperor still had to deal with the Turks, however, the war ended quickly. Francis I died in 1547.

Castle Bridge of Metz, known as the German Gate because of a nearby house belonging to the Teutonic Knights. Top and mddle: The two rear towers of the Gate belonged to 13th century city wall. The bridge crossed Seille River. The two towers in front of the Gate built in 1445. Bottom: City wall and towers adapted for use of cannons.

France started a new war in 1551 by invading Savoy while Pope Paul III's army was operating in the region around Parma. The army of Charles V took heavy losses on the French front in a failed siege of Metz that ended early in 1553. Siena was forced to surrender to Florence in April 1555. Charles abdicated in 1556, turning over his lands outside the empire to his son King Philip II of Spain. In 1557, a French army supported by the Pope advanced on Naples after which the war moved to France until a treaty was signed in April 1559.

During the remainder of the century, France became involved in a civil war of religion against the Huguenots (Calvinists) while the Holy Roman Empire concluded its struggle with Lutherans and engaged in the Eighty Years War of the Dutch Revolt led by Calvinists. The Hapsburg monarch also had to help Venice and other Italian states ward off the continuing Turkish threat. This was the age of large armies with muskets and pikes backed by field artillery. Most castles fell into obsolescence to be replaced by fortress cities.

New Walls for a New Era

The designs that replaced castles with forts and fortresses also brought major changes to city walls. Although the fortified town or city often can be called a fortress, the term is generally reserved for a major fort. Even though the terms fort and fortress are often used interchangeably, during the Renaissance and later the term fortress meant a large fort or a heavily fortified urban area ranging in size from a village to a city. The advent of the cannon forced communities to modify their old walls or build new ones. The new walls had to be thicker than the medieval ones and instead of a wall walk, they needed a wider terreplein to accommodate cannons. In most cases, however, the walls still had to remain high enough to deter scaling, but most of their height had to be concealed in a surrounding ditch. This meant that the depth of the moat had to be increased so that only a small portion of the wall was visible to the enemy. A glacis, especially one with steep slopes, helped mask the walls from direct artillery fire. By the end of the sixteenth century, medieval-style towers were modified or replaced with towers no higher than the walls. Many of those built in the middle of the century still used a circular shape. These new towers, often solid, are known as bastions or artillery towers. Walls and bastions were thicker than their medieval predecessors were because they had not only to accommodate gunpowder artillery, but also to resist it. The fortifications built during the fifteenth century still included medieval features, which did not disappear from military architecture until the end of the sixteenth century. Round bastions with casemates and platforms for cannons were gradually replaced with angular bastions during the sixteenth century. By the seventeenth century, the angular design that characterizes the *trace italienne* became ubiquitous.

Italians dominated the field of military architecture, and they were employed throughout Europe. Benedetto da Ravenna (1485–1556), Gabriele Tadini (1476–1543), Sangallo the Younger (1483–1546), and Michele Sanmicheli (1484–1559) led the development of the polygonal bastion, which began to replace the circular bastion in the 1530s and later. Benedetto worked on and off for Charles I of Spain from about 1520. His work included the improvement of the fortifications of Perpignan in the 1530s.[32] He was still designing circular bastions in the 1530s, but replaced them with angular bastions in the next decade. In the 1540s, Henry VIII of England contracted Girolamo Pennacchi (1508–44) to bring the new designs to England. Italians were also hired to build fortifications by the Spanish in the Netherlands and the French in Lorraine. Italian engineers and architects, however, did not monopolize the field. Albrecht Dürer (1471–1528) in the Holy Roman Empire and Francisco Ramiro López and Pedro Luis Scrivá (dates unknown) in Spain also made significant contributions.[33]

A fortress town or city posed a greater problem for the large professional armies, which could no longer live off the land. They blocked lines of communication and supply and they were more difficult to neutralize than individual forts, which could often be bypassed. They generally required a much greater amount of construction materials. Although the number of specialists needed was not much greater than during the previous era, a greater workforce was required because defences had to be built much more quickly than during the Middle Ages. The workers needed to be paid because feudal obligations could no longer supply the numbers of people needed for the construction, especially when it was for a town or city. This increased the need for taxes to finance the projects. In many cases, these massive projects began as temporary works akin to field fortifications of timber and earth. However, since the latter had a limited lifespan, it soon became necessary to add stone or masonry coverings. The addition of bastions with casemates required much more work than a simple solid bastion covered with masonry. The same was true of casemated walls and scarps. Moats, wet or dry, had to be more massive and deeper than those of the previous era were since they had to provide cover for most of the curtain wall. Wet moats made mining more difficult, if not impossible, and removed the chance of surprise attacks by escalade, but they prevented the defenders from launching raids. Counterscarps required sufficient revetment to prevent their collapse and further exposing the curtain. Covered ways were placed above the counterscarp from which the defender could protect an advanced position in front of the ditch from which the glacis could be covered. Ravelins in the moats protected entrances and curtains and caponiers defended the moat. Platforms for cannons called cavaliers were built slightly above the ramparts on bastions or walls. Other elements were added after this period. Even before the construction of these features, a great deal of work was required to create an adequate foundation, which had to be wider than the walls. In many cases, the ground was not sufficient to hold huge walls, so the foundations required piles to prevent subsidence to stabilize them.

As the cannon replaced the trebuchet and other types of medieval siege engines, siege machines changed as well. The heavy and cumbersome early bombards were largely replaced with cannons mounted on carriages by the sixteenth century. Scaling ladders remained an important tool for the besiegers, but the belfry and other types of siege towers lost their efficacy against the new fortifications. Even rams lost their importance since cannons could do a better job against most gates except dogleg entryways that did not allow a direct attack. A siege technique that became deadlier than ever was the mine, especially after the advent of gunpowder. The only remedy was the countermine, as ancient as the mine, which also became increasingly effective thanks to gunpowder. To approach the walls and move their cannon into range, the attackers had to negotiate the open area of the glacis. The only way to do this was to dig zigzag trenches in the direction of the moat and walls thus preventing the defenders from using enfilading fire along the approach trenches. This method remained in use for centuries.

Although there are many fortresses in the new style throughout Western Europe, three best represent the ongoing trends of the period: Sarzanello Castle in Italy, which became a fortress, Salses in France, and the coastal forts of Henry VIII in England. On a hilltop 120m (349ft) above the town of Sarzana, the Romans had built a castrum that became a medieval castle after various construction phases. During the fourteenth century, it became the main residence of the condottiere Castruccio Castracani (1281–1328), lord of Lucca. In 1421, Lorenzo de' Medici 'the Magnificent', the ruler of Florence, contracted Tomaso Fregoso to modernize the stronghold. After they fortified the town of Sarzana, the Florentines turned their attention to the old stronghold on the Sarzanello Hill. In 1487, Francesco di Giovanni (1446–98)[34] and Luca del Caprina (dates unknown) presented their plans for a citadel in the town of Sarzana and the fortress on the hill and began construction the next year. They used a square plan for the citadel that resembled Volterra and a triangular plan with 60m (197ft) sides based on Francesco di Giorgio's schemes for Sarzanello. The citadel (1488–93), emerged on the remains of the Firmafede Castle built by the Pisans during the thirteenth century. It is rectangular and includes six towers, two of which are located on the longest side dividing the citadel into two large courtyards. The construction method continued following medieval norms, consisted of rubble-filled walls that were, however, much thicker than in older castles. Both the citadel and the fortress have round artillery towers and their scarps were designed to resist artillery. The fortifications of the town of Sarzana were finished by 1493, but the fortress of Sarzanello was still unfinished when Piero de' Medici, whose father Lorenzo had died in 1492, turned both places and other Florentine fortresses over to the French invaders in 1494.[35] Construction resumed on Sarzanello under the direction of the engineers Pietro Biancardo (dates unknown) and Matteo Civitali (1436–1502), hired by the Genoese, after Charles VIII was driven back to France. They finished the work in 1502, having added an early version of a ravelin that covered the entrance.

This solid ravelin appears to have been built on the remains of an older tower.[36] Access to the ravelin is by a bridge from the fort, well covered from above, which passes between the ravelin and the fort before it turns into the stronghold. The fort had three large circular bastions and a keep on the wall facing the ravelin. All had machicoulis (none on the ravelin) and two of the bastions had thick ramparts while the third did not, but this may have been a result of modifications centuries later. A masonry counterscarp with a form of covered way was part of the outer defences. Probably at this time or later a couple of ravelins were added to the citadel in the town.

In 1497, as Sarzanello neared completion in Italy, the Spanish began the construction of a fort north of Perpignan, not far from the ruins of the village of Salses destroyed by the French in 1496.[37] The construction was directed by the artillery specialist and military engineer Francisco Ramiro López.[38] A huge workforce was gathered from around Spain and, despite peace with France in 1498, work continued at a rapid pace. López' design, with modifications made after the first siege in 1503, was revolutionary even though it became obsolete by the seventeenth century. What makes his work seem so different is that most of the vertical surface of the walls was concealed in the moat. The walls of the Salses fortress were not extremely thick and included galleries for firearms from which the defenders could fire into the moats. After 1503, López added a talus to them, thus covering the gun embrasures in the galleries, thickening the walls and reducing the effectiveness of scaling ladders due to the slope. The fort formed a rectangle about 110m by 84m (361ft by 262ft) with four circular corner towers for cannons. Like many other post-medieval fortifications, it still included a 26m (85ft) high seven-level keep that stood at the centre of the western enceinte, walled off the rest of the fort. It formed part of a reduit, which had its own drawbridges. The reduit included many of the important service features of the site, but it was unfinished. The artillery towers had casemate positions and, like the donjon, they were crowned with battlements similar to those of other Spanish castles such as Coca and La Mota. The 18m (59ft) high eastern towers consisted of three levels and the 21m (69ft) high western towers of four. An engraving of Salses made by the Portuguese Francisco de Holanda and dating from 1538, if accurate, clearly shows the merlons. If they existed, they were removed sometime after that date. The curved ramparts in front of the merlons were intended to deflect roundshot and the high donjon are also depicted in the illustration. The northern demi–lune appears in the 1538 drawing, but the cavaliers on the north and south walls do not appear.

The artillery towers at Salses could mount up to three cannons but no one is sure of the number actually mounted. The curtain walls did not accommodate cannons. The fort has a demi-lune in front of the middle of the eastern curtain and both demi-lunes, which have been referred to as ravelins even though ravelins are generally triangular rather than horseshoe-shaped. They are also linked to

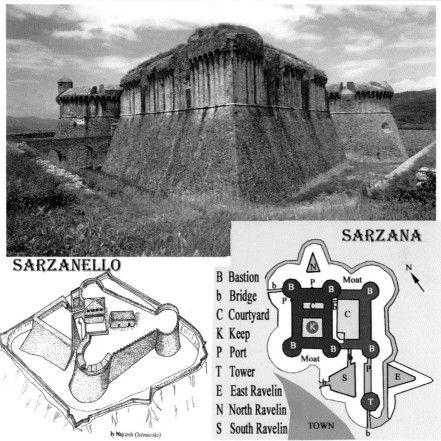

B	Bastion
b	Bridge
C	Courtyard
K	Keep
P	Port
T	Tower
E	East Ravelin
N	North Ravelin
S	South Ravelin

Sarzanello. Top: Sarzanello bastion and bridge to entrance. Centre: Sarzanello ravelin. Bottom left: Drawing of Sarzanello by W. Ostrowski. Bottom right: Plan of Rocca of Sarzana next to town and below the hill with the Rocca of Sarzanello.

Volterra: Top: Old castle known as Cassero begun in 1292 and expanded until 1432. Inset photo: View of the same feature from another angle by Pierre Etcheto. Bottom: New Castle built after Lorenzo di Medici 'the Magnificent' conquered the town for Florence in 1472 and supposedly finished with four high towers and a central keep in by 1474. Photo by Janericloebe on Wikimedia. Plan of the two castles with double walls added before end of the century to provide for barracks, stores and a refugee during a siege.

the fort by caponiers. In front of each entrance, one on the north side and the other the south side, were barbicans also identified as demi–lunes. After the siege of 1503, the northern entrance was sealed after its barbican was destroyed by a mine during the siege. There is no way to be certain when these demi–lunes and caponiers were added, like the sunken walls of the fort, they represent traits of modern fortifications.

In 1502, the fort mounted seventeen heavy cannons and thirty-nine light cannons and the garrison was equipped with over sixty arquebuses.[39] After 1503, a talus covered the galleries with the gunports, and then those galleries served as listening posts and positions for creating countermines. The round corner towers, much like those of Sarzanello, did not have machicoulis although the large keep and entrance did, but these were decorative and not functional, although from the 1538 drawing this is difficult to determine. The towers had flanking positions for handguns or very light artillery to cover the walls. Échauguettes or sentry boxes of brick occupied positions on the curtain walls and towers. The large 'place d' armes' or courtyard could be defended from the walls. The walls and towers included a maze of passages to confound the enemy. Posterns led into the moat and in the sixteenth century the southern entrance's protection included the demi-lune (or barbican) and a châtelet. The brick-paved moat, about 7m (23ft) deep and 12m to 15m (39ft to 49ft) wide, was designed to stay dry and included a stone-lined cuvette for drainage since the area is prone to great downpours and flooding. The curtain walls were approximately 4.7m (15ft) thick near the bottom by the gunports before the talus was added. The galleries included ventilation. After the addition of the talus the walls ranged from 7m to 11m (23ft to 36ft) thick. The scarp was twice the height of the counterscarp. The north, east, and south sides of the courtyard included stables on the lower level and barracks on the upper for a garrison of over a thousand men. The governor and family resided in the keep.

During the siege of 1503, which began on 3 September, the fortress' garrison of 1,000 infantry and 350 cavalry faced a French force of 15,000 men. The northern section of the fortress sustained heavy damage and part of the counterscarp was destroyed. The Spaniards pulled back and exploded a mine in the barbican killing about 400 to 600 French soldiers, depending on the chronicler who recorded the incident. When a relief force showed up, the French withdrew. López, who had been in the fortress during the siege, took advantage the period of truce that followed to improve and strengthen the defences.

The Achilles heel of the Salses may have been drainage system in the moat. During the Spanish siege of 1639, water backed up in the moat, swamping the lower levels of the fortress. Although early historians had thought that the Spaniards had deliberately flooded the moat, recent scholars have concluded that it was more likely the result of an act of nature. In the first place, neither the French nor the Spanish contemporary records mention such an act of sabotage. In the second place, French sources of the period report that a powerful storm system had prevented Frederick Schomberg's[40] army from coming to the rescue of the French garrison of Salses. It is therefore very likely that the massive downpours that had detained the rescuers had overpowered the moat's drainage capacity causing the flooding, something that occurs at Salses from time to time to this very day. In any event, the stagnant waters increased the misery of the starving French garrison and contributed to its capitulation.

A covered way appeared on top of the counterscarp of Salses at an uncertain date, probably after the mid–sixteenth century, but it was destroyed by Vauban in the next century. It consisted of an open area with a rampart from which troops could lay grazing fire along the glacis. It might have included traverses to block enemy penetrations, and artillery positions. The first description of the covered way is found in the 1554 treatise by the Italian Niccolò Fontana Tartaglia (1499–1557). However, it may have appeared prior to that at his home town of Brescia in 1438 and later in the moat of the castle of Milan about the time of his birth.[41] It seems that it became a standard feature in fortifications after the 1550s.

During the Renaissance, especially in the sixteenth century, many castles were converted into residences or palaces, as their military value had diminished due to the advent of artillery and/or location. Although many Renaissance engineers/ architects made innovative proposals in their treaties and books in the 1400s and 1500s, many of the buildings of that period continued to retain archaic features and lacked many of the defensive elements required for the new era. The more costly bastioned fortifications were large and concentrated in strategic locations, cities, and in some cases, as in England, for coastal defence. After Henry VIII broke with the Roman Catholic Church and founded the Anglican Church, the Pope Paul III negotiated a ten–year truce between Francis I of France and Charles V of Holy Roman Empire in 1538. Henry VIII of England feared an invasion. Thus, in the spring of 1539, he directed the creation of a chain of coastal forts that stretched from Cornwall to Kent to protect England from his religious opponents. The construction programme led to the creation of seventeen coastal forts and several smaller positions known as blockhouses that were often D-shaped and mounted a few cannons. Forts covered the entrances to ports such as Falmouth, Southampton or Portsmouth, and other possible landing areas. To say the least, their design was new, if not practical.

Henry's coastal forts, known as the 'Device Forts,' are not attributed to any single architect or engineer. Several Englishmen, a German, and the King himself may have had some input on their design. The 'Device Forts' have a number of common characteristic even though they have different layouts. They are all low to the ground and have thick walls with rounded parapets, numerous gunports and embrasures that would have would have provided formidable firepower, and include a circular central keep that mounted cannon. Most were surrounded by gun platforms usually in the form of semicircular bastions. The guns were mounted on several levels depending on the size of the fort, including the roof of the central tower. Gun casemates occupied the thick walls and included shutters and vents for the removal of smoke from the gunpowder. Some had merlons on the battlements that were merely decorative, but the murder holes in some of the gateways had a practical use.

Sandown, Deal and Walmer Castles, linked by earthen field fortifications and located between the towns of Sandwich and Dover, covered the Downs anchorage

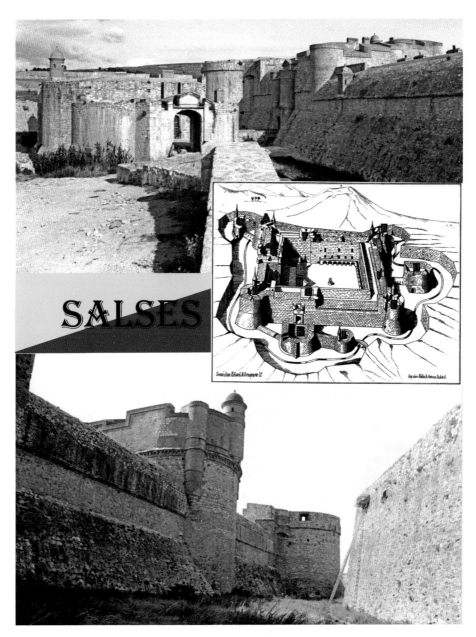

Salses: Two views of the moat of Salses Castle and 1860 plan. Plan: A, B, C & D – Artillery Tower; E & F – Cavalier; H – Interior defensive wall; G – Keep; I – Barracks; K & L – Barbican and Châtelet; M & N – Demi-Lune (the 1860 plan identifies K & L as a boulevard and N as a contre-guard).

off the Kentish coast. Walmer and Sandown are similar to, but smaller than, Deal with four semicircular bastions surrounding a keep. Deal has six projecting semicircular bastions that rise to the first floor level of the keep. The walls at

Salses: Key to plan and photos: A. Demi-lune. B. Caponier. C. Well. D. Stables (on lower level). E. Barracks (on upper level). F. Donjon. G. Entrance. H. Cavalier. K. Artillery tower. L. Barbican or Châtelet (depending on source). M. Moat. Top left: Photo of the north-west demi-lune (photo by Pierre Etcheto). Top right: Photo of the north-east section of the courtyard. Centre: Photo NW Demi-lune. Bottom left: Photo of the donjon (photo by Pierre Etcheto). Bottom right: Photo view from moat of entrance, south-east artillery tower and the lake in background. Drawing of Salses in 1538 by Holanda. Plan of Salses from 1693 includes Vauban additions.

Walmer are up to 4.6m (15ft) thick and made of Kentish ragstone and Caen limestone from nearby monasteries. The bastions form a gallery around the keep. At Deal, the quarters for a small garrison were on the ground floor of the keep were and food, supplies, gunpowder stores, the kitchen and a well were in the basement. In peacetime, the Deal Castle garrison numbered only two dozen men. Both had access to the bastioned gallery. The commander and his staff were more comfortably housed on the first floor. There were gun positions on the roof

Deal and Walmer: Top photos and centre right by Rupert Harding and aerial view of Deal by Lieven Smits (Wikimedia). Plan of ground level of Deal from O'Neil, 1966.

of the keep and its bastions. An outer curtain forms six bastions with cannons mounted above and embrasures below to cover the moat. A gatehouse with a drawbridge is located between two of the bastions. The medieval style entrance includes murder holes above, a portcullis, and an iron-studded oak door. The distance between the outer curtain and the keep with its bastions is not great and forms an inner moat or passageway. Beyond the outer curtain, there is a wide and deep moat with a masonry counterscarp. It is defended by the embrasures in the lower level of the outer curtain. The entire fort numbers 145 embrasures for firearms on five tiers and cannon on four.[42] It could mount sixty-six cannon whereas Walmer and Sandown[43] had positions for only thirty-nine guns in three

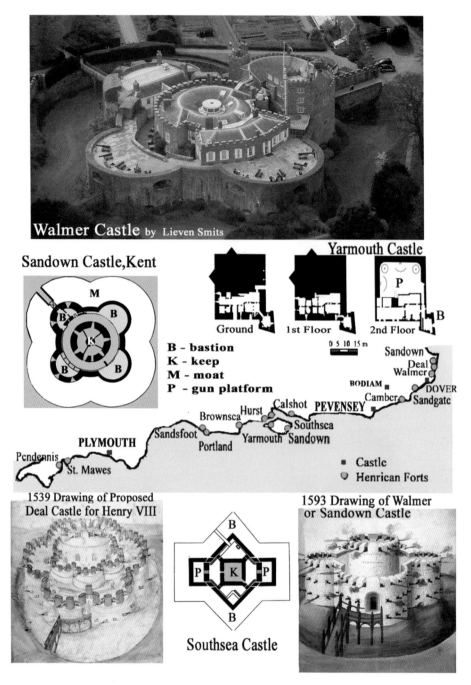

Walmer, Sandown, Yarmouth. Top: Aerial view of Walmer by Lieven Smits (Wikimedia). Middle: plans of Sandown and Yarmouth. Bottom: Southsea Castle and two 1539 drawings.

tiers and thirty-one embrasures for firearms at moat level in the basement. Vents in the casemates allowed smoke to escape. It took about 500 men to complete its construction between 1539 and 1540, before the winter when only about 100 men were employed. The workforce was increased to about 600 in June.

The other 'Device Forts' were smaller and required fewer workers, but that still meant that several thousand men were employed between 1539 and 1540 to build all these forts. Bricks were made at nearby kilns while wood, lead, and Caen stone was taken from the monasteries the King had shut down. Local Kentish ragstone, not as good as the Caen stone, was used for much of the work. The walls of Deal, Walmer, Sandown, and the other large 'Device Forts' were from 4.3m (14ft) to 4.6m (15ft) thick while the small smaller ones were about 3.4m (11ft) thick.

The invasion never came, but since another threat arose in the 1540s, a few additional castles were built between 1544 and 1547. In these new strongholds, round bastions began to give way to angular positions. Unlike Deal, they held fewer cannons; Yarmouth Castle, for instance mounted fifteen. Southsea Castle had two angled bastions with two gun platforms on each flank of the square keep with 30m (98ft) sides and an arrowhead bastion on its landward corner. Clearly, England was beginning to catch up with Continental trends. Most of the forts of Henry VIII remained in service for many years, but saw little to no action except during the English Civil War in the 1640s. After the 1550s, the transitional phase was nearing an end as round gun bastions were gradually replaced with angular ones and as many medieval features such as machicoulis became decorative rather than functional.

Chapter Six

Closing an Era

War Italian Style

Before the French invasion in 1495, warfare in Italy was changing from direct attack to manoeuvre and delay. The Italian condottieri preferred flanking attacks rather than direct assaults. Historian Frederick Taylor points out that 'Strategy may be defined as manoeuvring before battle in order that your enemy may be found at a disadvantage when battle is joined . . .' in order to defeat the enemy in the field.[1] The various Italian states tried to dominate their neighbours, which they achieved by occupying key strategic positions like cities and forts. When the numerous fortified cities in Italy adopted the *trace italienne*, they required larger numbers of men to defend the enceinte than they had in the past and sieges required even larger armies.

When King Charles VIII of France undertook the conquest of Naples, King Ferdinand avoided battles, dispersed his forces among several fortresses, and played for time, a stratagem known as 'Fabian'.[2] However, as Charles sought a decisive engagement, he discovered that his artillery corps, which had helped win the Hundred Years War, could quickly reduce Italian fortresses. Thus, he was able to swiftly drive Ferdinand from his kingdom. The diplomatic situation was in flux with changing alliances. Milan, Venice, the Holy Roman Empire, and the Papacy formed the Holy League, blocking Charles' lines of communication on land and sea. As its position in Naples weakened and disease took its toll, the French army began its long return march north.[3] Charles' enemies failed to engage him in the Apennines and allowed his army to reach the north Italian plains where he engaged the League's army of mercenaries in the indecisive battle of Fornovo in July 1495. Although both sides claimed victory, the outcome of the encounter allowed Charles' army to make it back to France. For centuries, the plains of the Po Valley became a battleground for Italian, French, and Germanic forces.

In November 1500, Charles' successor, Louis XII, formed an alliance with the Catholic monarchs of Spain and launched a joint invasion of Italy in 1501. The new king of Naples relied on his father's failed strategy of 1494 and again French siege artillery proved too powerful for medieval walls. In 1502, the Spanish forces led by Gonzalo de Cordova ended the alliance, but the French remained in control of Naples. In 1503, Cordova received reinforcements, defeated the French at Cerignola in April, and took Naples in May. In December, he blocked the route to Naples at the Garigliano River where he outflanked the French, blunted their direct assault across the river, and dealt them a decisive defeat.

Louis XII gave up his claims to Naples in 1505, but returned to Northern Italy in 1508 to engage the Holy League in a war that lasted until 1514. After the French took Bologna in 1511, they were besieged in the city by Papal and Spanish forces until they were rescued by a relief force. In February 1512, the French defeated the Venetians and took Brescia, thus gaining control of most of the north. Next, they laid siege to Ravenna. A combined Spanish and Papal army tried to break the encirclement, which led to the battle of Ravenna of April 1512. The French prevailed, inflicting about 9,000 casualties while suffering half that number. However, they lost their leader, Count Gaston Foix, during the battle. They took and sacked Ravenna shortly afterward.

At the battle of Garigliano in 1503, the French forces numbered about 23,000 men and their opponents 15,000, which shows the increasing size of field armies. In 1513, Henry VIII of England led and invasion of France from Calais with 28,000 men against 15,000 Frenchmen. The armies were much larger than they had been during the previous century. Infantry, increasingly armed with arquebus (harquebus) and pike, took on a greater role. At the battle of Ravenna in 1512, about 23,000 Frenchmen opposed the Holy League's 16,000, 5,000 of which were defending Ravenna. In 1521, the garrison of Milan, which numbered about 40,000 men, consisted of 25 per cent harquebusiers.[4] During the 1527 siege of Cremona, one-third of the Duke of Urbino's Venetian army of 29,000 men consisted of harquebusiers.[5] During the Renaissance, battles generally involved great numbers of men and artillery and fortresses grew in importance in campaigns. Cannons increased in size continuing to make it almost impossible for small garrisons to defend high walls. The addition of features like fausse-brayes and boulevards with artillery emplacements increased the need for additional defenders.

Cannons used in the field and against strongholds created the need for field fortifications on the defending as well as the attacking side. Before 1494, the cannons of the defenders had the mission of harassing the enemy during preliminary bombardment and breaking-up assaults. As a result, the besiegers had to shelter their guns in trenches. In 1495, during French and Neapolitan sieges of Castel Nuovo, the besiegers resorted to using trenches. That year, at the siege of Novara after the battle of Fornovo, the Italian used earth and fascines to protect their guns from the defenders. Trenches and gabions became standard in siege warfare.[6]

The first half of the sixteenth century witnessed a Machiavellian world in the Italian Peninsula as politics, religion, and war reached a crescendo. Wars continued to flare and the French and Germans returned to Northern Italy. Francis I of France, an unsuccessful contender for the throne of the Holy Roman Empire, was at war with Charles V (Charles I of Spain), the man who won the position. The French retreated to France after a defeat on April 1522, but they returned in April 1524 and they were decisively trounced near Milan. As a result, Charles V teamed up with Henry VIII of England and planned an invasion of France from Calais, Spain and Italy. Coordination, as King John of England had learned centuries earlier, was difficult. The Imperial forces led by Charles of Bourbon invaded French Provence from Italy, but they were stopped at the siege of Marseille despite support from the Genoese fleet led by Andrea Doria. Francis I riposted by leading an army of about 30,000 men into Northern Italy. He took Milan, but failed to seize its castle and had to pull back when disease spread among his troops. In 1525, he laid siege to Pavia but failed to take it and he was defeated and captured. In 1526, after Francis was released from captivity, he formed the League of Cognac, which included the Papal States, Venice, Florence, England, Navarre, and Milan. The league had little success during its first year while the unpaid Imperial troops it faced began to rebel.[7]

The cause of what happened next is open to speculation, but forces of the Empire, consisting of Spaniards and German mercenary landsknechts – the Empire's equivalent of Swiss pikemen – led by Charles de Bourbon marched on Rome in 1527. By the time they reached Rome in early summer, the unpaid troops were feeling rebellious. The Germans, led by Georg von Frundsberg, were Lutherans with little respect for the Pope and the Church he represented. The Eternal City was ill prepared for a siege. Few improvements had been made to the old Roman walls even though some defences had been extended around the Vatican. Renzo da Ceri, who had reinforced the walls of Marseilles to defeat the Imperial forces in 1524, organized the defences. The garrison consisted of about 3,000 largely untrained men, although some sources claim 8,000, and 189 Swiss Guards.[8] The enemy force included about 20,000 men mostly mercenaries.

The dawn attack on Rome of 6 May 1527 was recorded by Luigi Guicciardini, a Florentine government official. A large detachment of the Imperial army approached the city near Santo Spirito (on the west bank south of the Vatican) and the Landsknechts found inspiration in the plunder that awaited them. The Spanish troops began the attack from several directions 'trying to enter the city at a point near Santo Spirito above the gardens of Cardinal Armellini, since the walls were lower there than elsewhere'. At that location, 'the circuit of the walls incorporated the main wall of a small private house' which had a much wider than normal cannon port because it had been installed in a window. The defenders overlooked a small, unbarred window in the wall that was part of the house. A heavy ground fog limited visibility and prevented the gunners at Castel Sant'Angelo from seeing the enemy. Charles de Bourbon led the Imperial troops up ladders planted against the walls and was mortally wounded. The assault resumed in the heavy fog. The defenders, wrote Guicciardini, 'repeatedly threw burning liquids over the wall . . .' and aimed their cannons and firearms toward

by Martin van Heemskerck 1555   SACK of ROME 1527

Sack of Rome in 1527 by Martin van Heemskreck (1550).

the noise of the enemy obscured by the fog. While the fighting continued for over an hour, the attackers continually received reinforcements and fought with an unabated fury. The Spanish troops broke into the city at 10:00 am either after widening the cannon port or by entering through the unguarded cellar window. Renzo shouted for everyone to run for their lives. The Pope Clement VII and his entourage fled down the secret elevated passage called the 'Passetto' of about 800m (872 yds) connecting the Vatican to Castel Sant'Angelo to take refuge in the ancient stronghold.[9] About 3,000 people made it to the castle. Meanwhile, other Imperial troops burst into the city through the walls on the west side entering through Porta S. Pancrazio and through places where the walls had been abandoned. At 6:00pm, they found the gatehouse at Ponte Sisto abandoned. Before long, the attackers overran the city and went on a killing and pillaging spree.[10] The sack of Rome of 1527 was followed by the surrender of Castel Sant'Angelo and negotiations with the Pope in June.

The Turning Point

The transitional phase in military architecture was paralleled by a similar trend in weapons and tactics that brought about a turning point in modern offensive and defensive warfare. According to Frederick Taylor, this took place at the siege of Padua in 1509, which had been reconquered by the Venetians in mid-July 1509. The subsequent siege was 'a real trial of strength between the defensive and offensive tactics of the day'. Emperor Maximillian assembled 'the most formidable siege train of that generation,' with over 100 heavy siege guns, much greater than Charles VIII did in the 1490s.[11] Many inventors came to offer the condottiere Niccolò di Pitigliano (1442–1510), who commanded the Venetian forces at Padua, new engines of war. He ordered all the houses near the city walls destroyed, cleared the area around the city of all trees and structures for up to 2km (1.24 miles), and filled the deep surrounding ditch with water. Every gate and weak point was protected by enfilading fire from artillery mounted in projecting bastions. In a period of only two months, thousands of men laboured to create a new defensive system around the city. 'The old fourteenth century walls were lowered and reinforced. This included a continuous earthen embankment built against its inner face.' However, it is not now known if it actually was against it and exerted outwardly pressure on it, but the damage caused by the heavy bombardment seems to indicate it did have this negative effect. To the rear of the reinforced wall was a 'ditch thirty feet wide having sheer sides revetted with masonry and containing casemates and towers at intervals of a hundred paces'. Behind the ditch, another earthen embankment with a high parapet served as an assembly point for troops and a platform for artillery much like a boulevard, except it was behind the city wall instead of in front of it.[12]

In mid-August, the Imperial army destroyed the Venetian castle at Limena at the Brentella river junction a few kilometres north of Padua and tried to alter the course of the river waters feeding the Padua moat. In later August, they began siege preparations while the army swept through the area. Padua was the main position protecting Venice. When the Imperial troops reached the counterscarp of the ditch, they were subjected to intense artillery fire from the city and they were forced to dig trenches for both their infantry and artillery in the area the Venetians had left devoid of cover. On 3 September, the Imperial artillery began bombarding the bastions of Santa Croce and Pontecorvo on the south side of the city wall with stone balls, since the Empire had not yet adopted iron projectiles at this point.

On 7 September, a general mobilization took place in Venice since the situation appeared to be critical as the Imperial troops continued to advance throughout the region. The siege of Padua was only part of the ongoing operations even though it played a key role. The actual siege of Padua began on 16 September when the Imperial artillery was directed against the city. On 20 September, the Imperial troops were repulsed when they stormed the Bastione della Gatta on the north side of the city wall. Extensive stretches of the walls collapsed under Maximillian's bombardment and, apparently, the earthen embankment did not help. The Imperial troops could not tunnel beneath the deep moat and initially were unable to cross it without additional preparations. Undeterred, they pressed on and eventually got a foothold on the Bastione della Gatta, one of the bastions hastily added to the existing wall in the summer, only to be driven off. The defenders had prepared and detonated mines on this bastion, which successfully threw back the attackers. It included three palisades one of which ran across its 50m (164ft) diameter. Additional assaults took place on 26 September another attempt to take the Bastione della Gatta after it was almost completely destroyed by the bombardment. However, the Paduans had prepared a powder magazine in it to serve as a mine and the resulting devastating explosion killed hundreds and forced the Imperial troops to retreat.[13] On 28 September, one final mass assault lasted for over a day. Even though the Bastione della Gatta was reduced to rubble, the Paduans inflicted heavy losses on the assailants once more. Discouraged by another failure and supposedly unable to pay his mercenaries, the Emperor lifted the siege on 30 September and looked for other means to capture the territory of Venice. The Venetians recaptured Limena on 5 October and a few days later, water began to flow into Padua again.[14]

According to Frederick Taylor, the siege of Padua was a turning point in the history of fortifications because it inspired other urban centres in Europe to adopt similar defensive measures, which included clearing the surrounding areas and at a short distance behind the enceinte and creating trenches and ramparts like those of Padua. At Milan in 1516, for example, new defences popped up in 48 hours. They consisted of a massive terraced embankment bristling in front with the pikes of defenders on the lower level, arquebuses and other small arms on the middle level, and cannons to the rear on the highest level. The Milanese built strongpoints to enfilade the ditch and walls with flanking fire, caponiers in the ditch, and projecting earthworks, like the Bastione della Gatta at Padua, in the form of semicircular bastions.[15]

At Padua in 1509, the defenders behind cover used crossbows and a large number of arquebuses to inflict serious losses on the Imperial forces. The crossbow, however, fell into disuse as the arquebus took its place. Fortifications had to be adapted to this firearm and thought had to be given to the extraction of smoke. Even the importance of cavalry declined because, as in the past, foot soldiers served as storm troops at Padua in 1509 and elsewhere during sieges.

The attackers could only counter the new technology by creating an extensive system of trenches and gabions. They had to establish their camp beyond gunshot range and use sappers to create zigzag trenches to advance their artillery, a technique that endured for centuries. The Imperial army had tried to implement this method at Padua, but it lost because it required a massive labour force that the Emperor could not afford. In addition to deeper and more extensive trenches, the besiegers could opt to attack the walls in several places to stretch the resources of the defenders. Mining the walls continued to be a serious threat to the defenders, who responded with countermining. Now, however, instead of engaging the enemy underground, the objective was to 'dig air passages into the hostile mine and thus break the force of the eventual explosion'.[16]

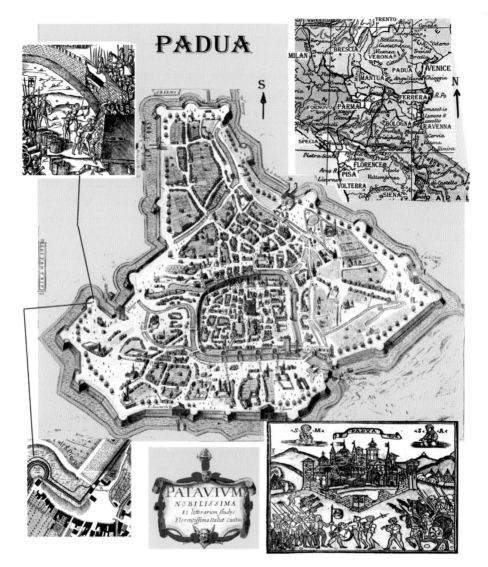

Padua: Map of north central Italy and plan of Padua during the battle.

Evolving Fortifications

Leon Battista Alberti's fifteenth-century treatise is credited with laying out the design for the *trace italienne*, but it was not until almost a century later that Girolamo Maggi and Jacomo Castriotto detailed its implementation in *Fortificazione Delle Città* and the angled bastion gained popularity. Most of the new fortifications of the transition period such as Sarzanello and Castel Nuovo included circular artillery bastions rather than angular ones. Earlier in the 1450s, at Castel Nuovo a low-level gun platform, like a fausse-braye, was actually added to the walls by the Aragonese to encircle the landward side. Between 1503 and 1519, the Spanish built a structure similar to a boulevard with three large circular gun towers and they added an anguled bastion to one of the landward corners in 1536.[17] When Sangallo the Elder worked on Castel Sant'Angelo in the early 1490s, he created octagonal gun bastions around the round towers that had been added to the corners in 1447. Fort Sangallo at Nettuno – attributed to Sangallo the Elder – was built for Pope Alexander VI and his son Cesare between 1501 and 1503. It has four anguled bastions at the corners of a quadrangle. The walls are 5m (16.4ft) thick and rise up to 25m (82ft). By contrast, most medieval walls were 2m to 3m (6.6ft to 9.8ft) thick. Sangallo the Younger designed Fort Michelangelo with its round bastions at Civitavecchia in 1507. He also began work on the city walls with angled bastions in 1515, but they took many years to complete. In the early 1565, Laparelli built an outer wall with three large angled bastions at Castel Sant'Angelo. The orillons that gave them an arrow shape and protected the flanking cannon positions were not added until 1630. Only the truly angled bastions associated with star patterns eliminated blind spots for enfilading fire from flanking positions.

After the siege of 1509, the Doge of Venice ordered the construction of new walls using the bastion system around Padua, which was important to the protection of the mainland possessions of his Most Serene Republic. A new bastion was built over the ruins of the famous and badly damaged Bastion della Gatta. Other earthen bastions became permanent masonry positions and the walls were strengthened with round bastions in 1513. However, work on the first angled bastions did not begin until 1526. Padua's fourteenth century walls built by the ruling Carrara family had to be replaced and/or modernized. The Cornaro and S. Croce Bastions, which had been among the first to be attacked in 1509, were replaced in the 1550s[18] with angled bastions with two faces and flanks, unlike most of the others, which were round or semicircular. The first of seven of the angled bastions at Padua did not appear until after 1526. The city never underwent another siege. The city of Ferrara, which was also under Venice's protection, added three angled bastions to its walls between 1512 and 1518. Verona, which had also suffered from sieges, like Padua, received only round bastions in 1516 and an angled bastion in 1527.

Many Italian cities replaced their walls or built new ones during the sixteenth century. Lucca, for instance, began rebuilding its walls in 1504 and continued into the middle of the next century. The new fortifications included two large angled bastions, four round ones and a rectangular one. Milan's new city walls included many angled bastions and an impressive moat and on the north side a citadel. Known as the 11km (6.8-mile) Spanish Wall, these defences were built between 1546 and 1560 when Milan was under Spanish rule and when the angled bastion finally became dominant. Historian J.R. Hale points out that the angled bastion on city walls was adopted more slowly than on forts.[19] Florence also built new walls on the north side of Fortress Basso. Construction of that fort, which included five arrow-shaped bastions, began in 1534. In the 1590s, the Fortress of Belvedere was added on the south side. Verona underwent two major sieges: one in 1509 and the other in 1516. Its old walls were in poor repair and had to be refurbished from 1520 onward. The renovations included additional round bastions and, in 1527, one angle bastion.

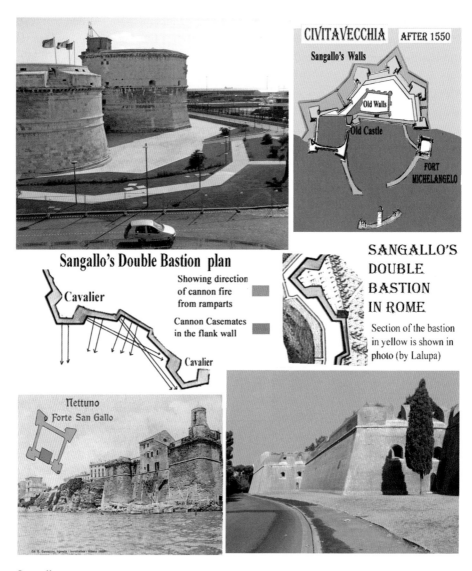

Sangallo.

In the mid-sixteenth century, the construction of angled bastions and the *trace italienne* increased as the transition period began to phase out. Despite the great expense, a growing number of cities and fortresses in the new style began to appear. They would be further refined in the next century by masters such as Vauban. Spain was involved in crushing a revolt in the Netherlands. Fortress cities in the new style began to sprout in the Dutch Lowlands where the low terrain favoured the construction of large wet moats. In Northern Italy, the Venetians built the fortress city of Palmanova as a star shaped position. As the old castles crumbled, new fortresses spread across Europe and even into the New World, Africa, and Asia.

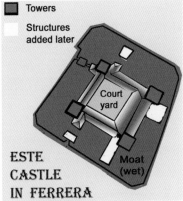

ESTE
CASTLE
IN FERRERA

Castello Estense in Ferrara – begun by Niccolo II of Este in 1385 as a refuge from the locals who revolted against him that year.

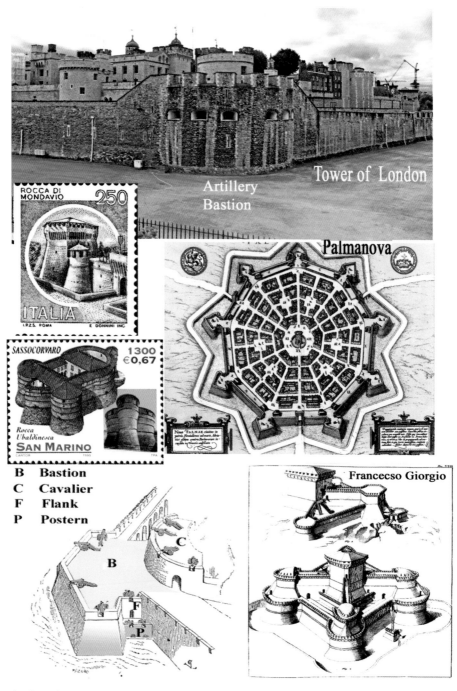

Artillery fortifications: Top: Tower of London showing bastion with arrow loops and cannon embrasures (photo by Lorenzo Mundo). Middle: Plan of star-shaped fortress of Palmanova. Stamps showing Mondavio and Sassocorvaro, both designed by Francesco Giorgio. The latter used rounded towers and curved walls and has a turtle-like shape. Bottom right: Example of Giorgio's symmetrical fifteenth-century designs. Bottom left: Bastion defensive system.

Bridges and Religious Structures

Key bridges such as those in Paris across the Seine and the Alcantara bridge at Toledo over the Tagus and those over smaller rivers such as at Cahors on the Lot River often received some form of defence that often included fortified towers on either side and/or additional positions. Many examples remain across Europe.

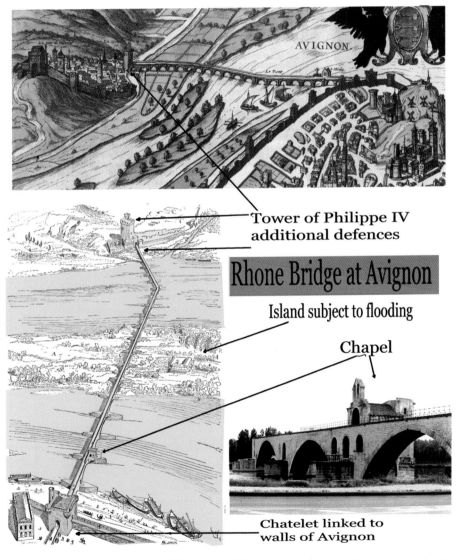

Fortified bridge at Avignon. Top: 1575 Braun and Hogenberg illustration of Rhône Bridge showing Tower of Philippe IV which included a set of fortifications behind it and the châtelet built into the walls of Avignon on the other side. Bottom: Avignon Bridge.

Late 13th Century

TOURNAI BRIDGE

CAHORS BRIDGE

© www.all-free-photos.com

Tower   Chatelet   Tower

Chatelet

mid-14th Century

Cahors Barbican   & St. John Tower

Fortified bridges: Top: The Pont des Trous, a fourteenth-century bridge at Tournai on the Scheldt. The tower on the left bank, the Bourdiel, built 1281 and right-bank tower, the Thieulerie built 1304. Arrow slits in connecting curtains on bridge. Middle: The Pont Valentré over the Lot at Cahors. Built between 1308 and 1378 with six Gothic arches and three square bridge towers. The two end towers have machicoulis. Bottom: Cahors barbican and St. John Tower (two photos at bottom — one on the right shows the Tower where connected to the barbican and left is the barbican).

Cluny Abbey Walls & Towers

Albi Cathedral

FORTIFIED RELIGIOUS SITES

Avila Church
in City Wall

Avignon
Palace of Popes

Fortified religious structures: Many abbeys and religious sites had walls around them or their own defences. The Cathedral of Ávila had its apse located in the city walls. The Palace of the Popes at Avignon was fortified and surrounded by a city wall.

Often churches and cathedrals in important locations that might be exposed to attack received some type of defences that might include defended entrances or even battlements on the roofs. Unfortunately, sometimes these battlements may only be decorative. The cathedral of Albi above the Tarn River is an example while the abbey on Mont Sainte Michel is fortified on its approaches and entrance and even includes some defences inside. Its elevated position offers protection and the island it is on is partially surrounded by a wall that covers the village on the approach to the abbey. Monasteries were often walled, but many of their walls did not offer a defendable position. At Caen some were used by the attackers to improve their own position during the Hundred Years War. The Cluny monastery included walls, but also had towers built for the purpose of defence.

Conclusion

This volume and its predecessor *Castrum to Castle* have centred on the fortifications built in the Western Roman Empire from the time of the decline of Rome through the Medieval Era to the early Renaissance. From the Italian to Iberian peninsulas and from Britain to Western Germany, Rome left a heavy imprint that endured through the Dark Ages into the Renaissance. This does not mean that Roman influence was not felt in other regions of Europe, but here Gauls, Britons, Iberians and many of the Germanic people merged with Latin culture leading to the emergence of modern-day states. The Germanic invaders that occupied Roman lands did not come in huge numbers and their kings learned Latin and adopted many elements of Roman law and culture instead of eradicating it. However, they found no need to maintain large armies like Rome had done and they continued with their own tribal institutions, which led to medieval feudalism. Noblemen provided a small mounted force of knights, but most armies consisted of unpaid militias that followed the later Roman practice of garrisoning and defending towns and local fortified sites, which remained the key to maintaining regional control. This arrangement did not change significantly until the High Middle Ages. In the eighth century, with only small mobile armies available to them, the Christian kingdoms in the West became vulnerable to the Islamic invaders who overran Iberia and penetrated into the Frankish Kingdom. Sieges rather than numerous field battles dominated the post-Roman era even in the Italian Peninsula where the Byzantine army of the Eastern Roman Empire attempted to reconquer the lands of the old empire.

During the last centuries of the Western Roman Empire, fortifications had become instrumental in the protection of its lands. The first defensive lines were the Limes on the frontiers. Later, the Romans resorted to fortifying cities, including Rome, to deter raiders. In the Medieval Era many of the most important castles and other fortifications were built upon the ruins of already well sited Roman castra. Roman walls remained around many cities and towns. They were maintained, like at Dijon, modernized, or simply rebuilt over old foundations. Roman architecture, whose influence persisted in the West until about the twelfth century, is reflected in the Romanesque style that included semicircular arches and heavy buttresses of the fortifications of this period. The Romanesque was gradually replaced with the Gothic with pointed arches and flying buttresses, which, however, were not of much use in fortifications. The massive Roman road system remained largely intact throughout the Western Empire in the Middle Ages.

During the High Middle Ages, the design of fortifications in the West improved due to contact with the Levant due to the Crusades; conversely, some Latin influence can be seen in the Holy Land. Castle and city walls rose in height and acquired a few new features such as machicoulis to ward off attackers at the

Fortress of San Leo. Top: View from cliff side: Insert: Photo (from Wikimedia) shows the entrance side of the fortress. Bottom: View of the entrance.

base of the walls. Ancient features such as the moat and the wall remained key features of medieval fortifications. The dominant earthen and timber walls of the Dark Ages were supplanted in the High Middle Ages with stone, which was the most effective though expensive. At the close of the Middle Ages and the latter half of the Hundred Years War, small castles lost their importance as fortress cities and larger fortifications rose to prominence. Throughout this period, sieges outnumbered battles.

The advent of gunpowder artillery brought the greatest change in the Late Middle Ages as fortifications started to included positions for gunpowder weapons. Italian architects like Leon Battista Alberti rediscovered the works of the Roman Vitruvius from the first century BC and applied his theories of fortifications to new designs known as the *trace italienne*. Renaissance masonry fortifications were reinforced with earthen positions. Their walls no longer projected high above ground level; instead they sank into deeper and wider moats. They also became thicker to resist gunfire and wider to accommodate 'modern' artillery. Towers were replaced with bastions. Fortifications continued to evolve during the next half of the second millennium as earth and masonry played a key role in their development. Military architecture culminated with the construction of the subterranean forts of the twentieth century like those of the Maginot Line.

Weapons of Siege Warfare

During the Middle Ages, the sword was the main weapon of knights and men-at-arms and many soldiers carried a dagger as well for hand-to-hand combat. Most troops also carried a buckler or shield for protection. During an attack on a castle, the attackers used their sword only when they fought on the ramparts or when they broke into the fortification. During a siege, knights on horseback were only effective if a gate was opened or smashed in or to engage an enemy raiding force. Javelins or spears were used as projectiles and were particularly useful for the defenders on the ramparts against enemy soldiers trying to scale the walls. However, their range was limited.

A more effective weapon was the bow because expert archers could fire several arrows per minute. A short composite bow was used until the twelfth century. The longbow, which came into use during the High Middle Ages, was a particularly effective weapon in siege warfare. Arrows shot from a yew longbow[1] could penetrate most armour. Opinions vary on whether the bowmen were more effective when they shot arrows in a mass volley or when they aimed individually. The defenders of castles and city walls could fire well-aimed shot from the cover of the fortification. The maximum range of the longbow was approximately 250m (273 yds) and the range for penetrating armour probably up to 200m (215 yds). However, during the Hundred Years War, English archers are said to have been effective up to about 370m (443 yds). Attackers would probably have been more successful shooting volleys and fire arrows.

The crossbow, used as early as the Roman era, was also a popular weapon in siege warfare. The Church banned its use against Christians at the Second Lateran Council of 1139 declaring it a brutal weapon, but it allowed it against non-Christians and heretics. Nonetheless, it continued to be used against Christians. The crossbow took longer to load than a bow, but it was more accurate and did not require a well-trained bowman to use it. It had the ability to shoot about two bolts[2] per minute as opposed to a maximum of ten to twelve arrows for the longbow. Its range was up to 360m (392 yds). Crossbows came in various styles, including one that required a windlass to pull the bowstring back.

Both defenders and attackers also used maces, which seem to have come into prominence in the twelfth century. These weapons came in various sizes and styles and could penetrate most armour, but their effectiveness depended on the strength of the men wielding them.

Slings were also part of the medieval arsenal, but they were not heavily used except in Muslim armies during this period. The halberd, which appeared in about 1300, had an axe shaped head and sometimes a hammer or spike on the opposite side. Like other polearms such as the billhook and the pike, it proved effective against cavalry and in the defence of ramparts. More deadly types of poleaxes appeared in the Late Middle Ages.

Mantlets and Pavises were shields to protect artillerymen and crossbowmen. Pavises, which were carried on the back of crossbowmen, were usually a little over a metre in high (4–5ft). They originated in the city of Pavia, hence the name. The crossbowmen stood behind them while they reloaded. The mantlet was a shield behind which an archer could stand. Some mantlets for artillery had mobile stands, which allowed them to rotate to a horizontal position for firing a cannon and then dropping it to a vertical position to protect the gunners as they reloaded.

Various forms of handguns came into use in the late fourteenth century. Some could fire a bolt-like apparatus and could serve as an incendiary device to set fire to wooden hoardings, thatched roofs, and other wooden structures in a fortification. The arquebus, which appeared around 1500, was a muzzle-loading gun fired from the shoulder with a lighted match.

Traditional artillery included the ballista, which looked like a giant crossbow and the mangonel, which was a type of catapult. The mangonel had a vertical arm that was pulled to a horizontal position through torsion and released to lob a projectile forward. It took from one to 100 men to operate mangonels, depending on their size. The smaller versions, called perrière or pierrie, required a dozen or fewer men to pull the ropes and had a range of 40m to 80m (44 yds to 87 yds) with 3kg (7lb) to 12kg (28lb) rocks. Estimates of the range of mangonels are from 40m to 130m (44 yds to 142 yds). The beam itself could consist of several pieces of wood lashed together to hurl heavier projectiles. The trebuchet, which appeared during the twelfth century in the Middle East, was much larger than the mangonel. The first models required manpower to launch the missile. Unlike the mangonels, which served mainly as anti-personnel weapons and could clear the battlements and even wreck wooden hoardings, the trebuchet was a wall buster. It was much larger than the mangonels and often referred to as a counterweight mangonel. The counterweight propelled the projectile. One or more men cranked the beam down into a horizontal position. Once released, the counterweight on the other end of the arm dropped down forcing the beam into a vertical position. The large trebuchets could throw rocks weighing 90kg (200lbs) to 140kg (300lbs) and even 450kg (1,000lbs) in the Late Middle Ages. The range of the mangonel was about 180m (196 yds) whereas the range of a large counterweight trebuchet might have been double that distance.

Most siege artillery was hauled in pieces and assembled on site, but some could be made on location. Trebuchets crews often had to haul their massive projectiles from elsewhere. Dozens of mangonels could be used to lay down a continuous barrage on a fortification. The defenders also used similar weapons for defence. Launching incendiaries or Greek Fire increased the havoc among the defenders. Dead animals or human bodies were sometimes launched in the hopes of spreading disease or for psychological effect. The trebuchet often received individual names like 'Malvoisine' (Bad Neighbour).

By 1400, cannons were commonly used in sieges. The first were small, vase or barrel-shaped, and often designed to fire arrows and stones. At the beginning of the fifteenth century, they were made of long strips of iron tightly bound and iron balls became standard. By the end of the century, they were cast as a single bronze piece, which was very expensive to produce. Thus, during the next century, many cannons were made of iron, which were of poorer quality. Modernizing armies with cannons became a major expense, causing taxes to rise.

In the fourteenth century multi-barrelled guns called ribauldequins appeared. They fired iron shot in volleys and served as anti-personnel weapons mainly to plug breaches in walls. The firing positions for most of these weapons had to be close to enemy walls to be effective. The largest cannons, known as bombards, were very heavy, relatively expensive, and difficult to move, but they could fire heavy balls, which is why they were almost exclusively siege weapons. Many bombards were given names like the large trebuchets. The Scottish bombard 'Mons Meg', built in 1449, had a range of about 1,500m (1,636 yds). Most large bombards had a range of only 200m to 250m (217 yds to 273 yds), which was less than the range of some of the large trebuchets. Moveable mantlets were often used to protect them since they were exposed to enemy fire due to their short range. In the sixteenth century, bombards were replaced with mortars and cannons. Culverins, small, long-barrelled cannons with a high muzzle velocity, were mainly used on the battlefield. In the sixteenth century, about a dozen types were developed. They had effective ranges of about 180m (196 yds) to 1,820m (1,984 yds). Several other types of howitzer-like cannons not classed as culverins were also developed at this time. They fired heavier projectiles and had effective ranges of 365m (394 yds) to 685m (747 yds). There were three types of mortars, short-barrelled high-trajectory weapons, the heaviest of which fired 90kg (200lb) projectiles at ranges of up to 1,820m (1,984 yds).

The belfry (siege tower) was another important siege engine. It was moved up to castle walls in order to drop its drawbridge for soldiers to cross onto the battlements. The preferred method for movement was with men pushing it and the using rollers instead of wheels. It varied in size and could sometimes hold several hundred men. Archer on the tower cleared the walls of defendants. Covered rams, which had been used as far back as the Bronze Age, were used to batter down gates or walls. The covering, often of skins, protected the assailants from enemy missiles and fire pots or rocks dropped from the battlements. There were various methods of repelling ram attacks. For instance, the defendants

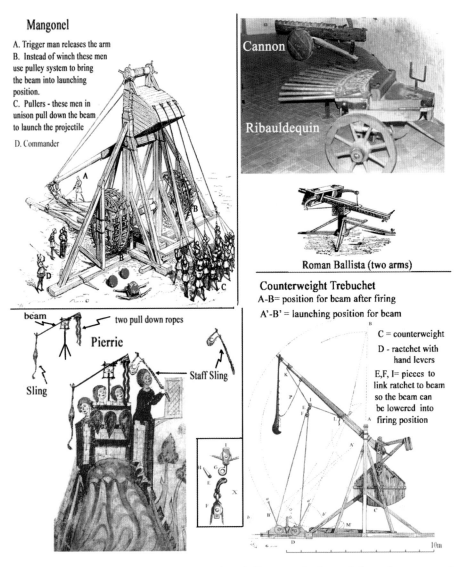

Medieval weapons: Various types of weapons from ballista to trebuchet and the early cannon and ribauldequin.

swung wooden beams from the walls to push the rams away or covered impacted walls with mattresses.

The simplest weapons were the miners' picks and shovels used to breach walls at the base or by tunnelling beneath them. The miners worked under mobile armoured sheds or began tunnelling at a safe distance from the walls. When the tunnel reached the desired area under the wall, they built a subterranean chamber, filled it with flammable materials and an accelerant like pig fat, and set it on fire. Once the props in the chamber down, the wall or the tower above crumbled,

Early cannons. Top: Examples of early cannons at Castel Sant'Angelo. Centre left: Some swivel mounted cannon and some breech loaders from the sixteenth century at Les Invalides. Right centre: A cast of a bombard found in the moat of Bodiam castle. Bottom: Bombard placed behind a swivel-mounted wooden shield, and some mobile wooden shields for troops at Castelnaud.

creating a breach. In the fifteenth century and later, gunpowder replaced the use of combustibles. The defenders, on the other hand, used a crane-like weapon to drop incendiaries or other objects on the miners working under the armoured shed at the base of the wall or they dug countermines to intercept the enemy tunnels. A deep and/or wet moat could also deter ram attacks and miners.

Despite all these weapons, the most effective way to reduce a fortification remained starvation, which no defender could overcome. Lack of water was even more damaging than a lack of food.

Appendix II

Vitruvius' Comments on Towers

According to the Bachrachs, authors of *Warfare in Medieval Europe*, the first-century BC Roman engineer Marcus Vitruvius Pollio's ten-book (more like chapters) series, *De architectura*, inspired the Italian architect Leon Battista Alberti to develop the *trace italienne*. Much of Vitruvius' work seems to focus on Roman building methodology. For instance, in Book I, in a small section dedicated to city walls, he recommends digging down to bedrock level or as far as possible to create the foundations of towers and walls. This foundation – he writes – should be much thicker than the walls resting upon it. The towers must project beyond the line of the walls so that the advancing enemy is forced to open his flanks and expose himself to missiles from towers on each side. Roads and paths leading to the gates should not follow a straight line, but run parallel to the walls. Towns and their enceintes should not be laid out in square grids or have salient angles. Instead – he argued – a circular form was much preferable because salient angles would be difficult to defend.

Vitruvius saw the disadvantage of square towers. Towers – he claims – must be either round or polygonal because square ones are more easily destroyed by siege engines. In addition – Vitruvius recommends – towers should be within bowshot of each other, a practice not always followed before the fifteenth century. Vitruvius also addresses other elements of fortifications. Moats, for instance, must be wide and deep and wall foundations must sink into the bed of the ditch in the places where attacks over level ground are likely. He also includes other details related to construction of the walls.

Vitruvius' main contribution is pointing out that the most effective enceinte will have round or polygonal towers projecting beyond the walls and within missile range of each other. During a good part of the Middle Ages, his principles were largely forgotten and square towers predominated until the end of the twelfth century. The Renaissance Italian engineers rediscovered his writings and adapted them to their designs or came up with their own similar solutions.

Notes

Chapter 1

1. Tariq was Musa ibn Nusayr's subordinate.
2. Assassination to eliminate a rival political leader was common.
3. The castle of Simancas was not built until the fifteenth century.
4. Each of these walls was 5m (16.4ft) thick and included a 5m (16.4ft) wide passage between them, according to David Nicolle in *The Moors* (p. 140). Descriptive plaques on the site state that during the reign of Abd al-Rahman III the Great Portico was constructed as the ceremonial entrance to the alcázar and was only a decorative structure that had fourteen open archways on the west side of the parade ground. Not long after its construction three archways were closed on the north side to create quarters for the guards. The gateways used the standard Islamic military feature of angled gateway passages. At this site two 90-degree turns were in the passage.
5. The term Moors generally referred to North African Muslims and those occupying Western Europe. Not all, such as the Berbers, were Arabs or from the same tribal groups. Some Berber tribes practiced Judaism. Yemenite and Syrian Arabs were rivals. The Yemenites, who controlled Seville, considered the Berber kings of Granada, Murcia and other taifas as semi-barbaric (Clissold, *In Search of the Cid*, p. 57).
6. Dynastic rule existed in the taifa states and by 1065 only about nine of the states remained.
7. Initially ribats were held by religious warriors and amounted to fortified outposts, similar to monasteries, on the frontier or the coast. Both Christian and Muslim raiding forces consisted of no more than 200 to 300 mounted troops and this was not sufficient to attack a major town or city.
8. The epic poem claims El Cid made the king swear he had not killed his brother, and this eventually led to his banishment.
9. Monte Hacho at Ceuta is often considered to be the southern 'Pillar of Hercules' and Gibraltar the northern pillar. Ceuta was the key base for controlling piracy and launching invasions of Iberia from North Africa.
10. Fletcher, *The Quest for El Cid*, pp. 168–9.
11. Fletcher estimates the Almoravid army at about 25,000 rather than the claimed 50,000. It was nonetheless heavily outnumbered El Cid's forces. Ibid., p. 173.
12. It is not clear if there was actually a castle in the Benicadell Range, although it did form a good defensive position. The poem of El Cid refers to Penna Cadiella, a castle in these mountains that has not been located.
13. After they were defeated on the Cuarte plain by El Cid, the Almoravids retreated to the safety of the walls of Játiva (Xátiva). It has two older forts, one pre-Roman (Castillo Menor) and one Roman (Castillo Major), each on a different peak and

surrounded by the same curtain wall. The Muslims rebuilt them, turning the larger fort into an alcazaba on top the hill with thirty, mostly square, connecting towers. The fortress follows the high ridge south of the city.

14. Today, little remains of the fortifications built by the Moors in the tenth century besides a wall of a keep. A fifteenth-century Christian castle now occupies the site.

15. Even though he is Spain's national hero, El Cid was accused of many cruel acts such as enslaving Muslim captives and even burning them. He ruled Valencia like a merciless despot. However, he was a man of his times and probably no better nor worse than his contemporaries.

16. A ribat might be considered a small fort or fortified monastery serving as a frontier outpost. On trade route travelers could find accommodations there.

17. Only the Moorish wall with its four towers (two forming the gate) and two corner towers remain. The other walls were a result of improvements made when it became a Christian palace. However, the site is famous for its Islamic architectural features. According to historian David Nicolle, the structure is typical of Andalusia. Its stone towers and brick walls reflect a tradition that dates back to the early Islamic era in Syria (*El Cid and the Reconquista*, p. 7).

18. Islamic-style work done by Muslim artisans under Christian rule

19. The longest remaining section of wall extends about 80m (262.4ft).

20. In the 1080s, Count Berenguer of Barcelona formed an alliance with the ruler of Denia, al-Hayib, son of al-Muqtadir the ruler of Zaragoza. After al-Muqtadir's death, Berenguer and al-Hayib tried to wrest Valencia from its puppet ruler al-Qadir and Castile. In 1086, Berenguer fortified Cebolla and Liria north of Valencia and laid siege to Valencia until El Cid forced him to withdraw. After El Cid laid siege to Liria, Yusuf invaded Iberia, creating a new problem. Shortly after his victory at Zallaca, Yusuf returned to Africa, Murcia rebelled against Seville. Al-Mu'tamid, al Haib's brother and ruler of Seville was forced to pay tribute to Alfonso VI until 1088 when he appealed to Yusuf for help. Yusuf returned in 1089. The Muslim leaders of Granada and Almería marched with the Almoravids against Aledo in 1092 bringing the small fortress into prominence.

21. The Cluniac Order was formed in France in the tenth century. Many other monastic orders joined its reform movement to clean up the political activities of the clergy and to improve moral standards among their members. Some of its most prominent members include Popes Gregory VII and Urban II.

22. A vassal could give fealty to more than one feudal lord for lands or titles, but the one he must perform homage for was the liege lord.

23. It is not clear if this mountaintop castle, located east of Teruel and between Zaragoza and Valencia, was simply a tower or a more complex outpost.

24. Navarre became independent again and no longer played a major role in the Reconquista. Ramiro II abdicated in 1137 and Ramón Berenguer IV of Catalonia, who married Ramiro's daughter, and his son, Alfonso II, united Aragon with Catalonia in 1164. Meanwhile, Alfonso VII (1126–57) ruled León and Castile from 1126 and claimed the title of emperor in 1135 working as an ally of Ramón Berenguer IV to form a united front against Muslim Iberia. They were soon joined by King Afonso of Portugal, but unfortunately, the three monarchs did not coordinate their offensive efforts.

25. Alfonso rebuilt the castle after the battle. Only a square tower and ruins remain today.

26. The Moors destroyed the castle and some sources claim the Templars took it over in the thirteenth century until 1312. In 1380 Archbishop Pedro Tenorio rebuilt the castle for use during the civil war in Castile.
27. The account is further detailed in Wolfe and Wolfe (eds), *The Medieval City under Siege*, p. 21.
28. A century later, in 1255, Lisbon became the capital.
29. Afonso I of Portugal took Santarém by surprise in 1147 when his men climbed over the walls at night and opened the gates.
30. Richard the Lionheart was among the Christian defenders.
31. The Order had lost Calatrava castle in 1195.
32. The caliph, who was in Morocco at the time, never sent the tribute (O'Callaghan, *Reconquest and Crusade in Medieval Spain*, p. 83).
33. The government rebuilt the tower during the twentieth century, but did not restore the medieval style.
34. Pedro won the battle of Nájera in 1367, but Enrique killed him in 1369 and took the throne.
35. The winter journey through mountainous terrain cut with ravines filled with swollen rivers was full of perils, especially since the Spanish force strove to avoid detection from the dozens of watchtowers that dotted the region. Every expedition was risky and ambush was one of the greatest hazards in hostile territory.
36. The so-called Roman bridge of Ronda is actually an Arab bridge. There were actually two, but the impressive high bridge spanning the gorge dates from the eighteenth century. The southern part (south side of the gorge) of the city included several sets of walls and fortified gates. Near the southern gate (the Almocabar Gate) was an alcázar, also known as the Laurel Castle, probably built by the Moors in the fourteenth century. Archers dominated the walls and approaches to the city from its towers.
37. Prescott, *Complete Works*, p. 385.
38. According to Prescott, in the 1480s there were more fortified sites in the emirate than in the rest of Iberia.
39. The Alcazaba of Almería was used for the shooting of Indiana Jones and Conan the Barbarian films in the twentieth century.
40. This type of low wall built to defend against artillery is called a 'falsa braga' or fausse-braye.

Chapter 2
1. Since early in the Middle Ages in Iberia both Muslim and Christian armies centered many operations on the capture of cities fortified since Roman times and for this both sides needed large numbers of troops. This was also the case in France during the Dark Ages, especially in the south in the Midi and Provence. Roman fortress cities simply did not disappear, nor did the road system allowing for the movement of large forces to besiege them when necessary.
2. Danielle Chadych in *Paris: The Story of the Great City*, p. 28, wrote that the wall did not encompass all the nearby boroughs and was to have twelve gates and that the towers were reserved for crossbowmen.
3. Chadych's numbers differ from Le Page who gives 2,500m (2,725 yds) of wall on the Right Bank and 2,000m (2,180 yds) on the Left Bank. Few sources agree on

numbers, including the number of towers and if they are counting gate towers. If the interval averaged 50m (164ft) between towers, then seventy-seven or more would have been present, while some sources and even Sebastien Munster's fifteenth-century engraving indicated closer to sixty-seven towers including those of gates. Unfortunately, Munster and even Viollet-le-Duc's artistry may not be accurate.

4. Jean and his son Phillipe became prisoners of the English. They were released in 1360 when a ransom was paid under the Treaty of Brétigny. Philippe became Duke of Touraine and in 1363 Philippe II the Bold, Duke of Burgundy. His older brother became Charles V, King of France, the next year.

5. Jean Froissart was a French clerk and wrote for English patrons. His chronicles cover much of the fourteenth century aspects of the war and are among the most extensive.

6. Froissart, *Chronicles*, p. 77. Edward marched on Calais afterward.

7. Bastides (see Glossary), temporary forts or Bastilles were added to give additional protection.

8. The kings depended heavily on militia for defending city walls, especially since for much of this era of feudalism large professional armies, like the old Roman army, did not exist since they required a heavy taxation system to be maintained. The kings still needed taxes to maintain their kingdoms and wage war.

9. Many cities like Bourges had their Roman-era walls, but by this time they needed improvements or major repairs.

10. Reims is an example of how the foundations of the old walls still remained. Michael Jones, 'War and Fourteenth-Century France,' in Curry and Hughes (eds), *Arms, Armies and Fortifications in the Hundred Years War*, pp. 117–19.

11. Ibid. p. 119.

12. This was a medieval raid, usually with mounted troops, to leave a trail of destruction so as to weaken an enemy.

13. Instability and factionalism in Rome prompted the Pope to move the Papal residence from Rome to Avignon.

14. This enceinte survives to this day.

15. Du Guesclin was a Breton knight who became Constable of France in 1370.

16. Most of the English expeditions began as chevauchées, but ended as sieges. The Crécy campaign included siege equipment, which would not normally be part of a raid since it made the army road-bound.

17. The figures vary from source to source. According to recent research, there were 5,000 (or as many as 10,000) longbowmen, 2,500 men at arms, over 6,000 infantry and light cavalry, and 5 ribauldequins (organ guns) vs. a French force of 6,000 crossbowmen, 12,000 men-at-arms and 12,000 infantry.

18. Henry Bolingbroke was the son of John of Gaunt, the Duke of Lancaster, one of sons of Edward III. When Richard II was overthrown, Bolingbroke became Henry IV, the first Lancaster king.

19. The faction representing Orléans was known as the Armagnacs. The Burgundians eventually became English allies.

20. Like other medieval battles the numbers widely vary with the English having 7,000 archers and up to 1,000 men-at-arms, but French numbers do not differ greatly for this battle.

21. Henry V died at Vincennes in 1422 and Charles VII soon after, leaving the nine-month-old Henry VI of England as king of both countries. The Armagnacs never

accepted the situation and continued to support the Dauphin, the future Charles VII. Henry VI was the son of Henry V and Catharine, the daughter of Charles VII. He may have inherited his grandfather's insanity, since he lost control in 1453, which led to the English War of the Roses.

22. This was one of the last major battles where the longbow proved decisive.

23. During this battle, cannon, which had previously had limited effect, played a major role.

24. Guyenne is an alteration of Aquitania or Aquitaine. Aquitaine was split into two parts in 1258 with Poitou and Auvergne directly under French control and Gascony and the southern part of Aquitaine under English control. Bordeaux became the capital and the English territory was known then as Guyenne. The region contained about 200 castles or fortresses.

25. Large armies in ancient and medieval times simply could not live off the land and used plundering to obtain food and supplies, especially in enemy territory. The leadership always needed to provide some type of logistical support.

26. There is some controversy regarding the nationality of the builders of this castle, known as Quat'Sos. Supposedly, the French began the work in the thirteenth century and the English completed it under Henry III. Located on a rocky outcrop overlooking the Garonne, it is square and originally had four towers, three of which remain today.

27. Froissart, *Chronicles*, p. 87.

28. At the same time, Hurepel worked on the fortifications of Boulogne. The château at Calais was incorporated into a new citadel in 1564.

29. The double moat may not have existed until sometime after the siege since there is no clear evidence of its existence on contemporary drawings.

30. These bastides may have been somewhat like those the English built in Aquitaine. Those built in south-west France were usually rectangular in plan and had either earthen walls with palisades or stone walls often with towers, and a moat. Like the French bastides they were to encourage settlement and provide a source of militia to hold the area. The English built over 300 of these in the south-west.

31. King Jean intercepted the Black Prince at Poitiers, blocking his route to the fortified port of Bordeaux. The Duke of Lancaster, who was leading another chevauchée from Brittany into Normandy, failed to link up with the Black Prince. Lancaster attacked the castle of Romorantin. His archers cleared the battlements while others 'swam over the ditch, and began to undermine the walls . . . [while] those within flung down upon them large stones and pots of hot lime'. The day-long attack ended in a retreat. Lancaster brought up cannons that somehow shot Greek Fire into the lower bailey of the castle setting a large thatch covered tower on fire, which forced the defenders to surrender (Froissart, *Chronicles*, p. 212). Next, he proceeded westward to burn the suburbs of Tours.

32. In 1349, Philippe negotiated with Rome for ownership of the territory of Dauphiné thus enlarging France and putting its borders on the Alps. His eldest son took the title of Dauphin. From then on, the crown princes of France were given the title of Dauphin. Similarly, the successors of the Kings of England have held the title of Prince of Wales.

33. Apparently Edward's ambition was to be crowned at Reims where French kings were traditionally anointed since he claimed the kingship of France.

34. The Lantern Tower became a prison in the sixteenth century.
35. This tower was badly damaged when it served as a gunpowder store in 1652.
36. As a result of the battle, Charles V of France was forced to accept the son of John of Montfort as Duke of Normandy.
37. In 1369 and after the 1375 raid, there were two more major outbreaks of the Black Death.

Chapter 3

1. The English had given up on the old feudal methods and improved taxing methods to finance the war.
2. Coucy included the largest donjon in Europe, 35m (114.8ft) wide and 55m (180.4ft) tall. It was built in the 1220s by Enguerrand III, Lord of Coucy.
3. The monastery town of St. Denis, now a suburb of Paris, was just a few kilometres from the centre of Paris. Sumption in *The Hundred Years War* (p. 15) refers to it as small, although its population may have been about 10,000 when the war began and less than half that when it ended. Some sources estimate Paris with over 200,000 when the war began and under 150,000 when it ended. France's population was about 15 million or more when the war began and was down to 14 million when it ended, but England's population of about 2.5 million rose to over 3 million. These figures are from B. Trianis, *Rost naseleniia v Europe* (1941) quoted on Wikipedia. The heaviest losses came from disease.
4. Known as the Great Tower, it was demolished in 1653.
5. In Gallic times, Bourges, known as Avaricum, was heavily defended. Caesar took it and sacked in in 52 BC after a long siege and refortified it.
6. According to Monstrelet, Henry V had to suppress an attempted coup in which some nobles tried to replace him with a relative of Richard II while he was at Southampton.
7. The Burgundians had already successfully used bombards, especially a huge one that could fire a shaped stone up to 1,000m (1,019 yds), at the sieges of Dun-le-Rois and Bourges.
8. There is no agreement regarding the length of the walls and some historians apparently do not include the walls around the harbour. Burne puts it at about 3.2km (2 miles) and Sumption at about 4km (2.5 miles) but the scale on his drawing puts it just over 2km (1.24 miles), including the harbour. According to an article in *Journées archéologiques de Haute-Normandie 2012*, archaeological work shows variations in the stonework, which indicates that the walls were built at different times. The town walls existing in 1415 dated from 1361.
9. Michael Jones, author of *24 Hours at Agincourt*, claims that the normal garrison of thirty-five men-at-arms and fifteen crossbowmen was reinforced by thirty soldiers brought by Raoul de Gaucourt.
10. According to Monstrelet, the English dug three mines.
11. According to some sources, Henry had twelve great bombards, but Sumption points out that even if he had that many, he had no way of bringing them to the siege and had to use his smaller cannons.
12. There is no agreement on the number of French troops and estimates of English troops range from 6,000 to 9,000.
13. Engennes, who took part in the battle of Agincourt, is only mentioned in Monstrelet's account and in nineteenth-century works. According to Monstrelet, he was at the siege

of Cherbourg in 1418; he was bribed by the French, and later beheaded by the Henry V. Monstrelet also claims that the siege of Cherbourg lasted six months rather than ten weeks (see Thomas Johnes, *The Chronicles of Enguerran de Monstrelet*, pp. 370 and 399). According to Wiley and Waugh, authors of in *The Reign of Henry the Fifth*, the story of Engennes was made up by the French to put the English in a bad light (p.110).

14. Few sources agree on the subject of the population of Caen. Monstrelet gives the high figure for civilians and soldiers while scholars today estimate there were only a few hundred soldiers. Monstrelet may have included militia. The city of Rouen only reached 40,000 by 1500, so a number closer to 8,000 for Caen is more realistic.

15. Most of the account that follows, which has several variants, comes from Abbot la Rue and is found in Pierre Carel's *Histoire de la ville de Caen* . . . (pp. 120–8) who points out that gaps in the Abbot's account were filled in by Léon Puiseux (see *Siège et prise* . . ., published 1848).

16. *The First English Life of King Henry the Fifth*, p. 89. The accuracy of this 1513 manuscript is often disputed, but it offers more detail than some other sources.

17. Livius is the name given to the anonymous author of *The First English Life of King Henry the Fifth*.

18. Charles V took the castle of Saint-Sauveur after a long siege that began in 1375. The northern curtain was rebuilt afterward. Its polygonal enceinte on high ground, which included a large square keep in the south-east corner, a round tower on the south-west corner, and an entrance in between consisted of a châtelet with two towers. The châtelet opened into the lower courtyard, which had a châtelet entrance in its south-west corner.

19. According to Livius, the castle had sixteen towers, double walls, and deep and wide ditches (p. 109). In the seventeenth century, Vauban ordered its demolition. Wiley and Waugh, who provide the only description in modern times, mention only the keep and four towers (p. 110).

20. Unfortunately, Wiley and Waugh are not clear on whether the shelters were within reach of the walls or if the metal claws were launched with catapults with ropes attached so they could be dragged back (p. 110).

21. In 1417, due to the civil war in France, Henry V had tried to forge an alliance with the Burgundians, but Jean the Fearless had lost interest in the negotiations.

22. It is not known how much the fifteenth-century châtelet actually resembled the illustration by Viollet-le-Duc. It was demolished in 1650.

23. One of eleven castles built by Philippe Augustus in Normandy, Bouvreuil was completed in 1210. Only the Tower of Joan of Arc (where she was imprisoned) remains since the castle was used as a quarry for other structures at the end of the sixteenth century.

24. Monstrelet gives a figure of 4,000 in addition to 15,000 militiamen (p. 307). Other sources cite about 20,000, including militia.

25. In *From Crecy to Assaye*, Clinton claims that the siege lasted seven months and ended on 5 June when the hated French commander was hanged (pp. 147–8).

26. According to Charles Oman, the Duke of Bedford was as skilled a soldier and administrator as Henry V.

27. East of Angers, on 22 March 1421, a Franco-Scottish army defeated the Duke of Clarence at the battle of Baugé. Only a third of his force of 4,000, which had been on a chevauchée, was deployed against 5,000. The French victory encouraged the

Dauphin to start a campaign to clear Normandy, but it ended years later with the defeat at Verneuil. Étienne de Vignoles 'La Hire' ('Wrath of God') and Count Dunois took part in this battle and several others that followed including the siege of Orléans.

28. Jean V, Duke of Brittany, entered an alliance with the Dauphin at Saumur in 1426 and then took and massacred the English garrison of Pontorson. In September 1427, he changed sides and accepted the Treaty of Troyes.

29. Although not a nobleman, La Hire was a Gascon mercenary who was one of France's most capable leaders. After 1419, he made a name for himself by taking the walled town of Crépy-en-Laonnais, located north-west of Laon, in a night escalade and advancing beyond Reims. In 1420, Philippe of Burgundy and the Earl of Warwick besieged him at Crépy where he surrendered after mines brought down a large section of the wall. He took part in the battle of Baugé in 1421 and led the vanguard in the victory at Patay in 1429. He took Château Gaillard by a direct assault from the English in 1430 (Sumption, *The Hundred Years War IV*, pp. 672–3, 722; DeVires, *Joan of Arc*, p. 188).

30. Le Mans had a 1.3km (0.8-mile) Roman wall with from a dozen to two-dozen towers that the populace maintained through the Middle Ages.

31. Earlier in March, Talbot had also driven the French from Laval, a town where the English had always failed to overcome French resistance before.

32. Boulevards were a form of advanced work of earth, timber, and stone that provided protection against cannon.

33. Meung, Beaugency and Châteauneuf, like Orleans, were all walled towns with castles on the right bank of the Loire.

34. The town, named for the Roman castrum, had Gallo-Roman walls. Improvements were made and the twelfth-century keep is 42m (138ft) high and 17m (56ft) in diameter.

35. See Vallet de Viriville (ed). *Chronique de la pucelle ou Chronique de Cousinot suivie de la Chronicque normande de P. Cochon*. Paris: Adolphe Delahays, 1864, pp. 260–2.

36. Contemporary sources, both French and English, do not agree on dates or details. Modern historians draw their own conclusions.

37. Killing prisoners was not unusual, especially if they were not nobility or had no value for ransom. Some historians also claim that wounded soldiers without status and lacking their own physician were often killed whether friend or foe.

38. Johnes (trans.), *The Chronicles of Enguerrand de Monstrelet*, p. 563.

39. According to Kelly Devries, author of *Joan of Arc: A Military Leader*, there were at least forty-four towers along the Oise side of the city. This number seems exaggerated because there would have been a tower every 20m (66ft), more towers than the enceinte of Paris and more closely spaced. Plans from the early seventeenth and eighteenth century indicate the entire enceinte may have had about forty towers. His other details appear to be correct in regards to heavily fortified gates on south side of the 140m (450ft) bridge and the length of the walls being 2.6km (1.6 miles). Devries also notes that within the walls there was a Louvre-like château palace on the south side (pp. 170–1).

40. This work included its own barbican, additions that were made in the next century, and an advanced position and modifications to the town walls. Emplacements for cannons were built on the walls.

41. The two bombards, known as michelettes, that were captured are on display by the main gate.

42. Formigny outwardly does not appear to be a massive battle, with about 5,500 English troops facing a similar number of French, but the English army in other major battles in France in that century were usually similar in size while at the great battles of Crécy, Poitiers, and Agincourt, the French far outnumbered them. French artillery wreaked havoc among the English archers just as it did against fortifications.

43. At Castillon the English army was again from 5,000 to 6,000 men while the French had an only slightly larger one, but with cannon.

44. The Combat of Thirty (1351) may be considered an engagement although it only involved thirty French and thirty English knights and squires in a challenge that took placed between the castles of Josselin and Ploërmel in Brittany.

Chapter 4

1. This is the present Dutch province of Gelderland (or Guelders) which was once a duchy that included some German territory.

2. When Louis the Pious died, the Carolingian Empire was divided among his three sons by the Treaty of Verdun in 843, ending a civil war between them. Lothair received the middle section of the empire, Middle Francia, which stretched from the North Sea to central Italy. When he died in 855, it was divided among his sons. One received Italy (northern Italy), another Provence, and Lothair II took Lotharingia and Suebia.

3. The Latin term Lotharingia was the name for Lothair's kingdom and did not refer to a single ethnic group. Since the division of that region into the Low Countries and French Lorraine, the French refer to their part as Lorraine, which is called Lothringen in German.

4. He took Jerusalem from the Muslims in a bloody victory resulting in the slaughter of many innocents and became ruler of the new Christian kingdom, but refused to use the title of king.

5. John became John III, Duke of Bavaria and Count of Holland and Zeeland, in 1417 and the following year Duke of Luxemburg. He was never ordained as a priest.

6. He died in 1191 in the Holy Land in an epidemic.

7. Van Artevelde, who became wealthy from the weaving industry and wanted to maintain neutrality for the sake of Ghent's economy, allied himself with Edward III. After driving out Louis, he became Captain-General of Ghent.

8. Floris' father was the Holy Roman Emperor who was killed fighting the West Frisians when Floris was two years old. When Floris came of age, he avenged his father, conquered much of Friesland, and built several forts to control the area.

9. Doornenburg Castle is not far from the later nineteenth-century Rhine fort of Pannerden.

10. The Brabant, a duchy created after the collapse of the Frankish Carolingian Empire, became part of the Holy Roman Empire. In the twelfth century, it included Brussels, Louvain, and Antwerp and its economy was based on the textile industry. Its southern section had a Walloon population while the region around Brussels and Antwerp was mostly Flemish. Today, Flemish Brabant only refers to the central region around Brussels while North Brabant is Dutch.

11. In 1309, the Crusade of the Poor assembled in the lands of Jan and prepared to march to Avignon to join a crusade planned by the Hospitallers. To raise money, they terrorized the region by looting and killing Jews, many of whom took refuge in

the twelfth-century castle (restored in 1850) at Genappe (in the Walloon Brabant). Jan came to their rescue and scattered the remnants of this would-be crusader group.

12. The son of Mary and Maximillian was Philip the Handsome who was married off to Joanna la Loca of Castile and their child Charles (Charles I of Spain who later became Charles V of the Holy Roman Empire) formed the Spanish branch of the Hapsburg family.

13. There are no battlements, only a wall walk, on the curtains on the east side that connect the gate tower with the southern tower.

14. The Eppstein family included four archbishops and electors of Mainz and one with the same position in Trier.

15. Maus (Mouse) Castle was located a short distance from Katz (Cats) Castle creating a 'cat and mouse' situation. The latter was owned by the Katzenlnbogens, the enemy of Trier.

16. The number of troops, and smaller proportion of cavalry, shows this was not a typical medieval battle, but belongs to the new era of the Renaissance.

17. In the 1470s, Charles the Bold of Burgundy also moved against Lorraine whose duke turned against him and regained the city of Nancy late in 1476. Charles' siege of Nancy was lifted when the Duke of Lorraine came to the rescue with Swiss mercenaries. Charles' army was defeated and he died in the battle. France took over most of Burgundy and its north-eastern parts went to the Hapsburgs of the Holy Roman Empire.

18. Landgrave was a title in the Holy Roman Empire that was the equivalent of a count.

19. Transalpine Gaul was modern southern France. Gaul included five parts in Roman times including Cisalpine Gaul in Northern Italy, the remainder of France and Aquitania, and Belgium and Flanders.

20. The Grimaldi family left Genoa during the political problems between the Guelph and Ghibelline factions and took over Monaco in 1297 expanding their control by acquiring Menton in 1346 followed by Roquebrune.

21. The southern part of the guardroom became a prison in the seventeenth century.

22. It seems there is little agreement for the dates of the construction for these two towers.

23. Some sources claim it was built in 1250 and others the 1270s.

24. The Renaissance began at different times across Europe and overlapped with the Middle Ages with no convenient time markers, although not accurate, such as those used to begin and end the Middle Ages.

25. The numbers vary widely from source to source. These seem to be the most reasonable as do others in this section.

26. Henry VI died about a week later, still a prisoner in the Tower.

27. Gillingham, *Wars of the Roses*, pp. 113, 152–5, 159–61, 171, 225–8.

28. Earlier, Francis I had detached a force of about 15,000 men and sent it towards Naples.

Chapter 5

1. Oillet slits made prior to the advent of firearms are straight vertical slits or in the form of a cross and have one or more round openings that may either have been decorative or improved the field of vision. The vertical slit with a small horizontal vision slit and round opening at the bottom is called a cross-and-orb slit. Most arrow

loops are vertical and thin and sometimes splayed at the bottom or have a cross slit. Slits for gunpowder weapons are called keyhole if they are round at the bottom, but there are also some shaped like a dumbbell, which are round at the bottom and have a smaller round hole at the top.

2. Some historians trace some of the new designs to the Islamic world.
3. Procter, *History of Italy*, p. 93.
4. Ibid., p. 97 and Manning, *Story of Italy*, pp. 115–19. This siege was recorded by the medieval chroniclers Matteo Villani and Leonardo Bruni whose descriptions disagree except for the outcome.
5. San Vincenzo (St. Vincent's) Tower was on an isle near Castel Nuovo.
6. The nature of the addition is still a matter of speculation. It may not have been a fausse-braye and some military historians tend to avoid using the term fausse-braye altogether and use the term boulevard.
7. According to F.L. Taylor, in addition to this achievement, the French supported Florentine troops against Pisa with twenty-two heavy guns and brought down 37m (121ft) of the city wall in a single day in 1500 (*Art of War in Italy*, p. 95).
8. Not to be confused with the Sant Elmo on Malta. The name of the castle in Naples appears to be a corruption of the name the church of Sant'Erasmo, which was on the same hilltop before the castle.
9. Lighting struck the powder magazine in 1587, causing considerable damage.
10. Frederick Taylor makes no mention of the outer ring, only the two moats. In addition, to de Hollanda's drawing, a 1566 illustration by Étienne Dupérac and Antonio Lafreri shows an outer wall. However, the bastions on the sea side are different from Hollanda's engraving. The outer walls were removed in the nineteenth century.
11. King Charles I (reigned 1516–98) was the first Hapsburg king of Spain (although some consider his father the first), son of Juana of Castile and the Austrian Philip of Hapsburg. He won the election for Holy Roman Emperor in 1519, defeating both Francis I of France and Henry VIII of England, and became Charles V of the Empire. Thus, he ruled both the kingdom of Spain with its wealth from the New World and the Holy Roman Empire. He was caught in the middle of Martin Luther's Protestant Reformation while he had to protect his empire and Italy from the Turks (who laid siege to Vienna in 1529).
12. The Italian trace is also referred to as 'bastion front', 'bastion fort' and 'star fort.' The last term refers to the star shape that ensues from the use of angled bastions consisting of two faces.
13. Alberti, *The Architecture* Book IV, pp. 239–44. He also mentions that the corniches (probably cordon or other mouldings) of the towers and walls, besides adding to their beauty, hinder the use of scaling ladders by projecting over the walls. He may also have believed that false machicoulis helped prevent escalade.
14. According to the Bachrachs, Alberti may have been inspired by Vitruvius, a first-century BC Roman engineer, who wrote *De architectura* (*Warfare in Medieval Europe*, p. 58). See Appendix II.
15. Lamarque and Nicolas, *Le Spectateur militaire*, pp. 131–2.
16. Alberti, *The Architecture* Book IV, p. 242.
17. Lamarque and Nicolas, *Le Spectateur militaire*, p. 122.
18. Tylden, 'Notice of the Military Portion of the Works of Francesco di Giorgio Martini', pp. 174–5.

19. Quentin Hughes, *Military Architecture*, pp. 70–1.

20. Pepper and Adams, *Firearms & Fortifications*, pp. 17–19.

21. Like Sarzanello, Caerlaverock Castle on the north edge of Solway Firth in Scotland was also built in the 1300s as a triangular castle. Its shape was determined by the high ground on which it was built. The original work at Saranza may not have been triangular since when it was rebuilt in the 1400s there was enough space to add a large ravelin.

22. Pope Clement VII formed an alliance to challenge Emperor Charles V for control of the Italian Peninsula after he defeated the French at Pavia in 1525. However, the Emperor did not attack Rome, but his large army mutinied and marched on Rome in May 1527 when he failed to pay its wages. Rome's garrison, which consisted of 3,000 largely untrained men (some claim 8,000) armed with gunpowder weapons, could not beat off the assault. The Spanish and German troops scaled the walls under cover of thick smoke from the guns of Castel Sant'Angelo. The unpaid troops pillaged the city. Although St. Peter's fell, Pope Clement VII fled to Castel Sant'Angelo using its now famous escape route, an elevated passage running about 800m (872 yds) created by Pope Nicholas III in 1277 that had been used by Pope Alexander VI in 1494 when King Charles VIII of France took the city. Pope Clement surrendered in June.

23. Pope Julius II commissioned the work while he was a cardinal in 1483. He became pope in 1503.

24. It is said that Leonardo da Vinci worked on Milan's castle in 1504 and 1506, but apparently his main contribution there was the art rather than the fortifications.

25. Roger Vella Bonavita. 'The career of Capitano Francesco Laparelli da Cortona', lecture.

26. Quentin Hughes in *Military Architecture* mentions that they plagiarized each other's drawings.

27. His book is a Socratic dialogue between Fabrizio Colonna and several Florentine nobles.

28. Although Italian, he served as a military engineer in the French army.

29. Hale, *Renaissance War Studies*, p. 24.

30. In *Siege Warfare*, Christopher Duffy refers to this as 'rampiring'. In some cases, to avoid the excessive pressure on the curtain wall, this earth bank was set slightly back from the wall (p. 2).

31. For many years, heavy artillery was synonymous with siege artillery. Early cannons had no wheels, and even when they did, they were heavy and difficult to move. They were mainly used against fortifications since it took too long to manoeuvre them onto a battlefield. Thus, they were designed specifically for use against fortifications during sieges.

32. Benedetto and Gabriel Tadini worked the defences of Rhodes in 1522 before they returned home. Tadini prepared plans for the defences of Perpignan in the mid-1520s and Benedetto made changes in 1530. Benedetto and Tadini mostly inspected and designed Spanish and Portuguese fortifications and took part in several campaigns.

33. López took part in several sieges including those of Ronda and Granada in 1492. He was an artillery specialist, but between 1497 and 1504, he rebuilt Salses into a transitional fort. Scrivá is considered 'Italianized' although his work was mainly for Spain.

34. Lorenzo the Magnificent employed Di Giovanni to design a new fortress at Volterra (1472–4) after he took the city. The Volterra fortress was built on a square plan with four circular corner bastions and a circular keep in the middle.

35. Piero was a weak ruler and when Charles VIII of France arrived, most of the populace of Florence was under the influenced of the fanatical Dominican Girolamo Savonarola, whom Pope Alexander VI did away with in 1498. The Medicis did not return to power until 1512.

36. Neri, 'Il Forte di Sarzanello', pp. 352–3.

37. The French also destroyed a nearby eleventh-century castle on a rocky outcrop.

38. Little is known about Ramiro López' life beyond the fact that he lived in the last half of the fifteenth century and early sixteenth century and took part in the Reconquista. Until recently, credit was given to Francesco Ramiro who died in 1501. However, it is now known that it was López who did the work at Salses.

39. The fort also had 224 spingardes, but it is not clear whether these cannon-like weapons fired arrows or small stone balls. Bayrou, *La forteresse de Salses*, pp. 23–4.

40. Schomberg was a German born in Heidelberg who successively served the Prince of Orange, the King of Sweden, Louis XIII of France (in 1635), the Portuguese king, Charles II of England, and next Louis XIV. He finally served the Elector of Brandenburg who allowed him to serve William of Orange in the invasion of England in 1688 during the Glorious Revolution.

41. Lamarque and Nicolas, *Le Spectateur militaire*, pp. 123–4.

42. The windows in the keep were added in the nineteenth century.

43. Beach erosion destroyed much of Sandown, while Walmer was modernized in the eighteenth century to serve as the residence of the Lord Warden of the Cinque Ports, later to include the Duke of Wellington. Deal was left largely without modifications to its defences.

Chapter 6

1. F.L. Taylor, *The Art of War in Italy*, p. 10.

2. The strategy used by the Roman dictator Fabius Maximus against the Carthaginian general Hannibal. He avoided major battles and held on to fortified sites that Hannibal was not equipped to besiege or assault. For Ferdinand, the problem was that Charles VIII had cannon that were highly effective against medieval fortifications.

3. According to David Nicolle in *Fornovo 1495*, one of those diseases was syphilis, which was brought by the Spanish from the Americas. It spread quickly to civilians and soldiers in Naples (p. 11). The disease would have spread with remarkable speed since Columbus only reached the New World in October 1492 and only over half of the eighty-eight sailors returned to Spain from that trip. His second voyage began late in 1493, and it was not until 1494 that some of his crew returned to Spain from that journey, while many remained in the New World. It is possible this epidemic was caused by an older European strain of the virus, but the American strain proved more devastating to Europeans.

4. The condottiere Prospero Colonna commanded the combined Imperial, Spanish and Papal army facing the French and Venetian forces in Northern Italy. On 23 November 1521, his troops took the city by storming a section of the walls held by the Venetian troops. After Colonna was drawn out of the city to engage the French, he defeated them at the battle of Bicocca in April 1522 in one of the first battles where firearms decisively in cut down charging French cavalry and Swiss pikemen.

5. The city of Florence in 1527 only had sixty arquebuses for its defence. Taylor, *Art of War in Italy*, Kindle e-book location 491.
6. Taylor, *The Art of War in Italy*, pp. 95–6.
7. The army included a number of Spanish troops since Charles V was also King of Spain.
8. No agreement exists on the numbers of defenders except most agree there was a Papal Swiss Guard of almost 200 men. The rest were militia, but the city defences had artillery while the attackers did not.
9. Pope Nicolas III had this passage created in 1277 and Pope Alexander VI used it in 1494 when Charles VIII took the city.
10. Guicciardini, *The Sack of Rome*, Kindle e-book location 1291 to 1451.
11. Taylor, *The Art of War in Italy*, Kindle e-book location 1366.
12. Ibid.
13. The name of this bastion was actually Codalunga, but the name of Gatta (cat) comes from a Venetian flag raised above it in which the lion was so poorly drawn it looked like a cat. A Spanish soldier was rewarded for capturing the flag, but the Imperial troops failed to take the bastion.
14. Details of the defence and siege of Padua come from Taylor's *Art of War in Italy* and extracts from Angiolo Lenci's *Il leone, l'aquila, e la gatta* that appear on the internet site 'Comitato Mura Di Padova' at http://www.muradipadova.it/lic/home.html.
15. Taylor, *Art of War in Italy*, Kindle e-book location 1385.
16. Ibid., Kindle e-book location 1421.
17. Pepper and Adams, *Firearms & Fortifications* p. 21
18. S. Croce, the last bastion to be built, was 88m (228.6ft) long with sides of about 49m (161ft) and 40m (131ft) and had gun positions in each flank. Pontecorvo, one of the first bastions built, was round and about 40m (131ft) long with connecting walls and a diameter of 43m (141ft). It included interior casemates for flanking fires with walls over 6m (19.7ft) thick.
19. Hale, *Renaissance War Studies*, p. 24.

Appendix 1
1. Spanish and English yew was preferred, but other woods could be used
2. Crossbows fire short arrows, more like darts, that are referred to as bolts or quarrels.

Glossary

Albarrana tower (from Arabic word barrani for exterior) – defensive tower attached to the curtain wall by a bridge or arcade called a coracha; a feature unique to Iberia.

Alcazaba – Moorish castle or citadel.

Alcázar – fortified Moorish palace.

Allure (chemin de ronde in French and camino de ronda or adarve [from Arabic] in Spanish) – wall walk behind the parapet of a wall.

Arrow loop (archère in French, saetera in Spanish) – Openings in walls or merlons for archers, see Loophole.

Ashlar – squared block of cut and shaped stone or freestone.

Atalaya (Sp.) – watchtower.

Bailey – enclosed courtyard or ward.

Bank – large mound behind the ditch of an Iron Age hilltop fort; palisades were often added to the inner bank.

Barbican (barbacane in French, barbacana in Spanish) – fortified outer gateway.

Barrel Vault – ceiling or roof consisting of cylindrical arches.

Bartizan – overhanging tower supported by corbelling or a buttress on a wall.

Bastide – (1) temporary fortification to support a larger complex; (2) thirteenth and fourteenth century fortified village and town in southern France. Also, called Villeneuve (new town) instead in northern France.

Bastille – isolated fort with tower placed in front of an entrance to an enceinte, not a barbican; generally, a temporary fort built by the besieger.

Bastion – tower like structure with thick walls to resist artillery and serve to provide flanking fire along the walls and as artillery platforms; usually not much higher than the walls; also any nondescript strongpoint of any type.

Batter – see Talus.

Battlement (almena in Spanish) – crenelated parapet at the top of a city or castle wall.

Beak or prow – angled projection forming a sharp sloping corner angle. Also, see plinth and talus.

Belfry – tall, mobile tower used in sieges.

Bergfried – freestanding fighting tower, usually associated with German fortifications.

Berm – (1) narrow path or flat area between a rampart and ditch; (2) raised bank of a canal or river.

Boulevard – the German origin of the word comes from bolwerk meaning a 'work of logs'. The French term is boulevard, balvardo in Italian, bolvarte in Spanish, boulevart in German,and bulwark in English. It is usually a low earthen rampart that may be covered by stone, and either placed in front of entrances or old walls and designed for use by artillery and intended to defend against enemy artillery.

Bretèche, also brattice in English – machicolation covering only a door or window.

Bulwark – an early English term for a bastion which is a forward defensive position, but also referred to a boulevard (see 'Boulevard').

Calahorra – the origin of the term is disputed. According to some interpretations, it originally referred to a castle on high ground, a red castle, and a public distribution place. The term is often used for keeps or 'homage towers' in Spain. One post-medieval castle near Granada is called La Calahorra.

Caponier – (caponnière in French and caponiera in Italian). It is a structure that protects the ditch of a fortification by extending into it or even across it.

Castellum – diminutive form of the Latin castrum, replaced the original word in Medieval Latin, and gave rise to the terms castello (It.), castillo (Sp.), castle (Eng.), and château (Fr.).

Castrum (pl. Castra) – Latin term for temporary and permanent fortified legion camps, or forts.

Catapult – a generic term for stone-throwing siege engines. It is mostly commonly associated with the Roman onager.

Cavalier – a work on a bastion or curtain that projects above the fortification. Also known as a raised battery position.

Châtelet (gatehouse in English) – French term for small castle; usually gateways consisting of two connected towers with a drawbridge and portcullis, became a prominent feature during the Hundred Years War and often took over the functions of the keep.

Chemise – from the French 'shirt', a wall surrounding a keep to protect its base; can be a shell keep surrounding a keep on a motte.

Cheval-de-frise (pl. Chevaux-de-frise) – originally, a tree trunk with projecting sharpened stakes. Later, wood and metal portable obstacles for blocking paths or confined areas; in modern times, wire replaced the sharpened stakes; also known as Frisian Horse and Spanish Rider.

Chevauchée (O.F.) – raid during which plundering and pillaging are employed to weaken the enemy.

Circumvallation – fortified line built around a fortification under siege and facing that position to keep the defenders from breaking out; see contravallation.

Cistern – water reservoir to collect rainwater.

Citadel – strongpoint that may be considered a small fortress within a fortified place; usually within city walls or part of the walls.

Civitas (pl. civitates, L) – township.

Contravallation – fortified line built around a line of circumvallation facing outward to prevent an enemy force from breaking through siege lines to rescue the defenders of a fortification.

Contrefort (Fr.) – buttress.

Coracha (Sp.) – wall extending from a fortified enclosure to protect access to a nearby point, such as a well.

Counterscarp (contrescarpe in Fr.) – outer side of a moat or defensive ditch.

Crenel – opening in a wall of a building or a rampart, often found between merlons on ramparts.

Crenellations – battlements of a castle, fort, or building consisting of alternating gaps (crenels) and merlons (see definition).

Curtain or curtain wall – usually referred to the wall surrounding a bailey, but later it referred to the wall connecting towers.

Demi-lune – an outwork similar in shape to a bastion, but with a crescent-shaped gorge (gorge is the rear face of a work).

Donjon (Fr.) – a keep, may derive from a Celtic term meaning 'lord's tower'.

Drawbridge, pont-levis (Fr.), puente (Sp.) – wood platform serving as a bridge and barrier.

Drum tower – circular tower.

Échauguette – enclosed sentry box usually placed at the corner of a wall.

Embrasure – opening in a wall, generally for weapons.

Enceinte – enclosing wall of a fortified site.

Escalade – scaling a cliff or a wall with ladders.

Fascine – bundle of brush and sticks used to fill ditches in preparation of crossing during an assault.

Faubourg – suburb.

Fausse-braye (Fr.), falsa braga (Sp.) – low wall in front of the main wall serving as protection against artillery fire by covering the lower part of the main wall. A ditch is found in front of the fausse-braye.

Forebuilding – extension or projection of a keep protecting the entrance, a stairway, and entrance.

Fossa (Latin) – defensive ditch.

Freestone – fine-grained stone that can be easily cut or shaped in any direction such as some types of limestone and sandstone; known as ashlar when cut.

Gabion – wicker basket filled with earth and/or stone to form a rampart to protect troops digging trenches.

Glacis – natural or artificial slope cleared of vegetation to allow clear fields of fire surrounding a fort or castle.

Gothic style – style that appeared in the mid-twelfth century and characterized by pointed arches, tall spires, and flying buttresses on buildings like cathedrals. The windows were larger than Romanesque and the style was elongated. This style dominated during the classical age of castles.

Groin vault – vault formed at the point where two barrel vaults intersect.

Hoardings, hourds (Fr.) – wooden projections with openings for dropping objects on the enemy below added to the battlements.

Kasbah or qasbah (Ar.) – fortress; also, oldest part of a city.

Keep, donjon (Fr.), torre de homenaje or calahorra (Sp.), Bergfried (Ger.), maschio or mastio (It.) – main tower found in most early castles, could be the entire fortified position in some cases; usually served as a residence for a nobleman.

Loophole, meurtrière (French) – firing position in a wall for archers, a round opening was added or widened later to accommodate guns (see oillet); called canonnière (Fr.), tronera (Sp.) when meant for a cannon.

Machicolation – opening in a projecting stone battlement for dropping objects on attackers attempting to climb or destroy the walls.

Machicoulis (Fr.) – machicolations along a wall and/or tower, not to be confused with bretèche, a single machicolation covering a window or door.

Mangonel – a beam-type sling siege engine that throws stones.

Mantlet – see chemise.

Matacán (Sp.) – machicolation, bretèche, or machicoulis.

Mine – tunnel dug beneath the wall of a fortification used that ended in a chamber where a fire was lit to collapse the wall; this technique had been used since ancient times; later, explosives were employed.

Moat, fossé (Fr.), fosa (Sp.) – broad ditch surrounding a fortification, often incapable of holding water.

Mudéjar style – architectural style combining Islamic and Gothic styles in Iberia during the High and Late Middle Ages.

Murage – toll in towns under English control in the British Isles and English-occupied France for financing construction or repair of walls.

Mural tower – interval tower on a curtain wall.

Oilet or oillet – arrow loop with a circular sight hole at one end, mostly meant for artillery.

Oubliette (Fr.) – chamber at the bottom of a tower accessed through a trapdoor, may have given rise to a nineteenth-century myth that it as a prison; actually served as a storage area, a cesspool for the garderobes, some type of aeration system, or an ice house.

Palisade – wooden fence, often made with timbers pointed at the top.

Plinth – see talus.

Poliorcetics (A. Gr.) – art of siege warfare.

Portcullis, herse (Fr.), rastrillo (Sp.) – latticed grille of wood and/or metal lowered to close a gateway sometimes used in conjunction with doors and drawbridges.

Postern, poterne (Fr.) – small, often concealed doorway or gate; called sally port when large enough to allow troops through.

Praetorium (Lat.) – commanding officer's house in a Roman fort or fortress.

Principia (Lat.) – headquarters in a Roman fort or fortress.

Prow – see beak.

Putlog holes – Holes located in walls used to support scaffolding during construction, also used for the horizontal beams supporting hoardings, sometimes called sockets when meant for hoardings.

Quoin – corner or ashlar-lined corner.

Rábida or ribat – Moorish fortified monastery on the frontier or the coast.

Ravelin – (rivellino in Italian). A triangular outwork usually located in the ditch in front of curtain. It can be used to cover a gate or the curtain and can also be known as a demi-lune.

Revetment – masonry facing or a retaining wall supporting a rampart.

Rib vaulting – intersection of two to three barrel vaults creating a ribbed vault.

Romanesque style – dominated from the eleventh to mid-twelfth century, it used rounded forms, semicircular arches, thick walls and buttresses, and small windows. Referred to as Norman architecture in England.

Barbican at southern entrance to Caen.

Embrasures for gunpowder weapons: Bottom left: Angers – A. Part of the rampart widened for artillery. B. Towers lowered to height of curtain and cannon embrasures added. Lower right: Fougères - Cannon embrasures added to tower at more than one level. M = Machicoulis remained, G = Embrasures for bow or crossbow. Top and middle left: Mont-Saint-Michel – F= Outer walls added with cannon ports, C = Letterbox-type embrasures for gunpowder weapons. Top and middle right: La Mota – H = Fausse-braye, E = Barbican with keyhole-type embrasures for handguns or small cannon.

Murder Holes in Entrance

Walmer Castle

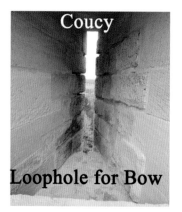

Coucy

Loophole for Bow

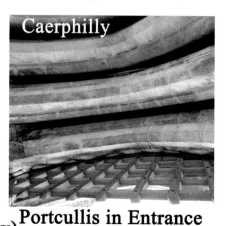

Caerphilly

Raglan Castle (below) Portcullis in Entrance

Exterior

Interior

Top: Murder holes. Middle left: Arrow loop. Middle right: Portcullis. Bottom: Interior and exterior view of unusual combination gun and arrow loops in lower level of the Great Tower of the fifteenth-century Raglan Castle. The walls were thick enough to resist artillery bombardment in the seventeenth-century Civil War. Photos by Rupert Harding.

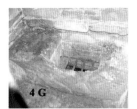

Bretèche and garderobe: Garderobes sometimes have a window slit for light and when they overhang a wall there are no windows or doors below them. With bretèche there will be a window or doorway below and a small bretèche may look like a garderobe except for that. 1 G – typical of many simple garderobes overhanging a wall. 2 G and 3 G - more stylish garderobes found at Castel del Monte where even the chamber is more spacious. 3 V - appears to be some form of vent since these garderobes appear to empty into some type of cess pool below (photos 2 and 3 by Gabriel Mundo). 4 G – simple garderobe in Ludlow castle (photo by Bernard Lowry). 5 G and 6 G – typical overhanging garderobes. 7 G – garderobe a Aigues Mortes. 1 B – bretèche at Aigues Mortes that looks like a garderobe, but it protects an entrance. 2 B and 3 B – examples of bretèche covering entrances. 8 G – 3 garderobes. 9 G – is a latrine block with several garderobes in one section of the wall for the garrison (9 D is where the effluent came out – if it did not drain away a peasant would shovel it out). 10 – drains for several garderobes concentrated on the same side of the keep of Orford (photos 9 and 1 by Bernard Lowry).

Top: Pyramidal spurs resulting from round towers built on square foundations. Center Right: Rib vaulting at Coucy (photos by Rupert Harding). Centre left: - remains of 'D' shaped barbican at Goodrich (photo by Gwyn Norrell). Bottom: Bastions at Ceuta (Spanish North Africa). The protected flanking cannon ports covered by the 'ear' or orillon can be seen in both photos.

Rubble – local stone of different sizes used in walls and various ways; the stones may be squared, laid out and held together with mortar or mixed haphazardly with cement or concrete to form the core of the wall.

Scarp, escarpe (Fr.), alambore (Sp.) – inside face of a moat or ditch.

Socket – in walls refers to a usually square hole for the insertion of beams or joists for floors or hoardings.

Solar – room above ground level, great chamber, or sitting room.

Spur – rectangular base forming a beak or plinth for a round tower; see beak and prow.

Tabby – see taipa.

Talus, batter, or plinth – outward slope that strengthens walls against siege machines; allows projectiles dropped from the top of the wall to roll towards the enemy.

Tapia (Sp.) – rammed earth or tabby; type of concrete commonly used for the walls of fortifications in Iberia and other regions; made of local raw materials such as earth, lime, chalk, gravel, clay, and/or bone.

Throat, gorge (Fr.) – rear of a fortification.

Torre vigía – see atalaya.

Tour (Fr.) – tower.

Tower of Homage (torre del homenaje) – term used for keep on the Iberian Peninsula.

Turf-and-Timber – fortification consisting of an earthen rampart and a timber palisade; the earthen rampart generally consisted of dirt and rock excavated from the surrounding ditch. Turf consists of sod or sections of soil with grass placed on the earthen ramparts to prevent erosion of the site; it was intended to last for an indefinite period.

Turret – small tower on a larger tower or on battlements.

Vallum (Lat.) – earthen rampart or stone wall in Roman fortifications; ditch behind Hadrian's Wall where it includes the mounds on either side of the ditch.

Voussoir – wedge shaped element used in building an arch or vault, each unit in an arch is a voussoir, the top one is the keystone.

Wall walk or rampart walk – walkway behind the battlements of a fort, fortress, or castle; also, called allure.

Yett (O. E. and Scottish) – gate of wrought iron bars forming a lattice; unlike the portcullis, it is hinged and opens like a door.

Bibliography

Académie Florimontane. *Montrottier Castle: History and Guide.* Annecy: Typo-Offset Gardet, 1987.

Alberti, Leon Battista. *The Architecture of Leon Batista Alberti in Ten Books* [English translation of *De re aedificatoriai* published in 1485]. London: Edward Owen, 1755.

Allmand, Christopher. *The Hundred Years War.* New York: Press Syndicate of Univ. of Cambridge, 1988.

Anderson, William. *Castles of Europe: From Charlemagne to the Renaissance.* London: Ferndale Editions, 1980.

Anonymous (often referred to as The Translator of Livius) and Charles L. Kingsford (trans.). *The First English Life of King Henry the Fifth.* Oxford: Clarendon Press, 1811 (written 1513).

Auvergne, Edmund B.d', *Famous Castles & Palaces of Italy, Illustrated in Colour from Paintings.* London: Warner Laurie, 1911.

Bachrach, Bernard S. and David S. *Warfare in Medieval Europe c 400 – c. 1453.* New York: Routledge, 2017.

Baudier, Joseph. *Le château de Joux.* Besançon: Les Éditions de l'Est, 1991.

Bayrou, Lucien, Nicolas Faucherre and René Quatrefages. *La forteresse de Salses.* Paris: Éditions du patrimoine, Centre des Monuments Nationaux, 2007.

Bernage, Georges. 'L'héroïque résistance des chevaliers du Mont', *Patrimoine Normand* No. 4, August–September 1995.

Bisson, Thomas N. 'Feudalism in Twelfth-Century Catalonia', *Publications de l'École Française de Rome*, Vol. 44, Number 1: 1980. pp. 173–92.

Black, Jeremy. *European Warfare, 1494-1660.* New York: Routledge, 2002.

Blay de Gaix, Gabriel-François de. *Histoire militaire de Bayonne.* Bayonne: Lamaignière, 1905.

Bonavita, Rober Vella. 'The Career of Capitano Francesco Laparelli da Cortona'. Synopsis of Lecture at Church of Santa Catherina d'Italia, Valletta (Malta), April 2017. https://www.um.edu.mt/newspoint/events/umevents/2017/04/thecareerofcapitanofrancescolaparellidacortonaintuscanyandthepapalstates

Borgominiero, Rutilio. *al segno di San Giorgio.* Getty Research Institute, Internet Archive.

Bottomley, Frank. *The Castle Explorer's Guide.* New York: Avenel Books, 1979.

Bradbury, Jim. *The Medieval Siege.* Woodbridge: Boydell Press, 1992.

_____. *The Routledge Companion to Medieval Warfare.* New York: Routledge, 2004.

Braun, Georg and Franz Hogenberg, Stephan Füssel (ed.). *Civitates Orbis Terraum: Cities of the World 1572-1617.* Berlin: Taschen, 2015 (reprint).

Brown, R. Allen. *Castles from the Air.* Cambridge: Univ. of Cambridge, 1989.

_____ et. al. *Castles: A History and Guide.* Poole: Blandford Press, 1980

Burne. Alfred H. *The Crécy War.* Novato (CA): Presidio Press, 1991 (reprint of 1955 ed.).

_____. *The Agincourt War.* Novato: Presidio Press, 1999 (reprint of 1955 ed.).

Burnod-Saudreau, V. *Dinan Castle Museum.* France: imprimerie régionale bannalec, 1985.

Bury, John Bagnell. *Cambridge Medieval History.* Vol. II. New York: Macmillan Co., 1913.

Bury, J.B. 'The early history of the explosive mine', *FORT 10*, Fortress Study Group, 1982. pp. 23–30.

_____. 'Early writings on fortifications and siegecraft: 1502-1554', *FORT 13*, Fortress Study Grop, 1985. pp. 4–48.

Cantor, Norman (ed.). *The Encyclopedia of the Middle Ages*. New York: Viking. 1999.

Carey, Brian. *Warfare in the Medieval World*. Barnsley: Pen & Sword, 2006.

Chadych, Danielle. *Paris: The Story of the Great City*. London: Andre Deutsch Ltd., 2014.

Chapman, Charles E. *A History of Spain founded on the Historia de España y de la civilización española of Rafael Altamira*. New York: Macmillan Company, 1918 (ebook reprint).

Charpentier, Bernard and Charles Cuissard. *Journal du Siège d'Orléans 1428-1429*. Orléans: H. Herluison Libraire-Éditeur, 1896.

Le château de Grandson Guide du Visiteur. Colmar: 1980.

Châtelain, André. *Châteaux forts images de pierre des guerres médiévales*. Paris: Rempart 1983.

_____. *Architecture militaire médiévale: principes élémentaires*. Paris, Rempart, 1970.

Clinton, Herbert R. *From Crécy to Assaye*. Great Britain; Warne, 1881.

Clissold, Stephen. *In Search of the Cid*. New York: Barnes & Noble, 1994.

Contamine, Philippe. *War in the Middle Ages*. New York: Basil Blackwell, 1984.

Cook, Theodore Andrea. *The Story of Rouen*. London: J.M. Dent & Co, 1899.

Corfis, Ivy and Michael Wolfe (eds). *The Medieval City under Siege*. Woodbridge: The Boydell Press, 1995.

Corroyer, Édouard. *Descriptive Guide of Mont-Saint-Michel*. Paris: General Library of Architecture and of Public Works, 1883.

Cortés, Javier. *Real Armería de Madrid*. Madrid: Editorial Patrimonio Nacional, 1963.

Cowper, Marcus and Chris McNab (ed.). *Encyclopedia of Warfare*. London: Amber Books, 2014.

Creveld, Martin van. *Technology and War*. New York: The Free Press, 1989.

Curry, Anne. *The Hundred Years War*. Houndmills (UK): Palgrave Macmillian 2003.

_____ and Michael Hughes (eds). *Arms, Armies and Fortifications in the Hundred Years War*. Woodridge (UK): Boydell Press, 1994.

Delbrück, Hans. *History of the Art of War: Medieval Warfare*. Lincoln (Neb.): Univ. of Nebraska Press, 1980.

Dept. of the Environment. *Scarborough Castle*. London: HMSO, 1960.

_____. *Tower of London*. London: HMSO, 1967.

_____. *Henry VIII and the Development of Coastal Defence*. London: HMSO, 1976.

DeVries, Kelly. *Joan of Arc: Military Leader*. Stroud (UK): Sutton Publishing, 1999.

_____. *Medieval Military Technology*. Toronto: Univ. of Toronto Press, 2010.

_____. et al. *Battles of the Medieval World. 1000-1500*. New York: Barnes & Noble, 2006.

Dienst Archeologie en Historische Monumenten van de Stad Gent. *Guide to The Castle of the Counts of Flanders: Ghent*. Gent: Snoeck-Ducaju, 1980.

Donnelly, J.A. 'A study of the coastal forts built by Henry VIII', *FORT 10*, Fortress Study Group, 1982, pp 104–26.

Donnelly, Mark P. and Daniel Diehl. *Siege: Castles at War*. Dallas: Taylor Publishing, 1998.

Dupuy, Colonel T.N. *The Evolution of Weapons and Warfare*. New York: Bobbs-Merrill Co., 1980.

Dupuy, T.N. and R.E. *Encyclopedia of Military History*. New York: Harper & Row, 1970.

Eggenberger, David. *Dictionary of Battles*. New York: Thomas Crowell, 1977.

Eltis, David. *The Military Revolution in Sixteenth Century Europe*. New York: Barnes & Noble, 1995.

Erlande-Brandenburg, Alain. *Cathedrals and Castles: Building in the Middle Ages*. New York: Harry N. Abrams Publishers, 1993.

Fa, Darren and Clive Finlayson. *The Fortifications of Gibraltar 1068-1956*. Oxford: Osprey, 2006.

Faucherre, Nicolas. *Places fortes: bastion du pouvoir*. Paris: Rempart, 1986.

Flenghi, Antonio. *San Leo Montefeltro of Old*. Bologna: La Fotocromo Emiliana, 1980.

Fletcher, Richard. *The Quest for El Cid*. New York: Oxford Univ. Press, 1989

Fortress of Gradara. Italy: Litografia Marchi, n.d.

France, Anatole and Winifred Stephens (trans). *The Life of Joan of Arc.* Project Gutenberg, 2006 (translation of 1909 text).

Frantzen-Heger, Gaby, et. al. *Château-Palais de Vianden.* Diekirch (Lux): Imprimerie du Nord, n.d.

Friar, Stephen, *The Sutton Companion to Castles.* Stroud (UK): Sutton, 2007.

Froidevaux, Yves-Marie and Marie-Geneviève. *Mont-Saint-Michel from the strand to the spire.* Paris: Le Temps Apprivoise, 1988.

Froissart, Jean, John Bourchier (trans.). *Froissart Chronicles.* London: Macmillan & Co., 1904.

_____, Geoffrey Brereton (trans.). *Froissart Chronicles.* New York: Penguin Books, 1979.

_____, Thomas Johnes (trans.) *The Chronicles of England, France and Spain: and the Adjoining Countries.* London: William Smith, 1844.

Garrard, William. *The arte of warre.* Ann Arbor (MI): Univ of Michigan, 2004 (copy or 1591 text).

Gaunt, Peter. *A Nation Under Siege: The Civil War in Wales 1642-48.* London: HMSO, 1991.

Gillingham, John. *The Wars of the Roses: Peace and Conflict in 15th Century England.* United Kingdom: Phoenix Press, 1981.

Godmond, Christopher. *The Campaign of 1346.* London: Edward Bull, 1836.

Goodall, John. *The English Castle 1066-1650.* New Haven: Yale Univ. Press. 2011.

Grabois, Aryeh. *The Illustrated Encyclopedia of Medieval Civilization.* New York: Octopus, 1980.

Gravett, Christopher. *Medieval Siege Warfare.* Oxford: Osprey, 1996.

Guadalupi, Gianni and Gabriele Reina. *Castles of the World.* New York: Metro Books, 2013.

Guicciardini, Luigi, James H. McGregor (trans. & ed.). *The Sack of Rome.* New York: Italica Press, 1993.

Harrington, Peter. *The Castles of Henry VIII.* Oxford: Osprey, 2007.

Ibn El-Athir, E. Fagnan (trans.). *Annales du Maghreb & de l'Espagne.* Algiers: Typographie Adolphe Jourdan, 1898 (translation of thirteenth-century edition).

Hale, J.R. *Renaissance Fortification: Art or Engineering?.* London: Thames & Hudson, 1977.

_____. *Renaissance War Studies.* London: Hambledon Press, 1983 (ebook).

Halle, Guy le. *Précis de la fortification.* Paris: PCV Éditions, 1983.

Haut-Koenigsbourg. Paris: Caisse National des Monuments Historiques, 1996.

Haute-Normandie archéologie. 'Les fortifications d'Harfleur (Seine-Maritime): diagnostic archéologique complémentaire'. *Journées archéologiques des Normandies 2012.* Universities of Rouen and Havre, 2013.

Hazard, Harry W. (ed.). *A History of the Crusades: The Fourteenth and Fifteenth Centuries (Vol III)* Madison (WI): Univ. of Wisconsin, 1975.

Hindley, Goefrey. *Medieval Sieges & Siegecraft.* New York: Skyhorse Publishing, 2009.

Hishop, Malcolm. *How to Read Castles.* London: Bloomsbury Publishing, 2013.

_____. *Castle Builders.* Barnsley (UK): Pen & Sword, 2016.

Hodgkin, Thomas. *Italy and Her Invaders: The imperial restoration, 535-553.* Oxford: Henry Frowde, 1895.

Hooper, Nicholas and Matthew Bennett. *Cambridge Illustrated Atlas: Warfare, The Middle Ages 768-1487.* New York: Cambridge Univ. Press, 1996.

Hughes, Quentin. *Military Architecture.* London: Hugh Evelyn, 1974.

Huijbrechts, Annick and Yvonne Molenaar. *Amsterdam Castle Muiderslot: Experience seven centuries of history.* Muiderslot: Stichting Rijksmuseum Muiderslot, 2013.

Jardillier, Armand. *Le château D'Harcourt.* Paris: Société Francaise d'Archéologie, 1984.

Johnes, Thomas (trans.). *The Chronicles of Enguerrand de Monstrelet.* Vol 1 & 2. London: William Smith, 1840.

Jones, Michael. *24 Hours at Agincourt.* London: Random House UK, 2015.

Jotischky, Andrew and Caroline Hull. *The Penguin Historical Atlas of the Medieval World*. London: Penguin Books, 2005.

Kantrowicz, Ernst. *Fredrick The Second 1194-1250*. New York: Ederick Ungar Publishing, 1957 (reprint of 1931 edition).

Kaufmann, J.E. and H.W. *The Medieval Fortress*. Mechanicsburg (PA): Combined Publishing, 2001.

Keen, Maurice (ed,). *Medieval Warfare: A History*. New York: Oxford Univ. Press, 1999.

Kemp, Anthony. *Castles in Color*. Arco Publishing Co., 1978.

Koch, Hannesjoachim Wilhelm. *Medieval Warfare*. London: Bison Books Ltd, 1982.

Lamarque, Jean Maximilen and François Nicolas. 'De l'ingénieur et de l'artilleur en Italie', *Le Spectateur militaire: Recueil de science, d'art et d'histoire militaires*. Paris: Bureau du Spectateur, Vol. XI, 1846, pp. 14–37.

Lamberini, Daniela. 'Practice and Theory in sixteenth century fortifications', *FORT 15*. Fortress Study Group, 1987, pp. 5–20.

LaMonte, John L. *The World of the Middle Ages: A Reorientation of Medieval History*. New York: Appleton-Century-Crofts, 1949.

Langins, Janis, *Conserving the Enlightenment*. Cambridge (MA): MIT Press, 2004.

Le Goff, Jacques and Julia Barrow (trans). *Medieval Civilization 400-1500*. New York: Basil Blackwell Ltd., 1988.

Lenci, Angilolo. *Il leone, l'aquila e la gatta: Venezia e la Lega di Cambrai. Guerra e fortificazioni dalla battaglia d'Agnadello all'assedio di Padova del 1509*. Padova: Il Poligrafo, 2002.

Lepage, Jean-Denis. *Castles and Fortified Cities of Medieval Europe*. Jefferson (NC): McFarland, 2002.

_____, *The Fortifications of Paris: An Illustrated History*. Jefferson (NC): McFarland, 2006.

Leroy, Marcel. *Bouillon et son château dans l'histoire*. Belgium: n.d.

Lewis, Archibald Ross. *The Development of Southern French and Catalan Society 718-1050*. Austin: University of Texas Press (The Library of Iberian Resources Online), 1965.

Libal, Dobroslav. *Castles of Britain and Europe*. Prague: Blitz Editions, 1999.

Lowry, Bernard. *Medieval Castles of England and Wales*. Oxford: Bloomsbury Shire, 2017.

Maggi, Girolamo, and Captain Jacomo Castriotto. *Fortificatione delle città*. Venice: 1564 (from Internet Archive of Getty Research Institute: digitalized in 2010).

Mallet, Michael and Christine Shaw. *The Italian Wars: 1494-1559*. New York: Routledge, 2012.

Manning, Anne. *The Story of Italy*. London: Richard Bentley, 1859.

Mantellier, Philippe. *Le Siège et la délivrance d'Orléans*. Orléans: A. Gatineau, 1855.

Manucy, Albert. *Artillery Through the Ages*. Washington D.C.: National Park Service, 1985 (reprint of 1949 ed.).

McNeill, William H. *The Pursuit of Power*. Chicago: Univ. of Chicago Press, 1982.

Mesqui, Jean. *Les châteaux forts: de la guerre à la paix*. Italy: Découvertes Gallimard Architecture, 1995.

_____. *Château Forts et fortifications en France*. Paris: Flammarion, 1997.

Monreal y Tejada, Luis. *Medieval Castles of Spain*. Cologne: Köneman, 1999.

Morgan, Morris Hicky (trans.). *Vitruvius: The Ten Books on Architecture*. Cambridge: Harvard University Press, 1914.

Morton, Catherine. *Bodiam Castle*. England: The Curwen Press, 1975.

Murphy, James Cavanah. *History of the Mahometan Empire in Spain*. London: William Bulmer and Co., 1816.

Neri, Achille. 'Il Forte di Sarzanello', *Archivio Storico Italiano*, Tomo XV. Florence (Italy): G.P. Vieusseux. Dec. 1885, pp. 345–53.

Newhall, Richard Ager. *The English Conquest of Normandy 1416-1424: A Study in Fifteenth Century Warfare*. New Haven: Yale University Press, 1924.

Nicholson, Helen. *Medieval Warfare: Theory and Practice of War in Europe 300-1500*. New York: Palgrave Macmillan, 2005.

Nicolle, David. *Medieval Warfare Source Book (Vol 1 and 2)*. London: Arms & Armour, 1995.

_____. *Granada 1492: The Conquest of Spain*. Oxford: Osprey, 1998.

_____. *El Cid and the Reconquista 1050-1492*. Oxford: Osprey, 1998.

_____. *The Moors: The Islamic West 7ᵗʰ – 15ᵗʰ Centuries ad*. Oxford, Osprey, 2001.

_____. *Orleans 1429: France turns the tide*. Oxford: Osprey, 2001.

_____. *Fornovo 1495*. Westport (CT): Praeger, 2005.

Norman, Vesey. *Medieval Soldier*. Barnsley (UK): Pen & Sword, 2010.

Nossov, Konstantin. *Ancient and Medieval Siege Weapons*. Guilford (CT): Lyons Press, 2005.

O'Callaghan, Joseph F. *A History of Medieval Spain*. Ithaca: Cornell University, 1975.

_____. *Reconquest and Crusade in Medieval Spain*. Philadelphia: Univ. of Pennsylvania Press, 2003.

Oman, Sir Charles. *A History of the Art of War in the Middle Ages* (Vol 1 and 2). London: Greenhill, 1924.

O'Neil, G.H. St. J. *Deal Castle*. London: HMSO, 1966.

_____. *Castles: An introduction to the castles of England and Wales*. London: HMSO, 1973.

_____. *Walmer Castle*. London: HMSO, 1975.

Ottendorff-Simrock, Walther. *Castles on the Rhine*. Würzburg: Universtsdruckerei H. Sturrtz, n.d.

Paris, Mathew, Rev. J.A. Giles (Trans.). *English History From to 1235-1273* (3 vols). London: Henry G. Bohn, 1854. Digitalized: https://archive.org/stream/matthewparisseng01pari#page/n5/mode/2up

Paris, Mathew, H.R. Luard (ed.) *Chronica Majora*. London: Longman & Co., 1876. Digitalized https://archive.org/stream/matthiparisien03pari#page/n9/mode/2up

Parker, Geoffrey. *The Military Revolution: Military innovation and the rise of the West, 1500-1800*. Cambridge: Cambridge University Press, 1988.

Pepper, Simon. 'The underground siege,' *FORT 10*. Fortress Study Group, 1982, pp 30–8.

_____ and Nicholas Adams. *Firearms & Fortifications: Military Architecture and Siege Warfare in Sixteenth-Century Siena*. Chicago: Univ. of Chicago Press, 1986.

Platt, Colin. *The Castle in Medieval England & Wales*. New York: Barnes & Noble, 1996.

Pohl, John. *Armies of Castile and Aragon 1370-1516*. Oxford: Osprey, 2015.

Prescott, William H., John Foster Kirk (ed.). *The Complete Works of William Hickling Prescott*, Vol 1. London: Gibbings and Co., Ltd., 1896.

_____, Albert McJoynt (ed.). *The Art of War in Spain: The Conquest of Granada 1481-1492*. London: Greenhill Books, 1995.

Prestwich, Michael. *Armies and Warfare in the Middle Ages: The English Experience*. New Haven: Yale Univ. Press, 1996.

Procter, Colonel George. *The History of Italy, From the Fall of the Western Empire to the commencement of the Wars of the French Republic*. London: Whittaker & Co., 1844.

Puiseux, Léon. *Siège et prise de Caen par les anglais en 1417*. Caen: Le Gost-Clérisse, 1848.

Ramsay, Sir James H. *Lancaster and Work: A Century of English History (A.D. 1399-1485)*. Oxford: Clarendon Press, 1892.

Ratheau, A. *Monographie du château de Salses*. Paris: Ch. Tanera, 1860.

Reid, Peter. *Medieval Warfare*. New York: Carol & Graf Publishers, 2007.

Ruaux, Jean-Yves. *Dinan*. Rennes: Ouest France, 1983.

Saalman, Howard. *Medieval Cities*. New York: George Braziller, 1968.

Sancha, Sheila. *The Castle Story*. New York: Penguin Books, 1979.

Saunders, A.D. *Deal and Walmer Castles*. London: HMSO, 1976.

_____. *Fortress Britain: Artillery Fortifications in the British Isles and Ireland*. Liphook (UK): Beaufort, 1989.

_____. *Channel Defences*. London: Bath Press, 1997.

Scaglia, Gustina. 'Francesco di Giorgio's chapters on fortresses and on war machine', *FORT 10*, Fortress Study Group, 1982. pp. 39–69.

Scott, Samuel Parsons. *History of the Moorish Empire in Europe*. Vol 2. Philadelphia: J.B Lippincott Company, 1904.

Seward, Desmond. *The Hundred Years War*. New York: Atheneum, 1978.

Snow, Dan. *Battle Castles: 500 Years of Knights and Siege Warfare*. London: Harper Press, 2012.

Stanton, Charles. *Medieval Maritime Warfare*. Barnsley: Pen & Sword, 2015

Sumption, Jonathan. *The Hundred Years War: Trial by Fire* (Vol. 1). Philadelphia: Univ. of Penn., 1990.

_____. *The Hundred Years War: Cursed Kings* (Vol. 4). Philadelphia: Univ. of Penn., 2017.

Taylor, Frederick Lewis. *The Art of War in Italy, 1494-1529*. Cambridge: Cambridge University Press, 1921 (also ebook - San Diego: Didactic Press, 2015 reprint).

Tendero, Elena (ed.), et. al. *Castillos y fortalezas de España*. Madrid: Susaeta, 2012.

Toy, Sidney. *Castles: Their Construction and History*. New York: Dover Publications, 1985 (reprint of 1939 ed.).

Tracy, James D. (ed.). *City Walls: The Urban Enceinte in Global Perspective*. New York: Cambridge University Press, 2000.

Turner, Hilary. *Town Defences in England and Wales*. London: John Baker, 1971.

Tylden, Captain Richard. 'Notice of the Military Portion of the Works of Francisco di Giorgio Martini, Architetto Senese, of the 15th Century', *Corps Papers and Memoirs on Military Subjects Complied from Contributions of the Officers of The Royal Engineers and the East India Company's Engineers*. London: John Weale, 1849.

Viollet-le-Duc, Eugène-Emmanuel. *Castles and Warfare in the Middle Ages*. Mineola (NY): Dover Publications, 2005 (reprint of 1860 ed.).

_____. *Dictionnaire raisonné de l'architecture française du XI au XVI siècle*. Paris: Edition Bance – Morel of 1854 to 1868. (https://fr.wikisource.org/wiki/Dictionnaire_raisonné_de_l'architecture_française_du_XIe_au_XVIe_siècle).

_____. *Military Architecture*. London: Greenhill, 1990.

_____ and M. Macdermott (trans.) *An Essay on the Military Architecture of the Middle Ages*. London: J. and J.H. Parker, 1860.

Viriville, Vallet de (ed). *Chronique de la Pucelle ou Chronique de Cousinot suivie de la Chronique Normande de P. Cochon*. Paris: Adolphe Delahays, 1864.

Vizcaino, Aureliano Gómez. *Castillos y Fortalezas de Cartagena*. Spain: AFORCA, 1995.

Wackerfluss, Winfried. *Burg Breuberg im Odenwald*. Breuberg: 1996.

Warner, Philip. *Sieges of the Middle Ages*. London: G. Bell and Sons, 1968.

_____. *The Medieval Castle*. New York: Barnes & Noble, 1993 (reprint of 1971 ed.).

Wenger, Daniel and Jean-Marie Nick. *Randonnées autour des château forts d'Alsace*. Mulhouse: Éditions du Rhin, 1996.

Wenzler, Claude. *Architecture du château fort*. Rennes: Éditions Ouest-France, 1997.

Wiggins, Kenneth. *Siege Mines and Underground Warfare*. Pembrokeshire: Shire Publications, 2003.

Wise, Terence. *Warfare Medieval*. New York: Hastings House, 1976.

Wolfe, M. *Walled Towns and the Shaping of France: From the Medieval to the Early Modern Era*. New York: Palgrave Macmillan, 2009.

Wylie, James H. and William T. Waugh. *The Reign of Henry the Fifth*. Cambridge: Cambridge University Press, 1914–1929.

Yonge, Charlotte Mary. *The Wars in France*. London: Macmillan & Co., 1880.

Index